Marlborough F & M School
Marlborough Hill, Harrow,
HA1 1UJ, Middlesex

First published in Britain in 1988 by
Young Library Ltd
45 Norfolk Square, Brighton
East Sussex BN1 2PE

Text © Copyright 1988 Young Library Ltd
Illustrations © Copyright 1988 Peter Pan Edizione, Modena
All rights reserved

ISBN 0 946003 95 5

Printed and bound in Hong Kong

There are two more Then and Now books

Kathy Then and Kathy Now
Nine-year-old Kathy compares her seaside holiday with a similar holiday enjoyed by her own great-grandmother.

Stephen Then and Stephen Now
Twelve-year-old Stephen compares his everyday life with that of his great-grandfather who lived in the same town.

Josette Blanco and Claude d'Ham
Translated from the German by Andrea Dutton-Kölbl

ANNA THEN and ANNA NOW

Seven-year-old Anna discovers an old photo album. It is full of photos of her great-grandmother's childhood in the country many years ago. Full of curiosity, Anna compares the pictures of bygone country life with her own life in the old family home.

YOUNG LIBRARY

This is a picture of my great-grandma when she was a child.
She was Dad's grandmother, and my grandad's mother.
Her name was Anna. She was seven when this picture was taken.

I am seven years old too, and my name also is Anna.
I love looking at the pictures of Great-grandma Anna and her family.
I compare the way she lived with the way we live now.

When she was a child Great-grandma lived in the country.
Her dad was a farmer, and she grew up on the farm.
Half their little house was a home, the other half was a stable.

My mother, father, brother, and I still live in the same house.
It has been turned into a pretty home with a garden all round it.
It is not a farm any more, and Dad drives to work in town each day.

Let us take a closer look at Great-grandma Anna's house.
There were stables for horses, with a hayloft above.
There was a dovecote under the eaves.

A shed for carts and ladders leaned against the end wall.
Behind the house stood a hen coop and a rabbit hutch.
A new wooden bench stood under the kitchen window.

Now the stables have become the entrance hall and living room.
The hayloft has been turned into Mum and Dad's bedroom.
Where doves used to coo, there is now my own little room.

The lean-to shed is now used as a garage for the car.
My swing stands where the hen coop and rabbit hutch used to be.
One thing hasn't changed. The old wooden bench is still there.

Families were usually bigger in Great-grandma's day.
With Anna at the table are her sisters and brothers, parents and
grandparents, and an unmarried aunt.

Today our kitchen looks very different.
I have only one brother. No aunts or uncles live with us.
My Granny and Grandad live nearly a hundred miles away.

Work was much heavier in Great-grandma's time.
Her father helped his men to harvest the corn.
Her grandfather spent hours chopping logs for the fire.

Her aunt had many jobs; plucking chickens was one of them.
Her mother cooked for a large family on the kitchen range.
Her grandmother gathered mushrooms and wild herbs in the meadows.

Today all heavy work is done by machinery.
My dad doesn't need to chop wood for the fire because
once a month a tanker delivers oil for the central heating.

My mum has never plucked a chicken. They are bought 'oven-ready'.
In modern kitchens the cooking does not take very long.
All Mum's groceries are bought at the new supermarket in town.

Great-grandma Anna always had to get up very early.
Every day she and her brother walked nearly two miles to school.
The narrow country road used to get flooded after heavy rain.

It is only a short walk from home to the school bus.
If it is raining Mum takes me to the bus-stop in the car.
My friends from the new housing estate join the bus at the next stop.

In those days the school was not much bigger than an ordinary house.
It had only one classroom and one teacher.
The teacher lived in the rooms above the schoolroom.

The children sat at wooden desks with hinged lids.
Each desk had a little inkwell which they dipped their pens into.
On cold mornings the teacher lit the wood-burning stove.

The town is much bigger today, so there are more schoolchildren.
Several new classrooms have been added to the old building.
Most of our teachers are women.

I sit near the window, just where my great-grandma used to be.
The classrooms look much more cheerful than in the olden days.
Today Miss Morgan is teaching us about sets.

Great-grandma and her brother used to pass the village blacksmith.
They could watch all sorts of metal tools being made.
Sometimes they would see a horse being fitted with new shoes.

Tools are made in factories now, so we don't need a smith.
Where the smithy used to be, there is a garage today.
Yesterday Dad took his car to be repaired.

Every day Great-grandma Anna had lots of chores to do.
In autumn she picked apples from the orchard.
Each day she fed the rabbits and carried milk home from the dairy.

After school there was more work for Great-grandma to do.
She fed the hens and collected their eggs.
Poor Great-grandma didn't have much time for playing.

Today there are not nearly so many jobs to be done.
After I have finished my homework I like to go roller-skating.
Or sometimes I play ball, or go for a cycle ride.

In the evening I get out my family of dolls.
Last year Mum and Dad gave me their old television, and
I am allowed to watch a programme before bedtime.

When Great-grandma was my age she could do beautiful embroidery.
Her grandmother spent hours teaching her needlework.
While they worked she used to tell my great-grandma wonderful stories.

Great-grandma's first sampler now hangs on my bedroom wall.
I'm not clever with my hands, and nobody tells me stories.
Thank goodness for my books and records.

On Sunday after church there was always a family outing.
Great-grandma's father would hitch the horse to the cart.
Lots of relatives would ride out from town to join them.

Everyone would be dressed in their best Sunday clothes.
Often they would go to the nearby lake for a picnic.
The men took turns showing off their strength in the rowing boat.

When we go on picnics we take the car.
There always seems to be heaps of things to pack.
We like to start early, before the roads are crowded.

We often go to the lake where Great-grandma Anna went.
Sometimes I wonder if we even choose the same picnic spot!
While we play in the water, Mum and Dad go windsurfing.

What a difficult way to wash hair!
Great-grandma had to bend over a metal bath.
There was no running water with pipes and taps.

I think the bathroom has changed more than any other room.
Last year Mum and Dad replaced our enamel bath with a shower unit.
Washing used to be quite hard work but now it is easy.

Some houses even in town had no running water.
There was a place where women could bring their washing.
Monday was always known as washing day.

Great-grandma Anna would help her mother hang out the washing.
The sheets were laid out in the field to be bleached by the sun.
It took all week to wash, dry, and iron the clothes.

There is no such thing as washing day any more.
Mum starts up the washing machine nearly every morning,
then goes off to work with her friend.

By the time she comes home the clothes are clean and spun-dry.
Mum and I hang them out on the line for a while.
With modern washing powders it is not necessary to bleach the linen.

In the evening Great-grandma Anna's family sat round the fireplace.
The children listened to the talk of the grown-ups.
The women did their knitting and sewing in the firelight.

My family usually likes to watch TV in the evening.
I like TV too, but sometimes I go off to my room to read a book.
It is nice when my grandma visits, because she reads me a story.

Doctors were expensive, so were called out only for serious illness.
When Great-grandma felt unwell she was sent to bed.
Then her grandma would set to work in the kitchen.

Her grandma knew a lot about natural medicines like herbs.
She would make herb tea and carry it up to her granddaughter.
Usually Great-grandma would soon feel well again.

I, too, get sent to bed if I don't feel well.
Then Mum goes to the telephone and asks the doctor
to call in to see me.

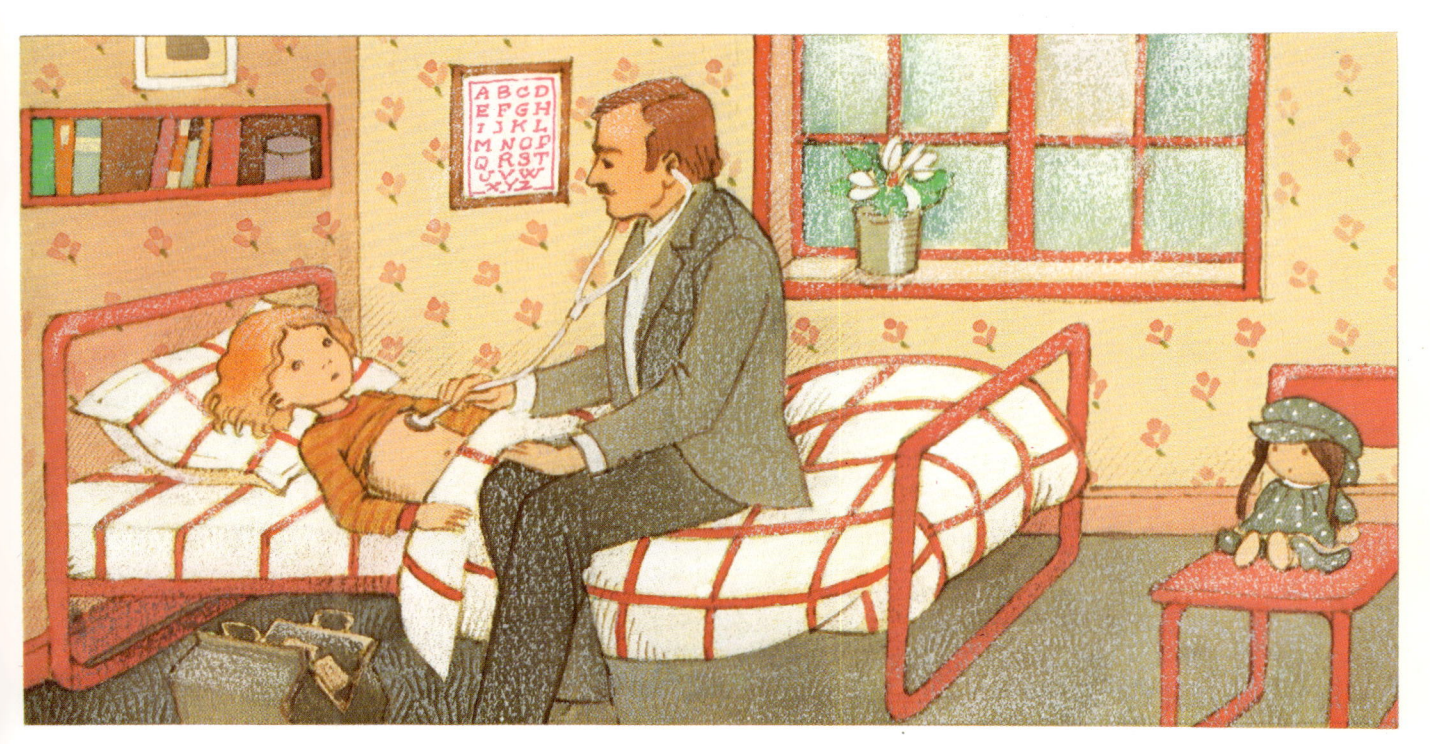

The doctor arrives and listens to my chest with his stethoscope.
Then he writes out a prescription.
Mum drives to the chemist and comes back with the medicine.

In Great-grandma's time there was no cinema, radio, or TV.
People would entertain themselves with dancing and music.
Sometimes there was folk-dancing to a fiddle and an accordion.

We visit the fête in the next village each year.
One of the most popular attractions is the folk-dancing.
People dress up and dance just like their grandparents used to do.

Index

References are to pictures as well as text

bathrooms 26/27
bedrooms 32/33
buildings 6/7, 8/9, 14/15, 16/17, 18/19

clothes 10/11, 12/13, 14/15, 16/17, 18/19, 20/21, 22/23, 24/25, 26/27, 28/29, 30/31
cooking 12/13

entertainment and play 22/23, 24/25, 30/31, 34/35

family life 10/11, 22/23, 24/25, 30/31
floors 10/11, 16/17, 22/23, 26/27, 30/31, 32/33
food 10/11, 12/13
furniture 10/11, 16/17, 22/23, 30/31, 32/33

heating 12/13
houses 6/7, 8/9, 10/11, 22/23, 26/27, 30/31, 32/33

illness 32/33

kitchens 10/11, 12/13

lighting 10/11, 22/23, 30/31, 32/33
living rooms 30/31

mathematics 16/17
medicine 32/33
music 34/35

roads 14/15

school 14/15, 16/17

vehicles 6/7, 8/9, 18/19, 24/25

washing 26/27, 28/29
wheels 6/7, 12/13, 24/25
work 12/13, 16/17, 18/19, 20/21, 28/29

Just for fun, did you see . . . ?
   a spinning wheel
   a pair of clogs
   a warming pan
   two washboards
   a crucifix
   a firedog and a fire-loving cat

TODAY'S WORLD
LIVING IN THE FUTURE

HOWARD TIMMS

GLOUCESTER PRESS
London · New York · Toronto · Sydney

CONTENTS

THE FUTURE HOUSE	5
COMPUTERS IN THE HOME	6
LIVING IN A COMMUNITY	8
HEALTH	10
LEISURE	12
AT WORK	14
COMMUNICATIONS	21
FUTURE EARTH	26
WORKING IN SPACE	30
FACT OR FANTASY	34
GLOSSARY	35
INDEX	36

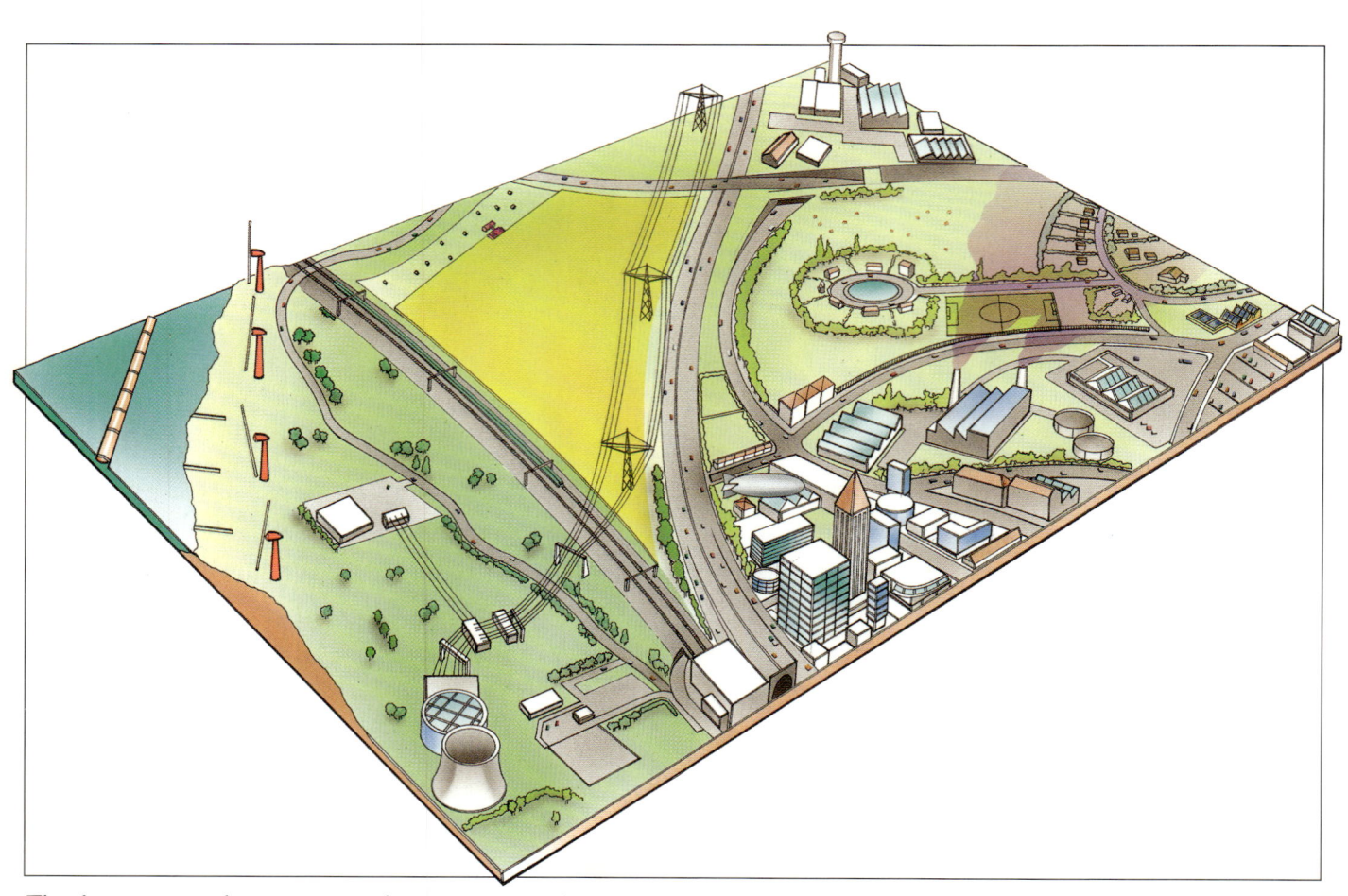

The front cover shows an artist's impression of a future space colony.

INTRODUCTION

With the exception of Australia, New Zealand and Japan, today's most highly developed countries are in the West. Collectively, all of these countries, including Japan, are known as the Western Nations. This book is about the way in which life and work in the Western nations can be expected to change within the reader's lifetime. It examines some of the latest developments, predicting the effect they will have on people's lifestyles in the next 20, 30 or 40 years. Similar changes will eventually take place in the developing countries, although they will take longer. Many machines now in homes are partly automatic, and in many countries this trend will continue so that before very long a whole home will be automatic. Computers are being applied ever more widely, and there will be further developments in homes, leisure, work and transport. Technological changes may cause problems, such as pollution and shortage of resources, and these are unlikely to disappear. Some new answers should develop soon. One possibility is to move people away from Earth into space, and to obtain resources from the Moon and other heavenly bodies.

A futuristic house in the American desert uses wind and solar panels.

Alternative energy
Methane gas, for cooking or heating, is produced by rotting organic waste, such as garden rubbish or waste food. Waste is dumped in a biomass tank which collects methane. Solar panels on the house warm water, which is stored in an insulated tank.

Communications
A dish aerial collects and transmits all the house's communications through telephone, radio, television, or computer networks. Radio signals connect the aerial with a communications centre.

Recycling
Household rubbish is collected for recycling. It will be taken to a recycling plant, where glass and metals will be separated for making into new bottles or cans. Alternatively, the waste is separated in the home before being collected for recycling.

Robots
Some household tasks can be programmed into robots. A garden robot can be programmed to collect leaves and other garden litter, or to mow the lawn. The robot takes the waste to the biomass tank. When it has finished its tasks, the robot plugs itself into the electricity supply to recharge its batteries.

Security
Callers at the front door are identified by fingerprints, or by their voice in a microphone. This is part of a system to maintain security and safety, which also acts as a fire alarm. When the house is empty, it operates as a burglar alarm.

THE FUTURE HOUSE

A hundred years ago, a few houses had servants who cleaned, and kept fires going for heat. Now many homes have machines which do cleaning, heating and other work. Increasingly, future homes will have robots and computer-controlled systems for running the home.

The house of the future will be easy to run. Already the time needed to look after the cleaning of a home, and to make it comfortable, is getting ever smaller. Machines such as automatic washing machines, dishwashers, and vacuum cleaners make household jobs quicker. In future, robots will be able to do more than one task, and will be able to move around. As already happens in some factories, robots will be controlled and programmed by a computer, making sure that the machines do exactly what the householder wants. Fuels such as oil and gas are getting scarce, and future homes will be built to produce some, or even all, of their own energy needs.

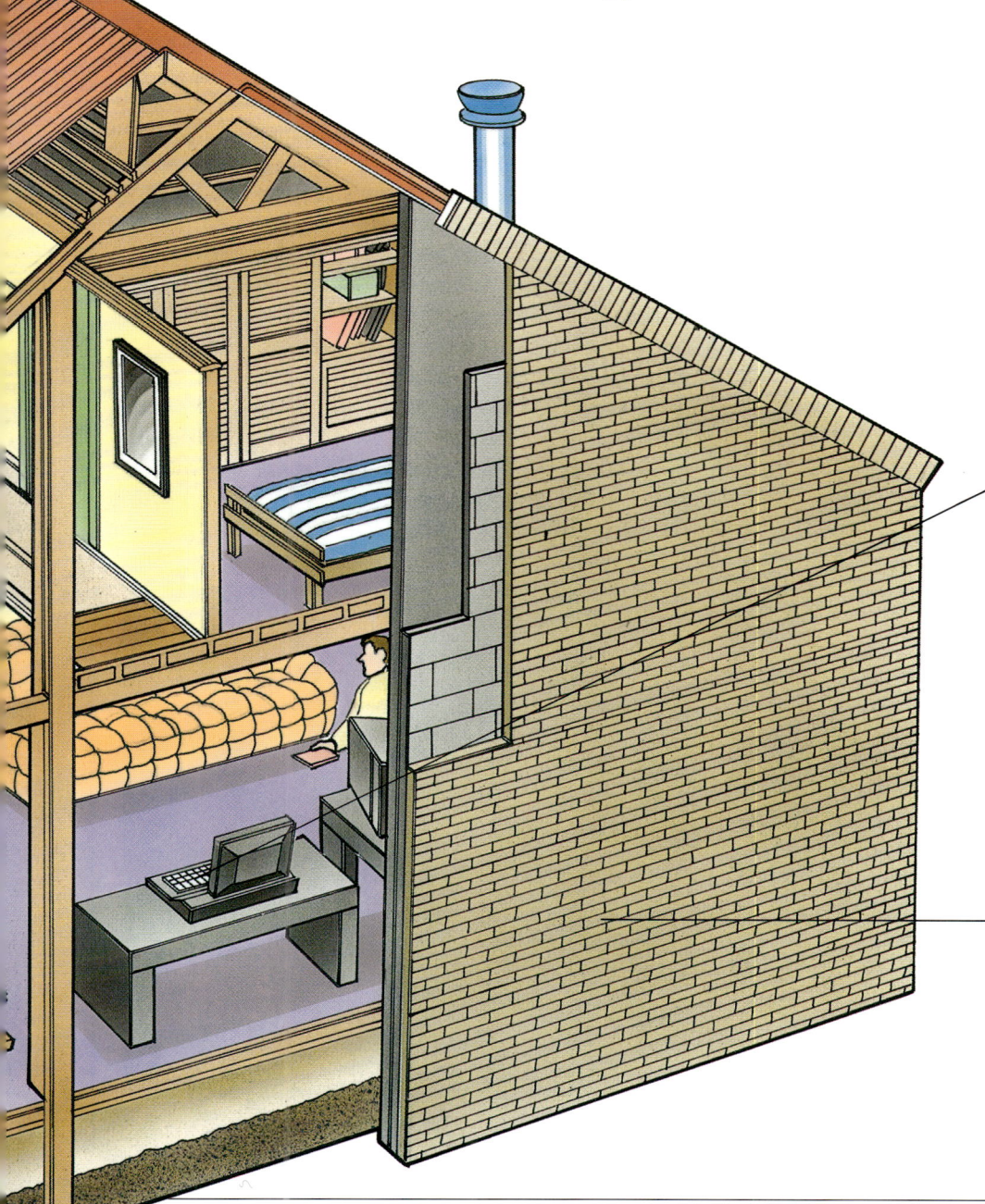

The house of tomorrow will run itself. A computer controls heating, safety, cleaning, conservation of energy and materials, production of energy, and communications. Robots controlled by the computer do household chores. The computer senses when the occupants are out, provides burglar and fire alarm systems, and keeps the place clean and tidy.

Computer control
A central computer controls the main systems, such as security, energy production, or internal heating and lighting. It controls the house temperature by altering things like the reflectiveness of window blinds, or air circulation, or by burning heating fuel when needed. The computer can switch lights on automatically when someone enters a room. It receives the householders' instructions for robots, and programs them.

Materials
Better building materials make the house cheaper and easier to run. An example is window glass, strong and long lasting, and with good insulation. Special glass can be made whose reflection properties are computer-controlled to stop glare from the Sun, or to absorb or reflect heat as needed.

COMPUTERS IN THE HOME

When electronic calculators first became available, they cost over a hundred pounds. But now they cost only a few pounds. Robots for the home will be very expensive to begin with. But one day perhaps as many homes will have a robot as have a washing machine today.

Day to day life in the home of the future will be different in many ways from that of today. Because tasks will be undertaken by computers and robots, people will have extra time for leisure and social activities. Computers will even help to plan each person's day. They will also start doing jobs that have not been done before, such as controlling the internal environment of the home – the heating, lighting and ventilation. Although life will be made easier in many ways, people will have to learn new skills so that they will be able to tell the machines exactly what they want them to do.

Central control

Occupants of future homes will not need to make decisions about turning on lights, or turning up heating or ventilation. A central computer will do it for them. It uses sensors, connected by wires, to find out if lighting levels are sufficient, or if the temperature is correct, and adjusts the lights or heating if necessary. Similarly, when the occupants are away, the computer's security sensors check whether there are any intruders. If there are, it contacts the police.

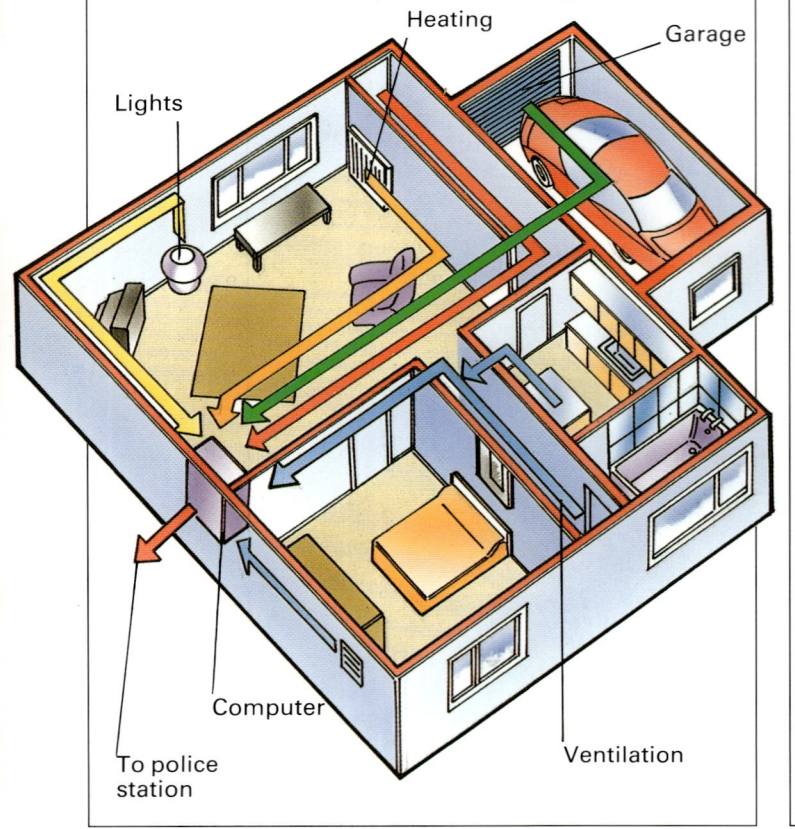

Computer management

Managing a home includes keeping check on the costs of running it, a job that computers make easy. But the range of home management jobs that computers can help with is growing all the time. Shopping by computer is possible for a wide range of goods and services. A customer at home shops by linking the home computer by phone to a large central computer. Information on goods and prices is passed to the home computer for the customer to study. Orders for goods are then passed to the computer network, which notifies shops to supply the required goods directly to the customer's home. Money to pay for the goods is deducted directly from the customer's bank account.

Ordering goods using a home computer

Robots

Any machine that controls itself is a robot. Many houses now have machines which are robotic – an example is an automatic washing machine. Each robot stores a program (a set of instructions) which it carries out whenever it is switched on. Generally, home robots carry more than one program, and users of the robot can select the program they need. More intelligent robots choose instructions depending on circumstances. An automatic vacuum cleaner, for example, controls its own movement. The robot's sensors tell it if something is in its way, and the robot decides whether to reverse or go round it. After a time, the robot learns the layout of the house and plans the best route round.

Pouring a drink is a simple task for a robot.

Less waste

A group of homes, such as a block of flats, can already have an economical system for re-using most household rubbish. A system which has been used in Sweden since the 1960s has a pneumatic pipe to carry rubbish along to a separator. Compressed air is used to push the rubbish along the pipe. The separator sorts out metal and glass rubbish into separate containers. The glass and metal are taken away to special factories where they can be recycled.

Any part of the rubbish which will burn is piped along to a heating plant. Burning the rubbish produces heat which is used to make steam. More pipes carry the steam, which is used for heating the building.

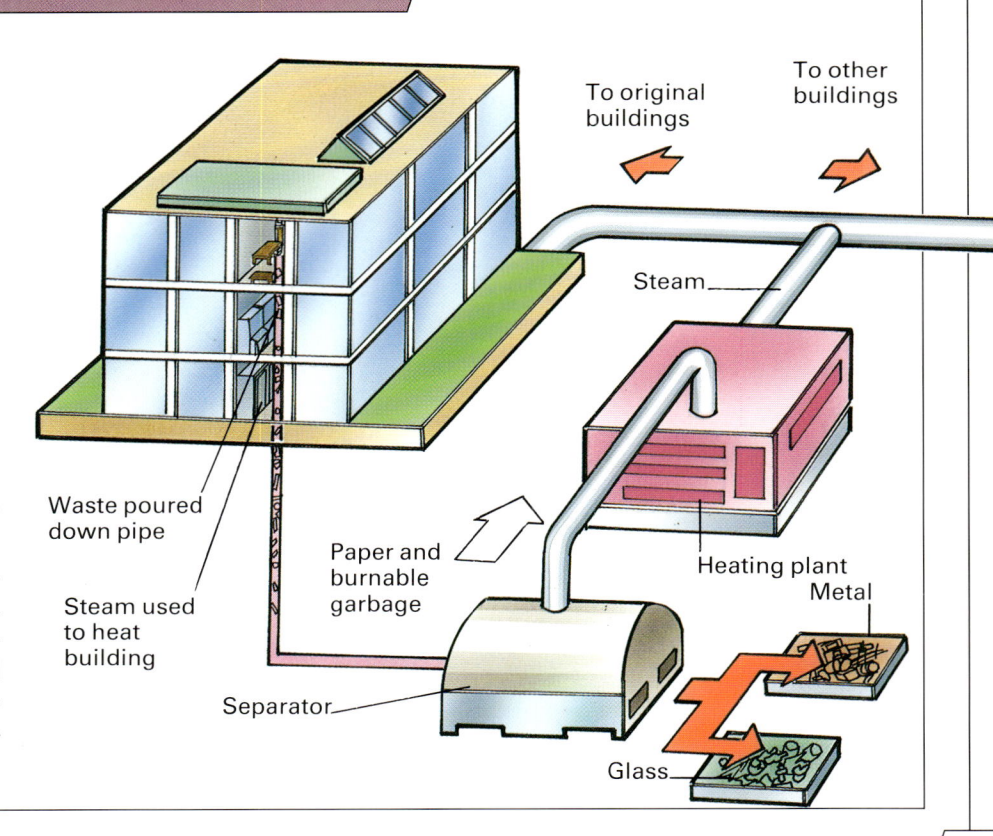

LIVING IN A COMMUNITY

Many of the world's largest cities provide homes for more than 10 million people. Within cities, individual communities consist of groups of only a few thousand people, similar in population to a small town. In remote country districts, a community may consist of only a very few families.

Homes are generally part of a community, such as a neighbourhood within a city or one of its suburbs. Most communities include some services such as shops or libraries. Many people want their home to be near the services or places that they visit regularly. But some people either cannot afford a home near a town centre, or prefer to live nearer the country. Others, such as farmers, have to live in the country. For these people, it is usually more convenient to be able to do a lot of varied shopping, or use several services, in one place on one trip.

Communities

The success of a community depends on the way that its planners arranged its parts in relation to each other. Planning for homes to be close together means that each will use less land and be cheaper. But the inhabitants may suffer noise and lack of privacy. Many tower blocks of flats built during the 1950s and 1960s were not supplied with services, such as shops and leisure facilites. Tower blocks consisting only of flats are rarely built now. The few that are built include services or have them nearby. Town layouts for the future allow for space around each home, with schools and services nearby, good transport connections, and amenities such as libraries, shopping centres, leisure complexes and parks within walking distance.

Old tower blocks are being demolished.

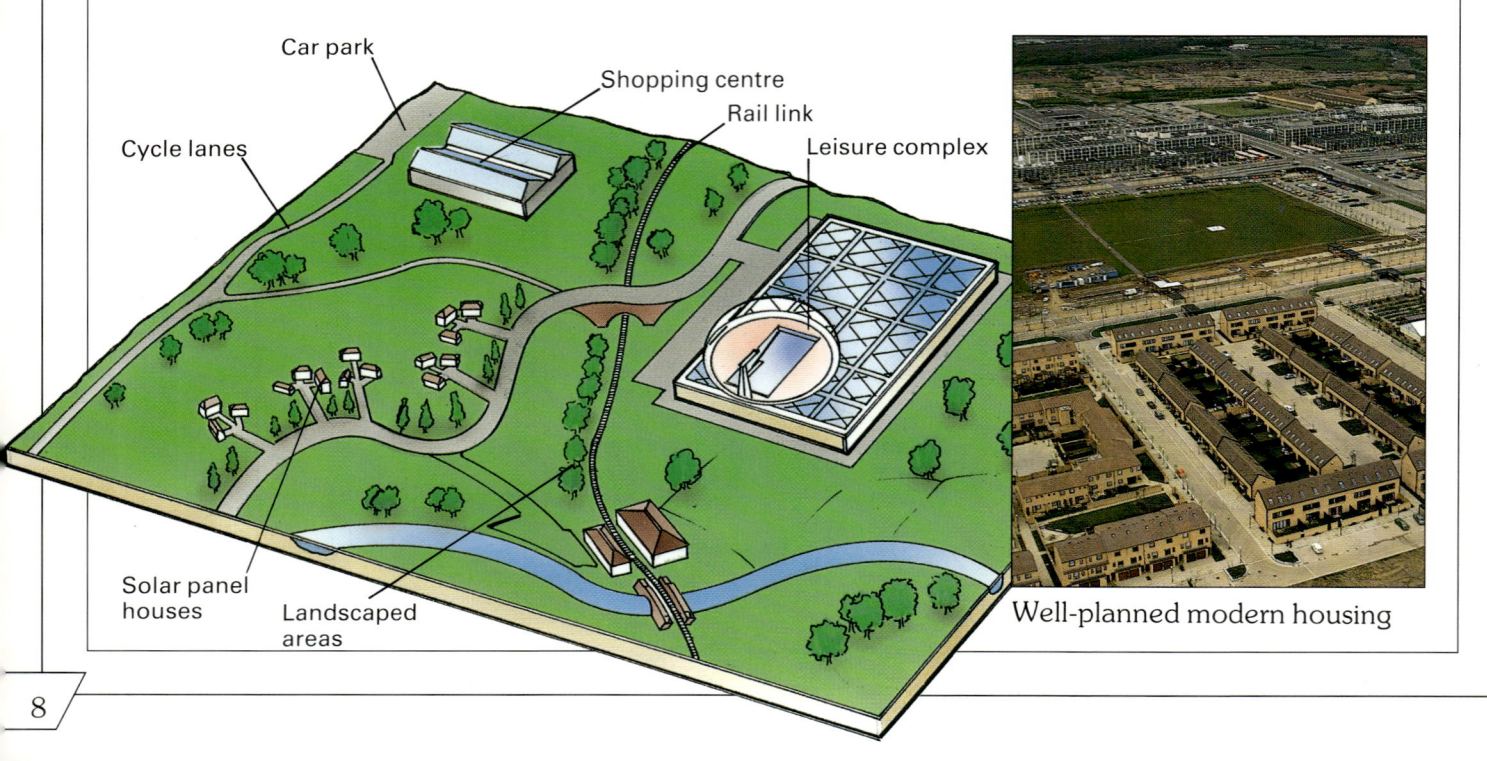

Car park
Shopping centre
Rail link
Cycle lanes
Leisure complex
Solar panel houses
Landscaped areas

Well-planned modern housing

Schools

In schools of the future, children will still have to be taught basic skills, such as reading, writing and counting. But many skills, such as dealing with money or crossing roads, will be taught partly by computer. By using programs which allow the individual to interact with the words or pictures, computers can help students to learn at their own pace. Some programs will use simulations to make situations seem like real life. Because computers will be such a major part of school life, they will affect the ways in which many subjects are taught. Teachers will have more time for individual tuition, and students will have more time to study a wide variety of subjects.

A student doing homework on a computer

A computer helping to teach languages

Shops

Shopping in bulk, or for a variety of goods, becomes increasingly easy with the development of shopping arcades and malls. A shopping mall includes many small shops, which sell a wide variety of goods, as well as larger stores. In future, a customer visiting a shopping centre will be able to use a centralized delivery service. Goods from various shops will be taken to a central collection area, packed and delivered together. They will also be charged for together, with a computer system reading bar code numbers on each item. The computer will arrange for payment for the goods to each of the shops from which they were bought.

A large shopping centre in Toronto, Canada

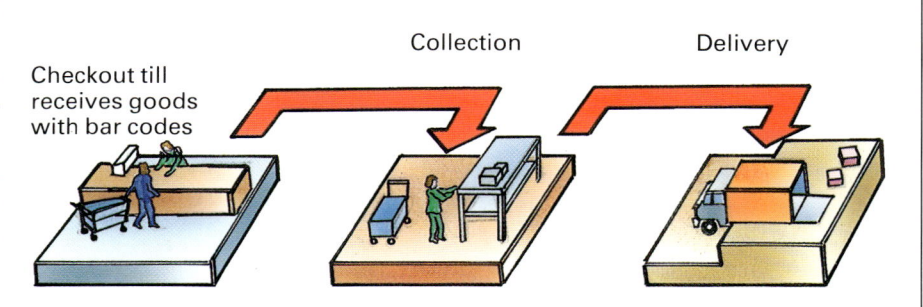

Checkout till receives goods with bar codes

Collection

Delivery

HEALTH

Healthcare has improved greatly over the last 50 years. Much of this is a result of advanced technology. Surgeons can now use lasers to perform operations that could not be carried out before. Computer technology is used to detect illnesses before they become serious.

Improvements in medicine have led to people being fitter and living longer lives. New techniques in biotechnology, such as genetic engineering, allow the production of "tailor-made" drugs and vaccines. The benefits will continue in the future through developments such as automation in surgery, which will use computer control and robotics to perform operations.

People's health is also improving because of better preventive medicine, which involves monitoring a patient's state of health, and encouraging healthy activities. More and more people regard preventive medicine as something they can take advantage of without a doctor – for example, by eating a balanced diet of healthy foods. A keep-fit plan is one area in which computer technology is likely to bring continuing improvements.

Keeping healthy

Keeping fit through exercise is best done to a plan, and figures need to be worked out for the correct amount of exercise at each stage. Progress in health terms can be measured through pulse and breathing rates, and blood pressure. A computer is ideal for taking and recording all these measurements and planning future exercise. Another approach to better health involves routine screening, in which a person is examined regularly to detect possible signs of a disorder before it becomes difficult to treat.

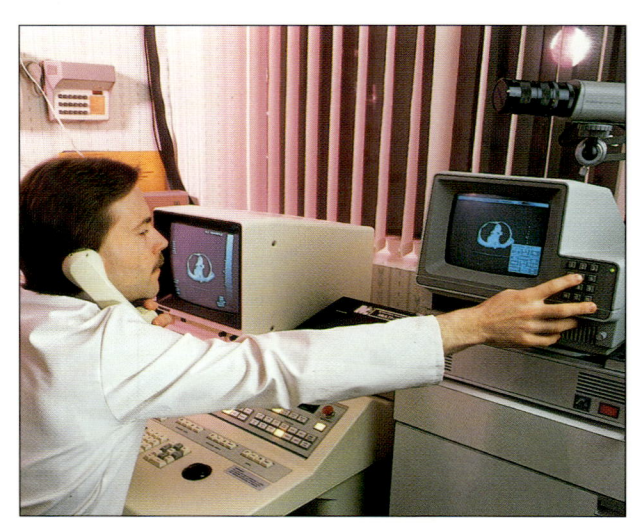

1.

2.

A doctor sends a CAT scan by videophone.

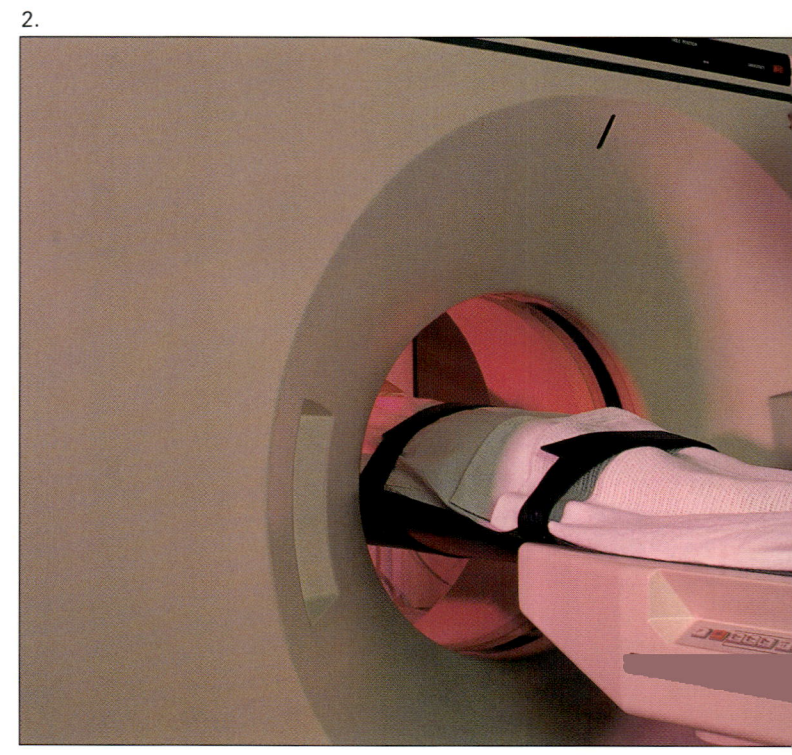

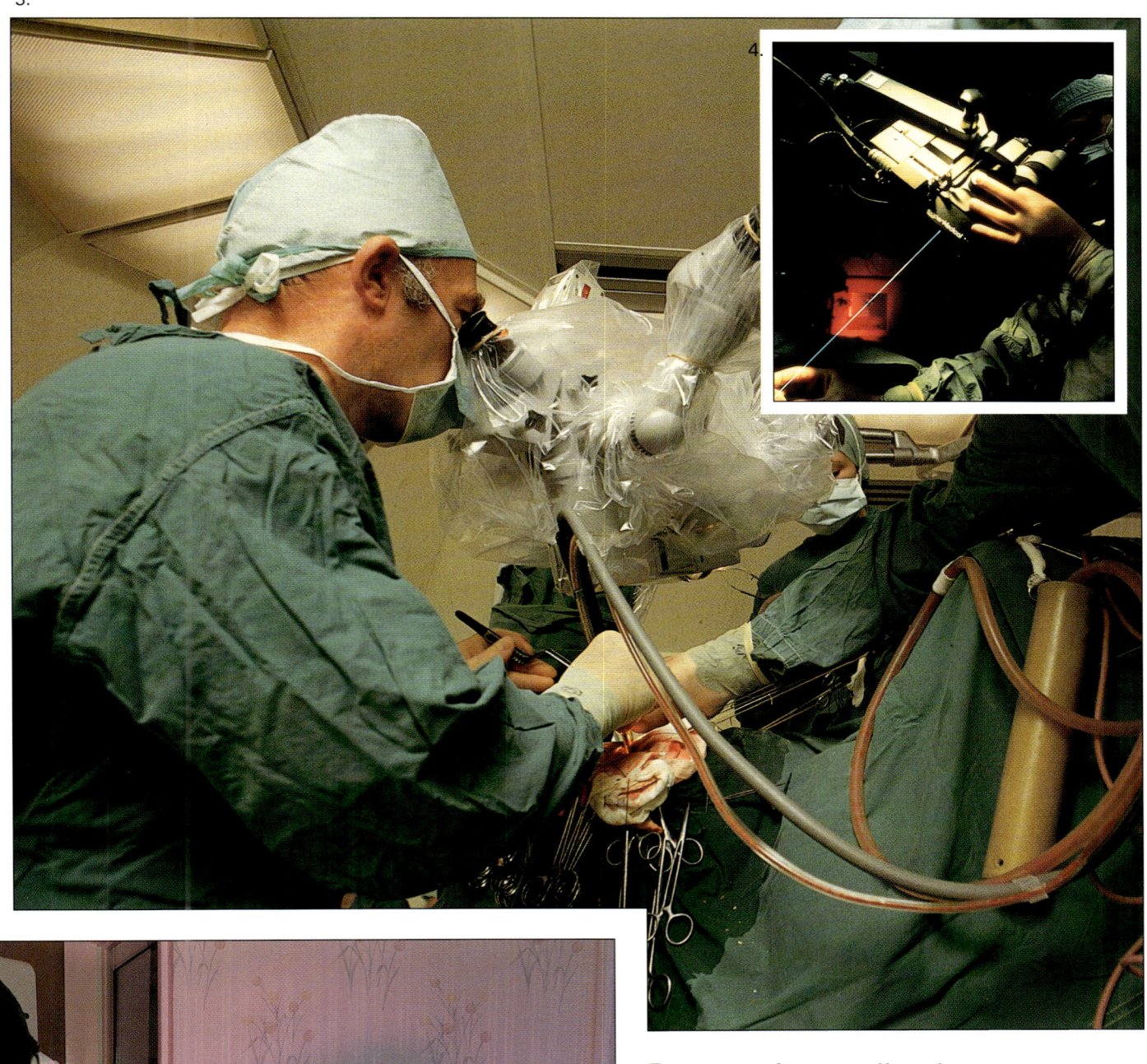

Future medicine will make increasing use of high technology for the investigation and diagnosis of illnesses, as well as for their treatment. 1. An operator uses a computer system to analyse data about a patient's bone structure. 2. This patient is having a CAT scan. CAT stands for computerized axial tomography, which is a technique for taking "pictures" of tissues inside the body. The scanner moves around the patient and takes very detailed X-rays of cross-sections of the body. 3. In microsurgery, the surgeon uses a microscope to perform delicate operations on nerves and other small structures. 4. A laser beam is being employed to treat tumours inside a patient's ear.

LEISURE

Future developments in computer games will include new output devices. These enable the computer to make special images such as holograms (a three-dimensional image made using laser technology).

In your own home you can tour the Universe, fight a dragon, or fly an aeroplane, by playing computer games. Even better is a three-dimensional image, or a chair that gives you the feeling of a moving spacecraft. This kind of realism is now available in pilot training simulators, and will soon be available in homes for learning a whole range of skills, such as learning how to sail a wind-surfer.

For leisure out of the home, more people will visit theme parks. And with faster and cheaper air travel, tourism will expand as more people take holidays abroad.

Home entertainment

A link between a computer and a videodisc produces interactive video (IV). When used as part of a video game, interactive video could show actual moving images of real places as part of the game. Another use of IV could be choosing a holiday, with the opportunity to explore as you wish the places that you are considering visiting. After choosing a place, you might decide to use IV to learn the local language. You could practise asking people for directions. When you try following the directions in an IV simulation, you'll soon know if you understood them.

Other educational uses of video enable people to learn about the arts. Paintings can be studied, and holograms would display sculpture and architecture in realistic three dimensions. Using IV, it will be possible to learn how to play a musical instrument. Many games and sports can be simulated, for example to improve a player's skill at chess or pool before taking on a human opponent. Three-dimensional war games using holograms (right) will replace today's flat-screen versions.

This computer responds to a child's spoken instructions.

Control joysticks
Projectors
Moving hologram

Total sensory simulation

You are an airline pilot, making your first landing at Hong Kong. As the runway lights come nearer, you move the throttle controls to reduce engine power. You feel the aircraft respond, and engine noise decreases. You are in a real cockpit, and your senses tell you just what they would tell you in a real aircraft, but you are in a simulator. A computer responds to your actions in the cockpit, and provides total sensory simulation of flying. The images of Hong Kong are on a screen in front of you, hydraulic rams move the cockpit, and loudspeakers provide the sound. All the seats in a cinema can be similarly controlled (right) to give a sensation of movement.

A pilot "flying" an aircraft simulator

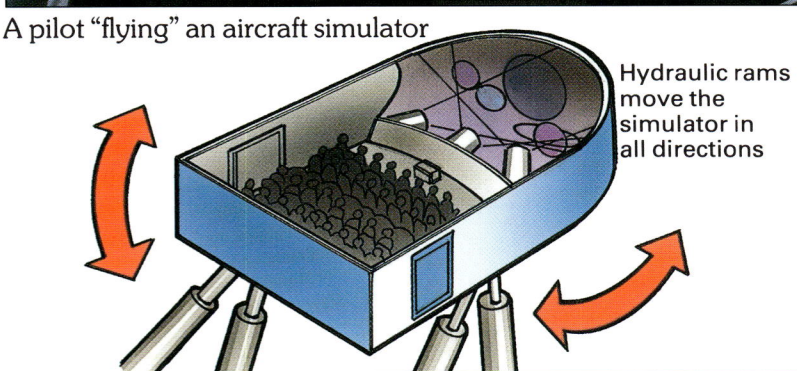

Hydraulic rams move the simulator in all directions

Container holiday

Caravans are a popular method of cheap, mobile holiday-making. But caravans sit idle and unused for much of the year, while their owners are at home, sometimes short of space. The solution is to link the caravan onto the home, with a connecting door, and plug-in electrical and plumbing services. The house then has one more bathroom, and another living room or guest room. The caravan would be moved on a transporter to its holiday site.

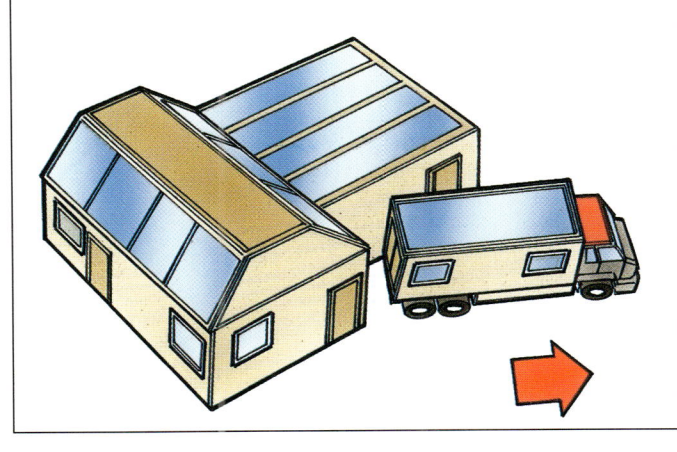

Theme holiday

Theme parks use technology similar to that in pilot training simulators, and give holiday-makers the thrill of realistic trips to exciting or dangerous places. As well as projected images, sound effects and simulated movement, theme parks may use realistic moving models and androids – robots that look like humans. Computer control ensures that effects are timed for maximum impact, or to provide interactive response to the holiday-makers.

Theme park Alton Towers, England

AT WORK

Factories with complete automation, where no people work, already exist and will probably soon be common. Raw materials and components are fed into one end of the production line, and finished goods come out at the other end. Offices, too, make increasing use of computers and electronic equipment. As a result, people can do office work from home, and send out the results of their work as "electronic mail" using data links.

A completely automated factory can make a variety of products, all literally untouched by human hands. Automatic hover platforms carry materials round the factory. Machines do the assembly, and can work 24 hours a day if necessary. Occasionally they may stop for repairs and maintenance, but even that work they may do themselves. Although no people work in manufacturing, human beings still do the most important work of all – managing the factory and deciding what to make. Managers monitor the factory's output and customers' needs, and plan the type and quantity of product to be made. Plans are fed to the main factory computer, and are processed into instructions for the machines in the factory. Managers also ensure that raw materials and components are available, normally ordering the quantities suggested by the computer system.

Robot technology

Robots are machines that continually carry out instructions stored in their memory. Like human beings, robots have ways of sensing what they are doing. They may use their sensors to take measurements, or to discover if a stage of production is complete. The information from sensors goes back to the robot in a process called feedback. The robot uses the feedback to decide what to do next to carry out its instructions. Robots are well suited to doing boring and repetitive work. Some can be programmed to do a variety of different tasks.

Car bodies being welded by robots

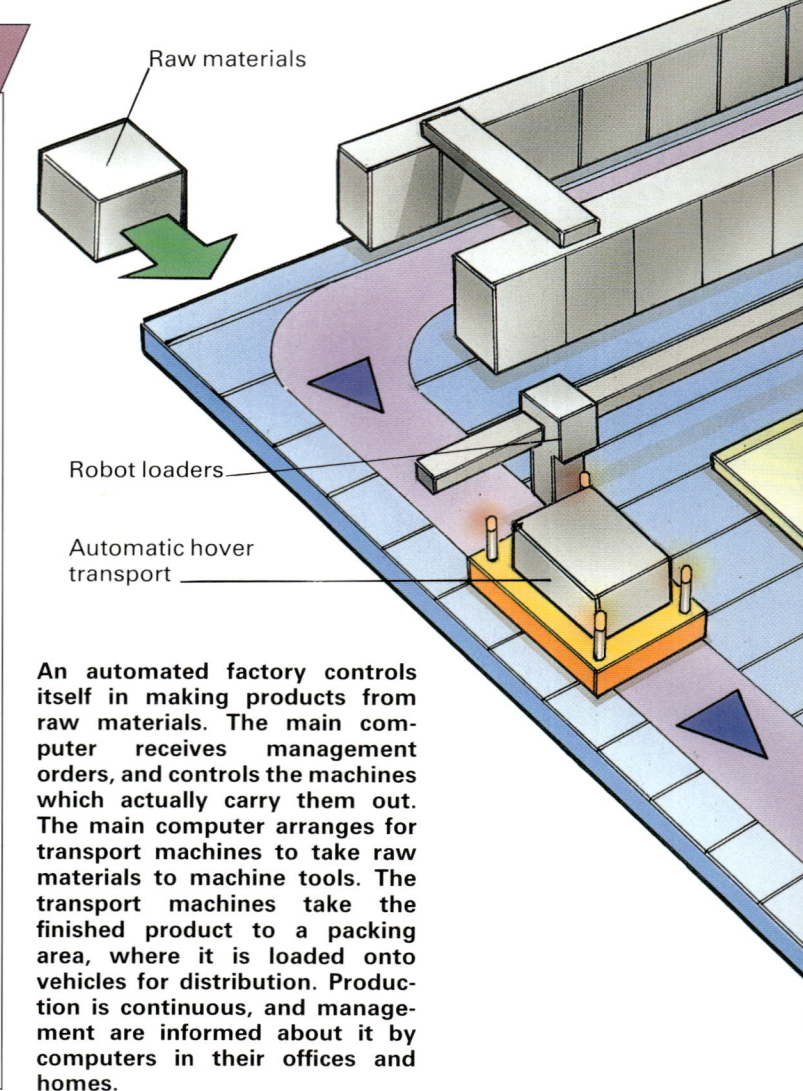

- Raw materials
- Robot loaders
- Automatic hover transport

An automated factory controls itself in making products from raw materials. The main computer receives management orders, and controls the machines which actually carry them out. The main computer arranges for transport machines to take raw materials to machine tools. The transport machines take the finished product to a packing area, where it is loaded onto vehicles for distribution. Production is continuous, and management are informed about it by computers in their offices and homes.

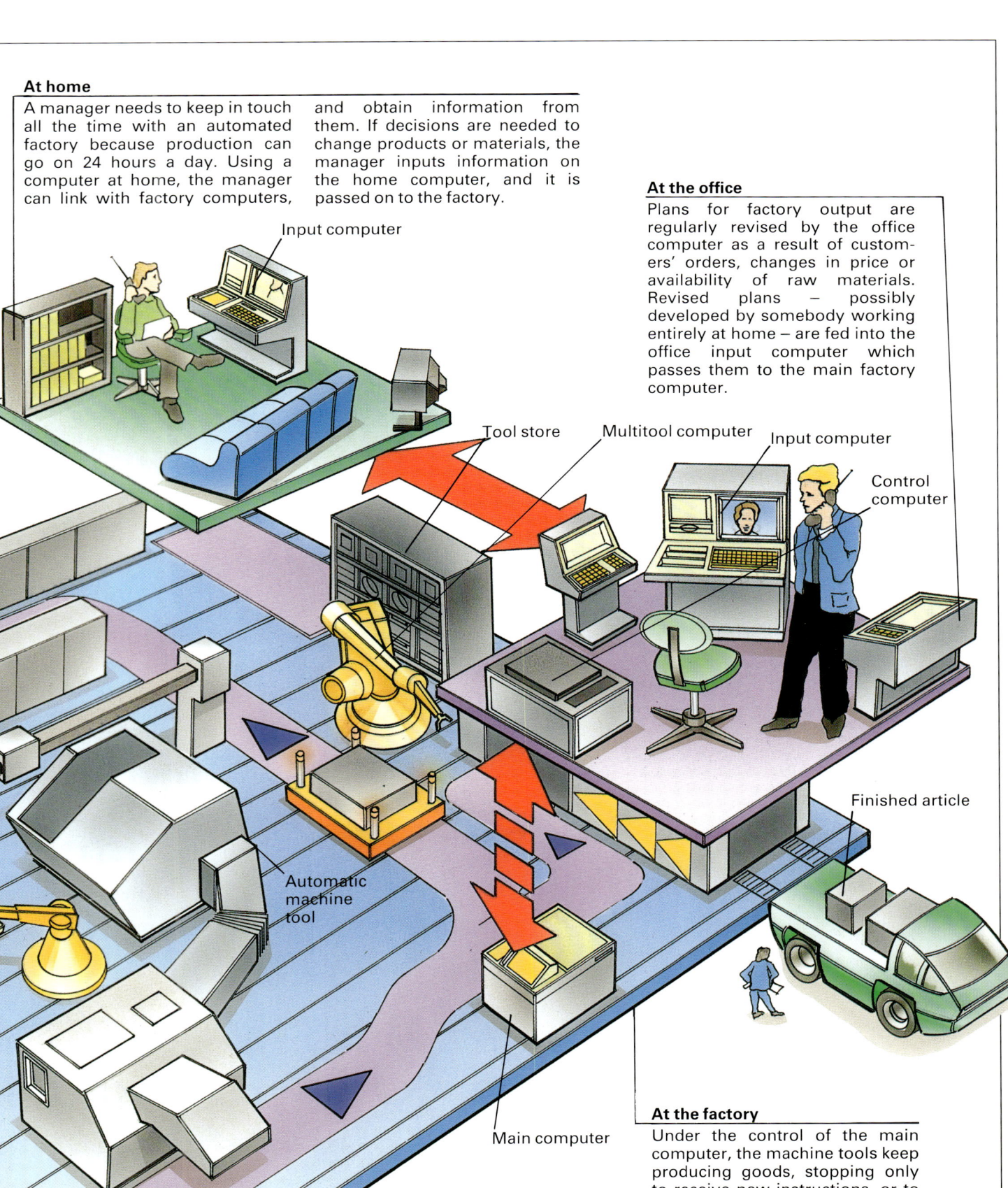

At home
A manager needs to keep in touch all the time with an automated factory because production can go on 24 hours a day. Using a computer at home, the manager can link with factory computers, and obtain information from them. If decisions are needed to change products or materials, the manager inputs information on the home computer, and it is passed on to the factory.

At the office
Plans for factory output are regularly revised by the office computer as a result of customers' orders, changes in price or availability of raw materials. Revised plans – possibly developed by somebody working entirely at home – are fed into the office input computer which passes them to the main factory computer.

At the factory
Under the control of the main computer, the machine tools keep producing goods, stopping only to receive new instructions, or to be given different tools when a different type of product is to be made. A multitool computer works out the tools necessary for individual tasks, and selects them from the tool store. Hover transports automatically carry everything that travels to or from the machine tools.

Growth of service industries

Using robots frees people for jobs that only human beings can do. Many such jobs involve providing a service for other people, and these workers are said to be in the service industries. They provide services such as cleaning, selling or retailing, hotels and catering, as well as banking, education, law and government, and many others. Most workers in these areas meet customers or clients, and provide a service for which they charge money. For example, a lawyer charges a fee for giving advice or representing you in court. Computers and other technology already make service industries more efficient, and in future robots will probably make them even more so.

Interior of a modern American hotel

Dangerous jobs

Some work is impossible for human beings to do, like assembling radioactive parts of a nuclear reactor. Such work can only be done by remote control, using robots which can operate without damage in a radioactive place. The work is supervised from behind protective screens or walls by technicians who watch progress by television and control the equipment. Another example of risky work done by robots is mining in very narrow seams, where robots can extract coal or other minerals in places too cramped or unstable for people to be safe. Bomb disposal robots approach a bomb without any risk to the robot operator. They can pick up a bomb and place it in a bomb-proof container, to be defused.

A bomb disposal robot picks up a suspect suitcase

Vital services

In an emergency such as a fire, accident, or crime in the home, people's safety depends on how quickly they can contact the emergency services. Fire, ambulance, and police services will leave their base to help as soon as they receive a message. A vital part of the message is the exact location of the emergency, and much time may be lost giving addresses, and working out the best route. One way of saving time is a radio transmitter attached to a fire or security alarm. In an emergency it will automatically transmit details of the location. A fire engine with a radio receiver will be able to take the location message and its on-board computer will show the location of the fire and the best route to it. Ambulance crews will radio the hospital to give details of a victim's injuries.

Control centre at a police station

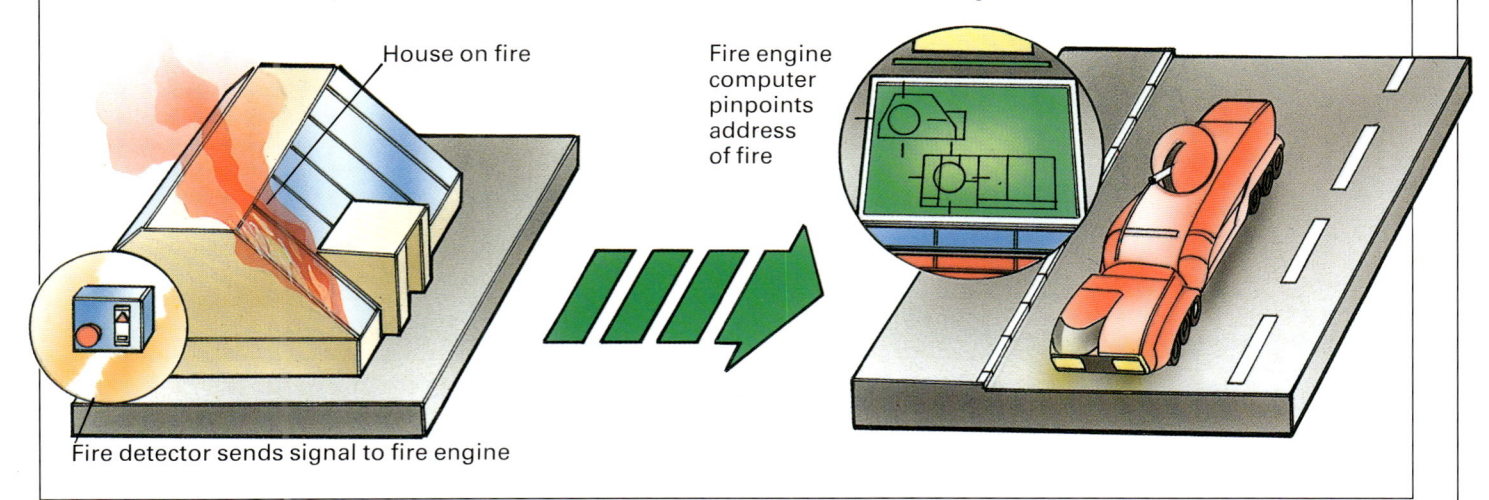

House on fire

Fire engine computer pinpoints address of fire

Fire detector sends signal to fire engine

Criminals

Electronic tagging is a way of restricting criminals' freedom with less expense than putting them in prison. A belt, fitted round the criminal's ankle, carries an electronic device which sends out a coded radio signal. The receiver for the signal is a special telephone fitted in the criminal's home. If the criminal tries to leave home, the signal is broken, and the telephone automatically contacts the police. Electronic tagging is particularly useful for people awaiting trial for crimes, and who may be found innocent. The police can ensure that they will come for trial with no risk of imprisoning innocent people.

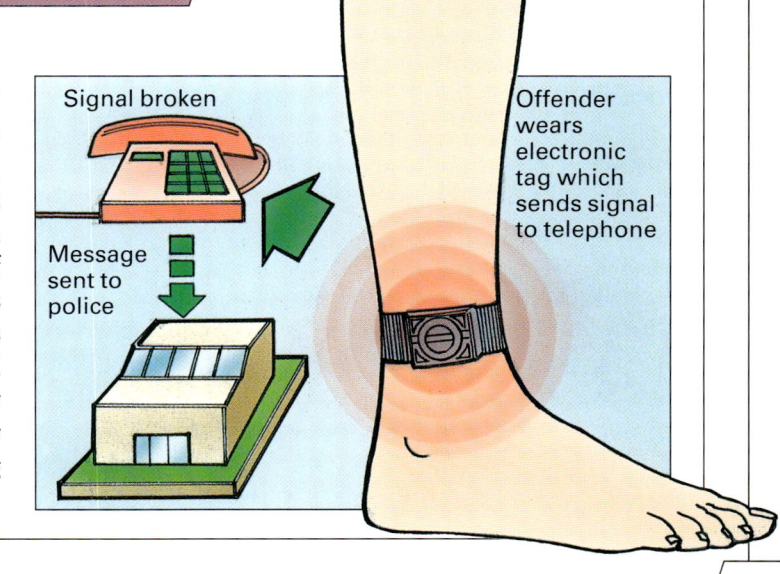

Signal broken

Message sent to police

Offender wears electronic tag which sends signal to telephone

17

Farming and food

Farming was one of the first industries to be mechanized, with machines for threshing and harvesting. It was also one of the first to use solar power, in greenhouses. In recent years, many advances have come from the development of better livestock and types of plant through the use of genetic engineering. The results include food animals that mature more quickly, and crop plants that tolerate cold climates or poor rainfall. But it looks as if the next developments may be computerization and automation, already widespread in manufacturing industries. Future farms will use robots for harvesting, milking cows, or monitoring grain in store.

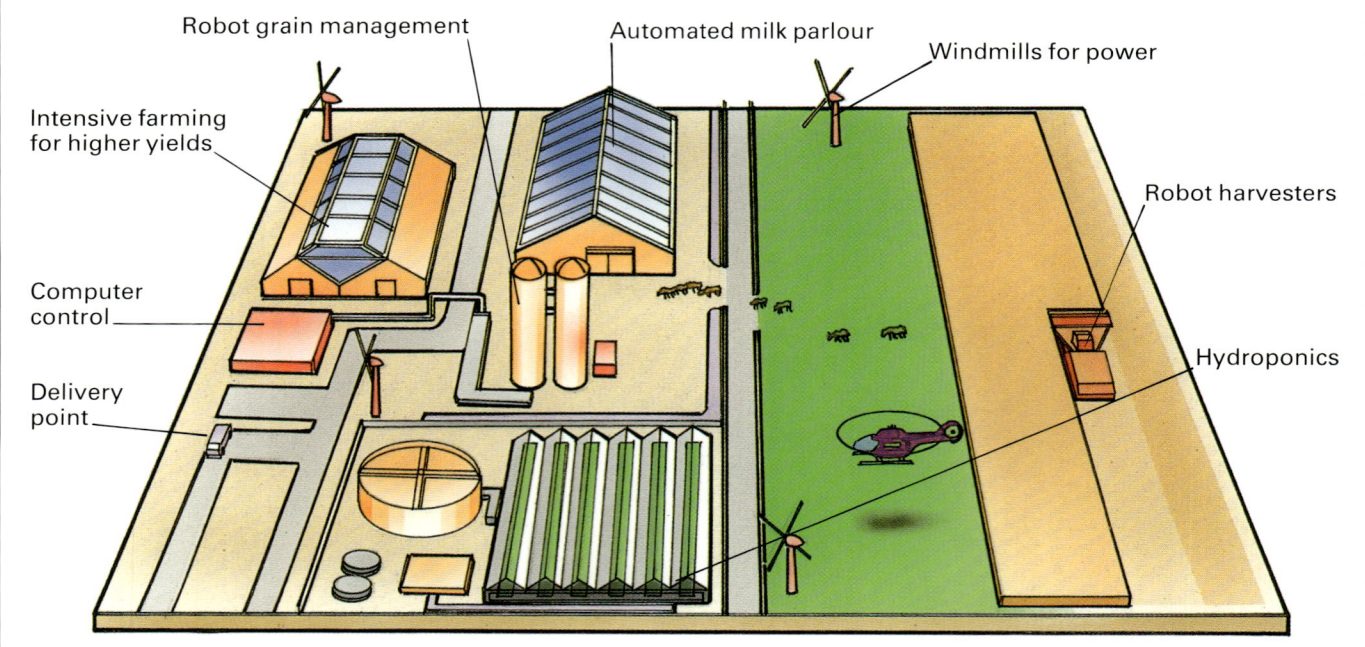

- Robot grain management
- Automated milk parlour
- Windmills for power
- Intensive farming for higher yields
- Robot harvesters
- Computer control
- Hydroponics
- Delivery point

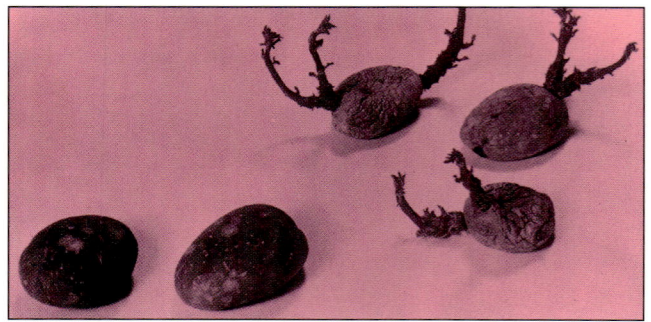

Irradiated potatoes do not sprout in store.

Growing plants without soil using hydroponics

Applying new technology to farms may include a form of electronic tagging, by which a computer will record not only a cow's location, but also its activity and health. Intensive crop farming will include hydroponics, growing plants without soil. The plants are supported in a wire mesh and are fed entirely by water containing a computer-controlled mixture of chemicals. Preserving farm produce may be done by irradiation, in which radioactivity kills bacteria, bugs and mould, also slowing down ripening and sprouting.

Cows wearing collars with electronic tags

The city

A vertical city with homes, offices, factories, shops and recreational facilities all under one roof is perfectly possible with skyscraper technology. Many buildings and developments already have enough space to house a small town, especially in the United States. Homes, shops and offices are together, linked by corridors and lifts. The whole building can efficiently be kept warm in winter and cool in summer, so that travel to work within the building will be easy and pleasant. Alternatives, especially in countries such as Japan that are running out of living space on land, include floating cities built on artificial islands and underwater cities in watertight domes on the sea bed. The island would be connected to the mainland by a causeway or a bridge carrying a road and a high-speed rail link. An underwater city would have lift shafts up to the surface, with a landing platform for helicopters or vertical take-off aircraft. Eventually it may be possible to construct a city in space or on the Moon.

A design for a mile-high skyscraper

Computer future

The rapid pace of developments in computers in the 1970s and 1980s is almost certain to continue right through the 1990s and into the 2000s. As the memory chips become more efficient, the average size of computers will continue to decrease. Wristwatch computers will soon combine timekeeping with a diary, address book, and notepad. Higher priced watches will also give the user a link to other computers and to the telephone network. They will use voice communication. Human speech will tell the computer what to do, and the computer will report back to its operator through a speech synthesizer.

Improved memory, and new software, will soon give computers artificial intelligence, so that they can think, ask questions, and solve problems without having to be given detailed instructions. Computers will also be able to automatically translate from one language to another. This development will greatly improve communications throughout the world.

Another *very* futuristic idea involves connecting nerve cells directly to a computer's memory.

How a nerve cell might grow on a silicon chip

City of the future
Some passengers fly direct to an inner city interchange by vertical take-off and landing aircraft (1) or by airship (2). Not far away, short take-off and landing aircraft land at an inner city airstrip (3). Serving the airstrip is a monorail (4) which has a central station (5). From an autotaxi terminal (6) an autotaxi (7) travels, guided by underground cables. Motorists travel on a highway (8) while pedestrians move round the city on a fast three-lane walkway (9). Shorter walkways (10) carry passengers from other transport to the super train (11), which they board at a special terminal (12). Transport systems, and their passengers, communicate by radio through a communications dish (13) or by using the network of fibre-optic cables (14).

COMMUNICATIONS

A busy inner city interchange of the future combines all forms of transport with road, rail, and air transport systems, that are as free of pollution and noise as possible. A wide variety of choice enables travellers to pick a form of transport that they can afford and that best suits the distance they are travelling. People with luggage, or disabled people, will be able to move between vehicles on the kind of walkways now seen only in airports. Traffic will no longer be a mass of separate vehicles, but part of a system in which each vehicle is in constant communication with a network. This will help avoid traffic congestion, and warn drivers of likely hazards. Communications systems will be flexible too, using varied methods of linking with fibre-optic cables or radio networks. They will carry telephone messages, television signals and computer data.

Automation

Automatic pilots on aircraft have increased safety and made a pilot's job very much easier, especially on long flights where the pilot's concentration might otherwise falter. Railways have benefited from automation through computer-controlled signalling, allowing higher speeds and more trains along a section of track. Machines can automatically produce a traveller's choice of ticket, and other machines can check the ticket at stations, and collect the ticket if necessary.

Driverless trains, widely used on some London Underground lines, are spreading to other railways. For example, they are used to provide a shuttle service round airports and exhibition centres. A computer controls a network, varying each train's speed as necessary, and stopping it at each station. Sensors tell the computer where each train is, and it makes sure that the trains do not crash into each other.

Machines for issuing automated train tickets

Driverless monorail train (yellow) at an airport

Bullet trains

The original Japanese Bullet Train is a very fast, conventional train. The future bullet train will be much more efficient – it will overcome the problem of a high-speed train's movement being affected by resistance from air in the atmosphere. The bullet train uses air pressure to push it along a sealed tunnel. Pumps in the tunnel create a vacuum in front of the train, and the air pressure behind pushes the train into it. When the train is in a station, special airlocks allow passengers to enter or leave without leaking air into the tunnel. The train itself is pressurized, to stop air leaking from it into the vacuum in front. But building tunnels is very expensive indeed, and this will limit the number of bullet trains.

An experimental Japanese bullet train

Autocars

Autocars are a development of the passenger transporters and robots now used for transport round factories and other large sites. A control track under the road passes signals to and from the autocar about other vehicles, and the route to be taken. The autocar computer interprets this information, passing instructions to the engine, steering, and brakes. In this way the car is controlled, it is kept at a safe distance from other vehicles, and it turns onto other roads when necessary, perhaps to avoid a traffic jam or to divert round roadworks. A radar sensor at the front of the autocar watches for obstructions or emergencies. In an emergency, the autocar computer will quickly stop the vehicle.

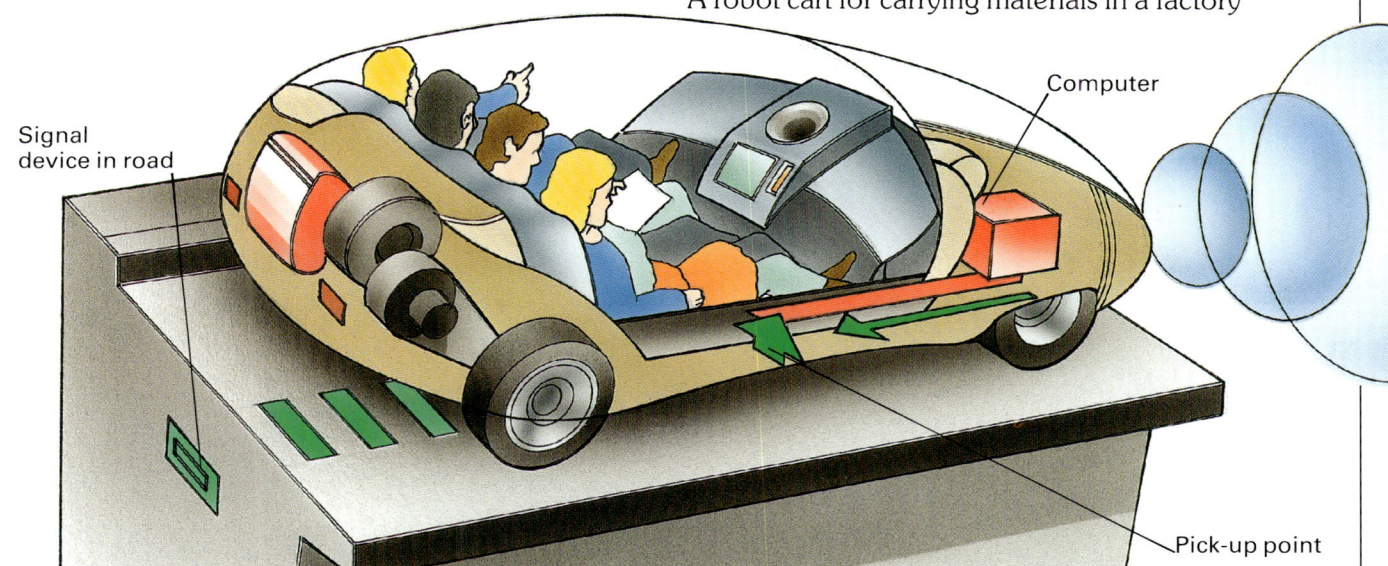

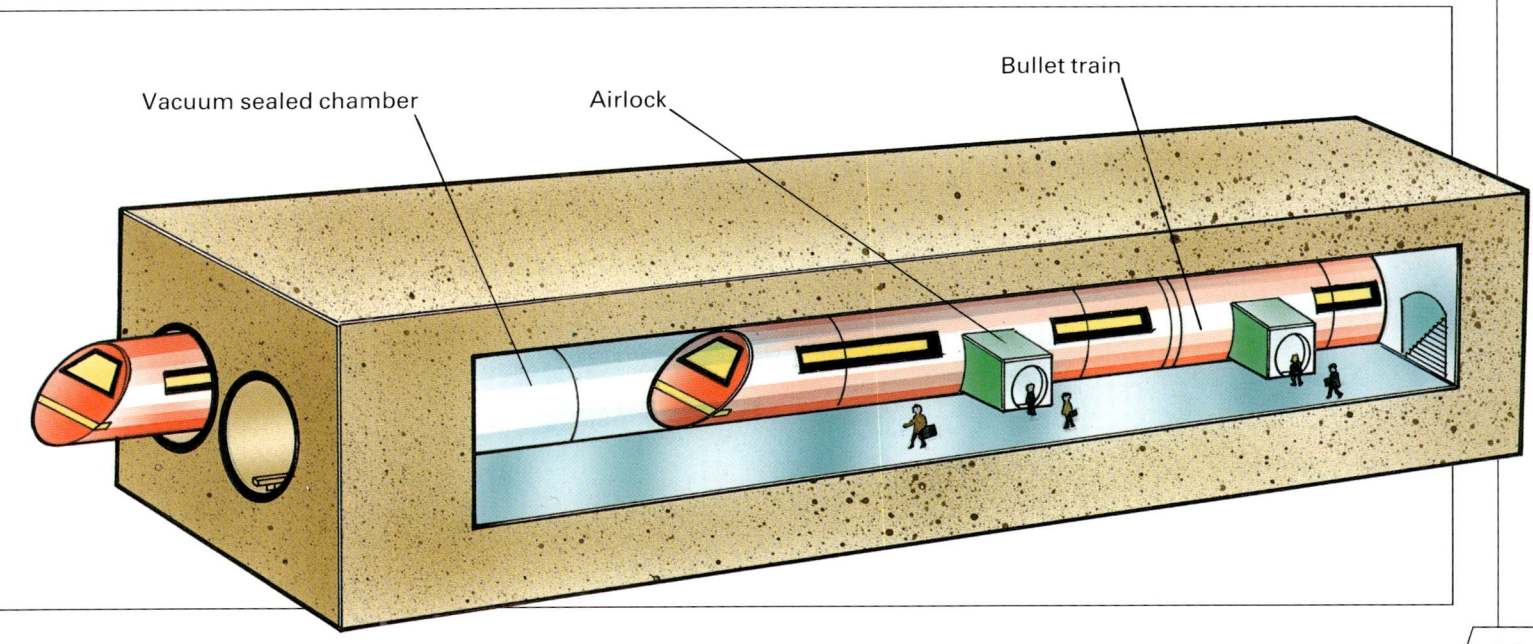

A robot cart for carrying materials in a factory

Signal device in road

Computer

Pick-up point

Vacuum sealed chamber

Airlock

Bullet train

Access to the skies

Vertical take-off and landing (VTOL) aircraft make more city-centre airports likely. They avoid or replace long journeys to airports outside cities. VTOL aircraft tilt engines upwards for take-off, and turn them horizontal for normal flight. Short take-off and landing (STOL) aircraft have big engines and great lift, and can use very short runways. Airships were once dangerous because they used inflammable hydrogen gas for lift. Modern ones use safe helium instead, and new, light engines. They are not very fast, and may be used more for carrying cargo than passengers.

A vertical take-off and landing aircraft

Optica, a short take-off and landing craft

A modern helium-filled airship

Space hop

Planes have been proposed that will fly between airports on opposite sides of the Earth, but go into space on the way. The key to their technology is their engines, which will power winged flight in the atmosphere, burning fuel in air. As the aircraft moves out of the atmosphere, the engines start using oxygen, carried on board, instead of air. Soon after reaching space, the aircraft can stop its engines, and coast round the Earth in orbit. When it nears its destination the engines push it towards Earth and guide the aircraft to its landing. The idea combines the advantages of a modern airliner and a space shuttle, using existing airports.

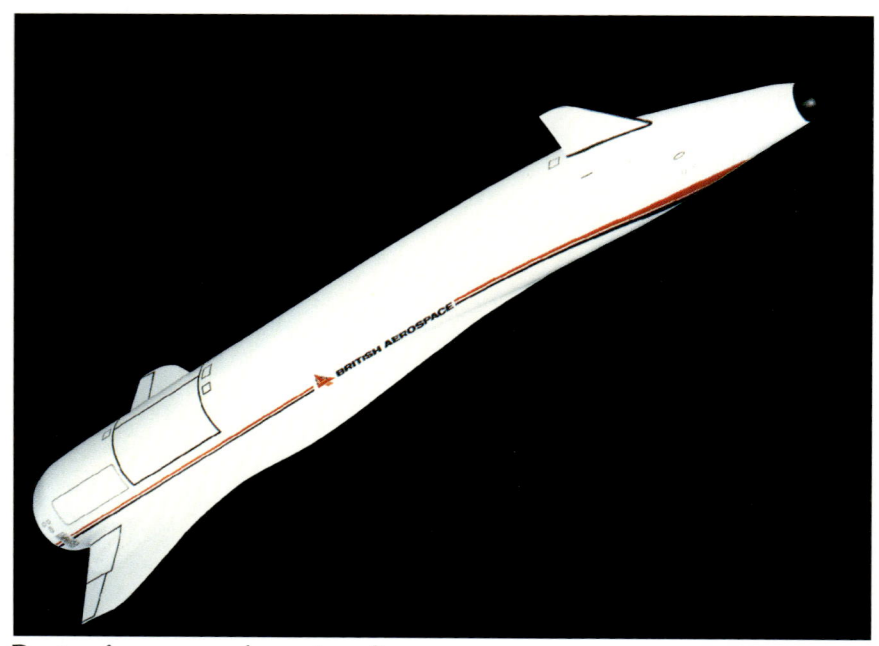

Design for a space-hop aircraft

Communication

For more than 100 years, the telephone has provided voice communication for people who are apart. Recently, fax technology has enabled people to send documents, using telephone lines. Telephone links can now provide full visual communications, as well as sound, and videophones are being used in some places. Each videophone has a small video camera and television screen, corresponding to the microphone and earpiece in a conventional phone. Just as conventional telephones can be used for "conferencing", so videophones can be linked for several people in different areas to communicate with each other. Each videophone sends signals by radio to a communications satellite, which sends the signal on to each of the other videophones in the conference. To see and hear the other conference members, each person will need extra screens and loudspeakers. In a conference involving four videophones, each participant will need a total of three screens and speakers.

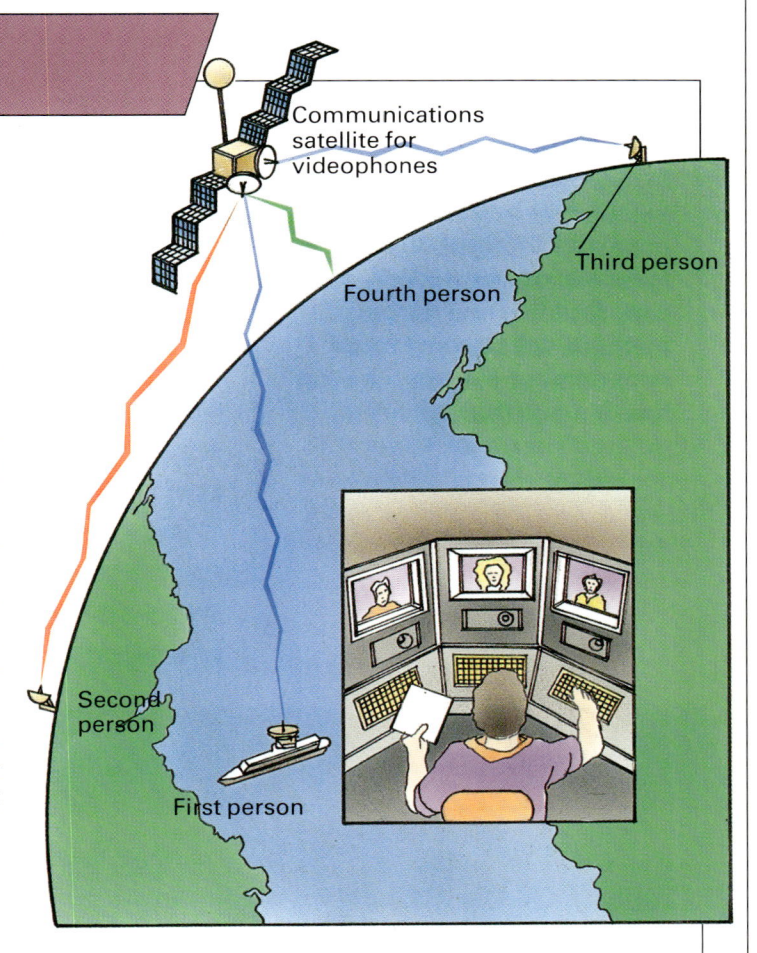

A child using a compact videophone to see and talk to his father

FUTURE EARTH

Keeping the Earth clean will be a growing concern for many years to come. This means reducing pollution from factories, power stations, and cars. Building and transport methods will become more environment-friendly, causing less damage through noise, pollution or waste. Current sources of energy will become scarcer. New, cleaner ways of producing it will develop.

New technology will improve people's living standards in many ways. Machines will continue to bring greater comfort, longer lives, more wealth, and greater choice in entertainment. But the machines will also increase some of the world's problems, and greater emphasis will be needed on solving problems that result from changing technology. For example, machines use energy, particularly as electricity, so more machines will use more energy and make energy scarcer. But years of generating electricity have made the Earth polluted, and electricity generation will have to be done in cleaner ways in future. Other problems to be tackled centre on the world's steadily growing population which will produce more mouths to feed, and which will require more use of land for housing and farming.

Future problems

Car pollution will continue to be a problem for many years. Car exhausts are made cleaner by catalytic converters, which will become compulsory in more and more countries. Making cars smaller and lighter makes them burn less fuel, saving energy. But all petrol-driven cars pollute the atmosphere with carbon dioxide gas. This gas increases the greenhouse effect, making the Earth overheat through retaining more of the Sun's energy. Electric cars do not burn fuel, are quiet, and are environmentally friendly. They look likely to replace many petrol cars.

This car produces little carbon dioxide.

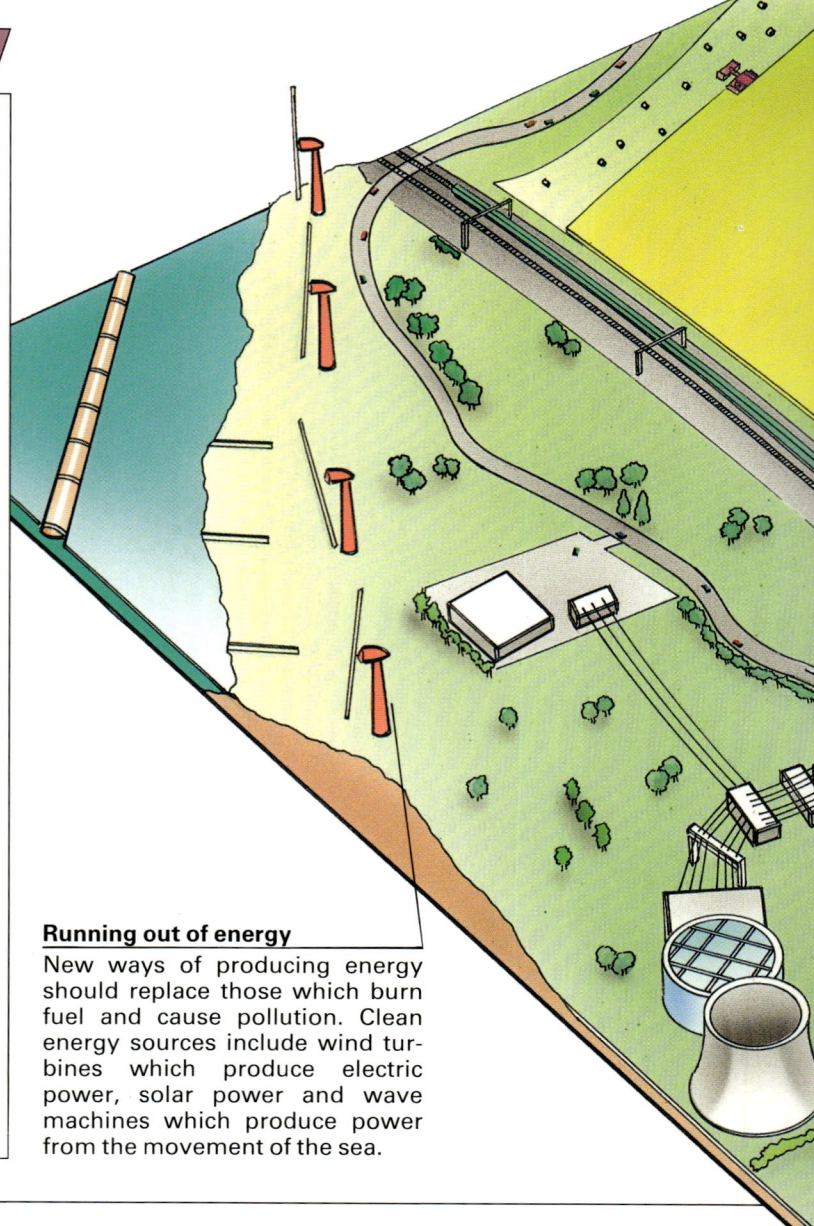

Running out of energy
New ways of producing energy should replace those which burn fuel and cause pollution. Clean energy sources include wind turbines which produce electric power, solar power and wave machines which produce power from the movement of the sea.

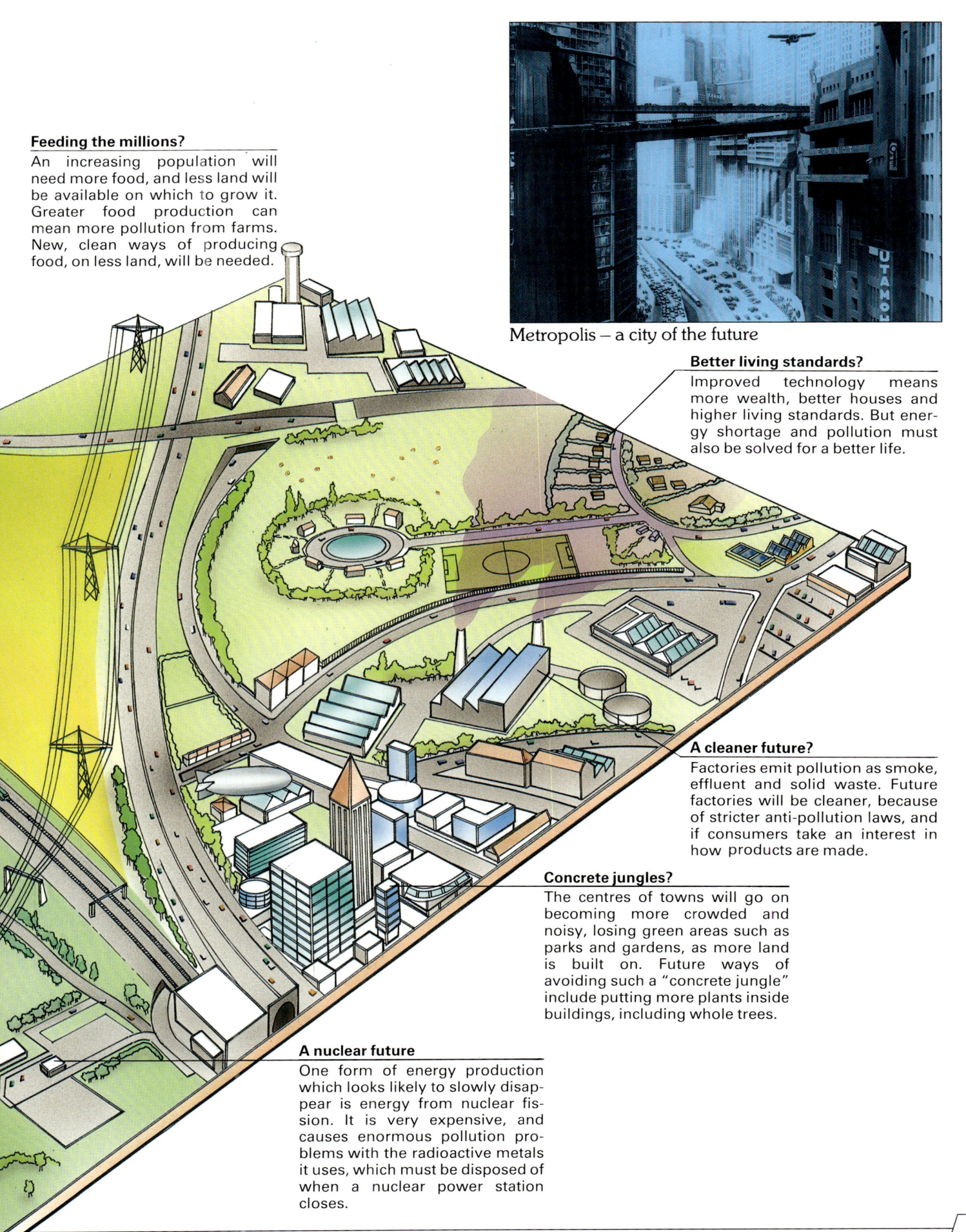

Feeding the millions?
An increasing population will need more food, and less land will be available on which to grow it. Greater food production can mean more pollution from farms. New, clean ways of producing food, on less land, will be needed.

Metropolis – a city of the future

Better living standards?
Improved technology means more wealth, better houses and higher living standards. But energy shortage and pollution must also be solved for a better life.

A cleaner future?
Factories emit pollution as smoke, effluent and solid waste. Future factories will be cleaner, because of stricter anti-pollution laws, and if consumers take an interest in how products are made.

Concrete jungles?
The centres of towns will go on becoming more crowded and noisy, losing green areas such as parks and gardens, as more land is built on. Future ways of avoiding such a "concrete jungle" include putting more plants inside buildings, including whole trees.

A nuclear future
One form of energy production which looks likely to slowly disappear is energy from nuclear fission. It is very expensive, and causes enormous pollution problems with the radioactive metals it uses, which must be disposed of when a nuclear power station closes.

Future energy

Much electricity comes from burning fossil fuels such as coal or oil, supplies of which may eventually run out. The burning produces pollution, causing problems such as acid rain. This can be avoided by making power without burning. Tides and waves in the world's oceans contain energy which can be converted to electricity. Tide turbines across a river mouth or a narrow channel turn tidal energy into electricity. Wave machines make electric power from wave motion. Sea thermal power comes from the Sun's heat on oceans. On land, geothermal power comes from steam created by heat within the Earth. Wind turbines produce electricity, and solar power units turn sunlight into electricity.

Nuclear power comes from nuclear fission, and is the most widely used alternative to fossil fuels. But at present it is expensive, and has pollution problems. A possible future alternative is nuclear fusion, which harnesses the power of the hydrogen bomb.

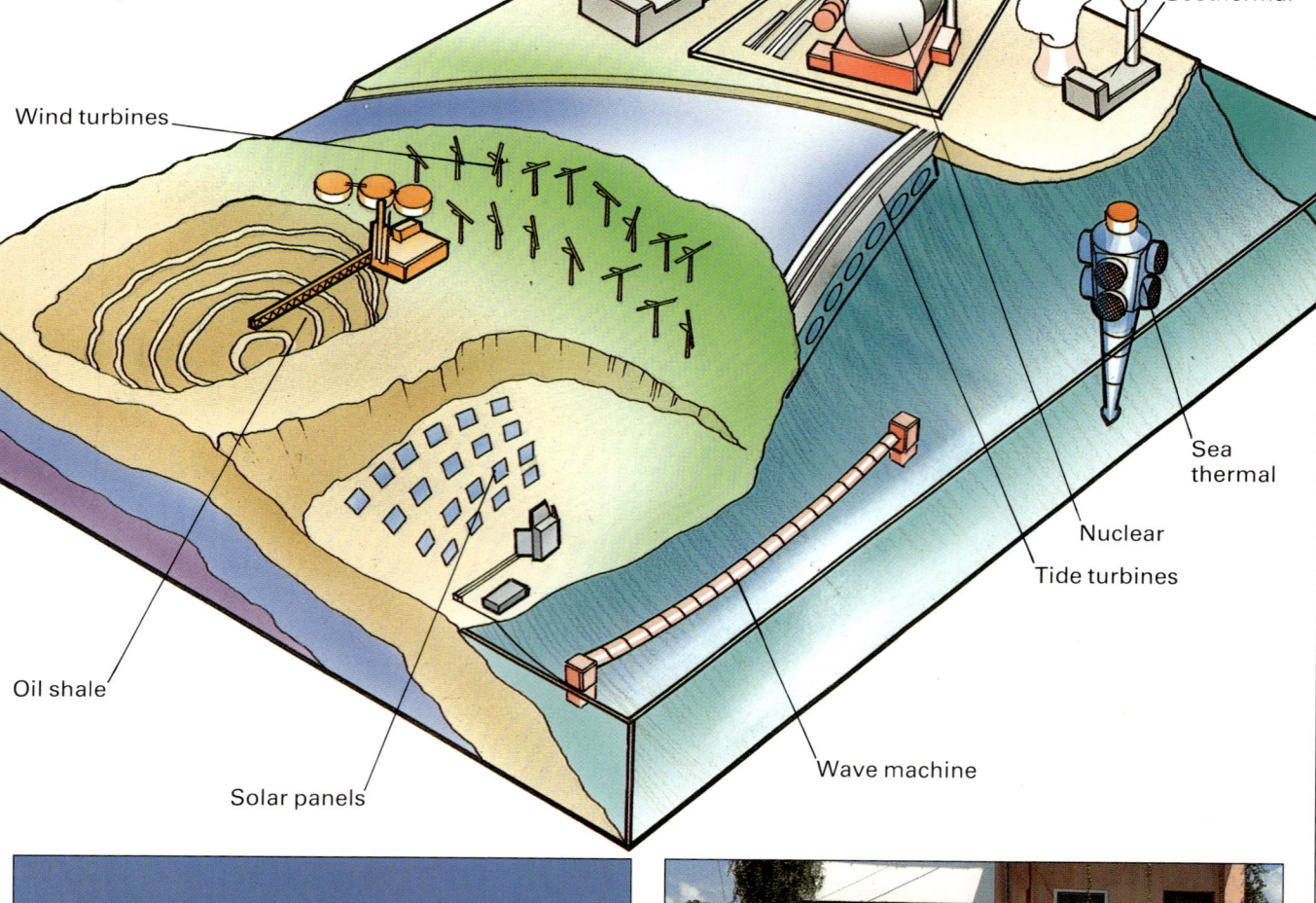

Windmills for generating electricity

Solar panels for heating water

Better use of land

Much of the Earth's land lies empty and unused. Some is waterlogged by being near a river or the sea. Other land is derelict, having been used for mining, industry or disposing of waste. Much more land is unused because it is mountainous, desert or in very cold parts of the world. Unfortunately, land that can be used for the first time, such as tropical rainforest, is running out and there are great problems in using it. Deforestation destroys animal habitats, and increases the amount of carbon dioxide in the atmosphere. The need to make better use of land, because of increasing population, is steadily growing. Answers to these problems include making more land by building dikes to reclaim low-lying areas that at present are under the sea.

A farm with crops growing on reclaimed land in the Netherlands

Cleaner atmosphere

The most dramatic example of the need for the Earth to be cleaner is what is happening in the atmosphere. Industry, power stations and transport all pour out pollution such as sulphur compounds. The sulphur compounds dissolve in raindrops which fall as acid rain. Much carbon dioxide is converted into oxygen by plants, particularly trees. But the number of trees is falling as forests are cleared for building or farming, or trees are killed by acid rain. So the amount of carbon dioxide in the air is growing. This dirtying of the atmosphere increases the greenhouse effect. Extra carbon dioxide and dust in the air make the atmosphere reflect heat down again. This leads to global warming and to changes in climate.

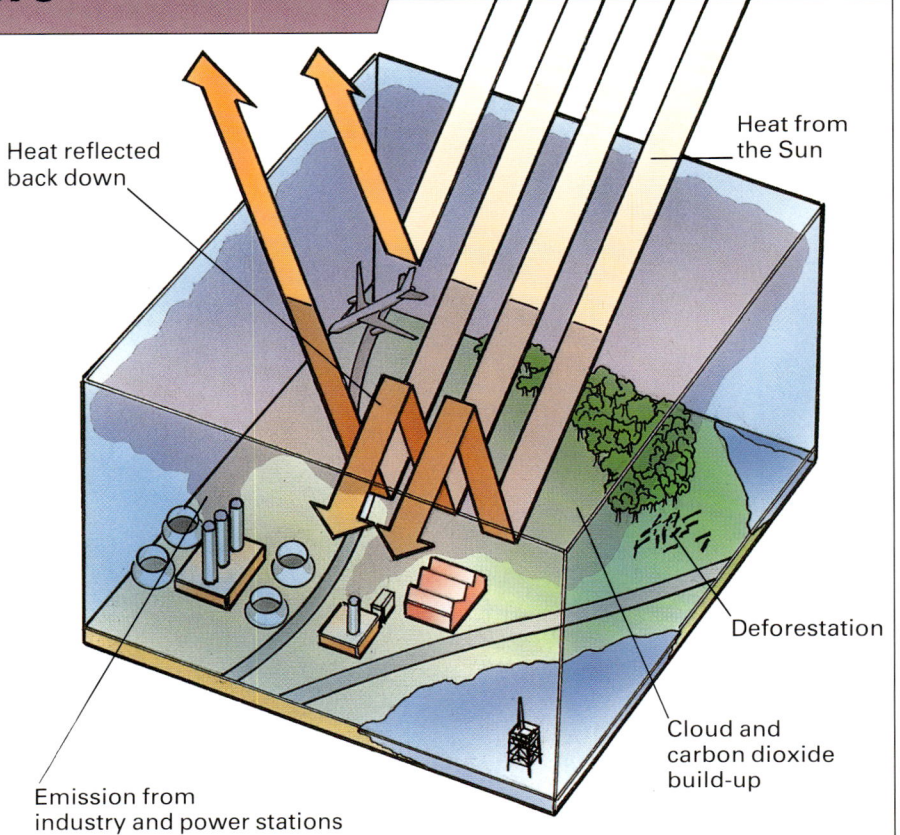

WORKING IN SPACE

People have already spent more than a year living in space, and construction techniques have been developed for assembling space stations. Provided that the cost of shuttling material into space can be brought down by developing better rockets, these techniques will be used to make orbiting space stations and Moon bases. Some stations will become factories for producing new materials and products that can only be made in zero-gravity conditions, or in a vacuum. Such factories will be automated, running themselves with computer links to Earth. Human beings will be used for activities such as constructing space stations and bases, and carrying out scientific research.

So far, space has been used mainly for research, gaining information about the Moon, Solar System and the Universe. Future possible uses include manufacturing in zero-gravity conditions, mining in space, or even disposing of pollution such as the waste from nuclear reactors. This will need cheap vehicles for transport into Earth orbit and for travelling the long distances between planets.

Working at a space station

A space vehicle (1) constantly shuttles materials and people from Earth (2). Most space stations and space craft will be assembled in space (3). People working outside vehicles wear extra-vehicular activity (EVA) suits (4) to keep them alive in space. Space construction includes welding parts together (5). Living modules (6) spin to give people artificial gravity. Mining activity on the Moon will be automated (7). Major transport work, like moving an asteroid (8) towards Earth for mining (9), will need nuclear-powered rockets such as the NERVA.

NERVA

Liquid hydrogen

NERVA reactor

Adjusting thrusters

Nozzle

Resources

Much of the material for building space stations is available in space. The Moon, for example, has more iron and titanium than the Earth, and has plenty of aluminium and silicon. Much of the material needed to build a large Moon station could be mined and refined there, avoiding the expense of carrying the materials from Earth. On the Moon, solar energy could be used to convert ores into metals for sending back to Earth.

The greatest resource from space is constant sunlight. Huge solar-powered satellites will be able to beam down energy that can be converted into electricity on Earth.

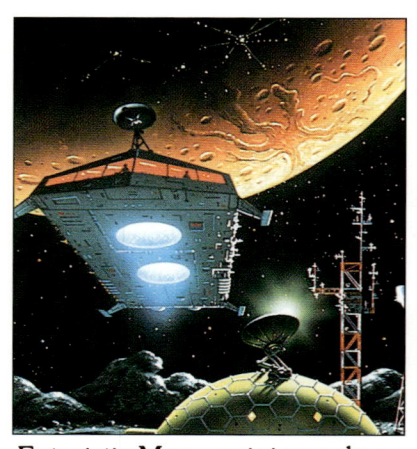

Futuristic Moon-mining colony

A sample of Moon rock

Biosphere

For people to live permanently on the Moon, an artificial biosphere would be built, following the pattern of the Earth's biosphere. The biosphere consists of air, soil, water in rivers and oceans, and the plants and animals they support. Each part of the biosphere is in balance, and the same balances would be needed on the Moon. As the Moon does not have enough gravity to hold an atmosphere, the air of the biosphere would have to be contained within an envelope or cover. The most likely materials to build the envelope are metal and glass, both easily extracted or made from minerals obtained on the Moon. The envelope, like the Earth's upper atmosphere, would have to shield the lower parts from the Sun's ultraviolet light. Water, nitrogen and carbon, all essential for life, would be transported from Earth, and constantly recycled within the biosphere. Water evaporating in the lower biosphere, for example, would form clouds or condense on the envelope at night, running down it to form streams at its base. Plants would be grown within the biosphere to produce oxygen and food. To avoid pollution, energy could be produced outside the biosphere from solar panels, and all machines, including transport, would be electric-powered.

Volunteers leave an artificial biosphere built on Earth

Space colonies

Colonies in space, orbiting around the Earth or another planet, would need to be huge to be able to support permanent inhabitants. There would be plenty of energy from solar panels, but all materials for building and for sustaining life would have to be transported to the colony from Earth or the Moon. Once the space colony was operational, all its contents would be carefully conserved and recycled. Plants would be grown in sunlight to make oxygen from carbon dioxide breathed out by human beings. Water could be recycled and distilled to purify it using solar energy. For the comfort of inhabitants, and for their convenience in working and moving around, artificial gravity would be created by making the space colony spin about its axis. Once started, it would keep spinning. Stations with a larger radius or a faster spin would have greater gravity.

Artist's impression of a future space colony

Work on the Space Shuttle

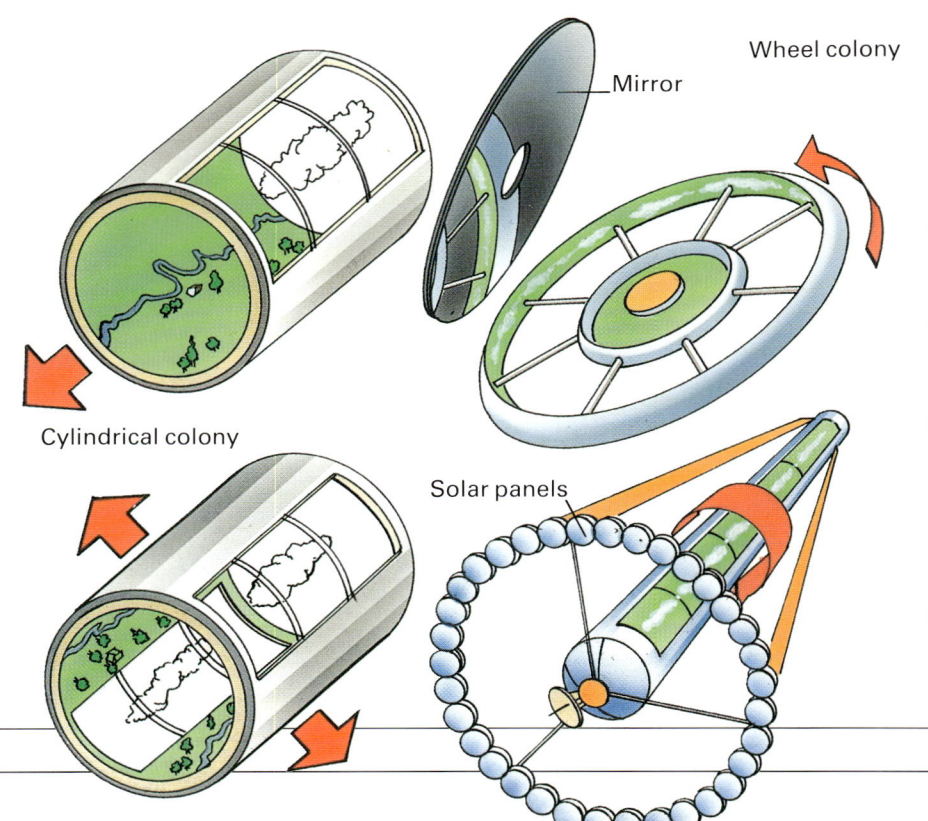

Cylindrical colony

Wheel colony

Mirror

Solar panels

FACT OR FANTASY

Looking into the future to guess what will happen is not easy. Most of the items in this book simply assume the technology – ways of doing things – that is already developed will be used more widely in the future. No doubt the new products that appear in the next 25 years will affect people's lives as greatly as the changes brought by video machines, robots in industry, or air travel have in the previous generation's lives. But predicting changes is a matter of guesswork.

Computers – a safe bet

It is easy to assume that computers will be used more and more widely, and will be built in to more and more appliances, and even into buildings such as homes. For 20 years or so, computers have been steadily improving, becoming cheaper, and have been ever more widely used. Cheap new input devices such as a joystick or a mouse have been added. It seems reasonable to expect that input direct from the human voice will follow shortly, making a keyboard unnecessary. Size will go on reducing. With wallet-sized computers available at the beginning of the 1990s, it seems likely that watch-sized computers will be common by the end of the 1990s.

Guessing about computer application is more difficult. Ten years ago, the Prestel system was just starting up in Britain, using telephone lines to link offices and homes with information computers. Anyone looking at the system then would have seen quite a cheap system allowing families to communicate with each other on their television screens, or order goods at any time of the day or night. They might have guessed that by now millions of homes would have installed one. In some countries, such as France and Japan, that has happened, but in Britain the proportion of homes on such a system is small.

Fact: the Soviet MIR space station in orbit

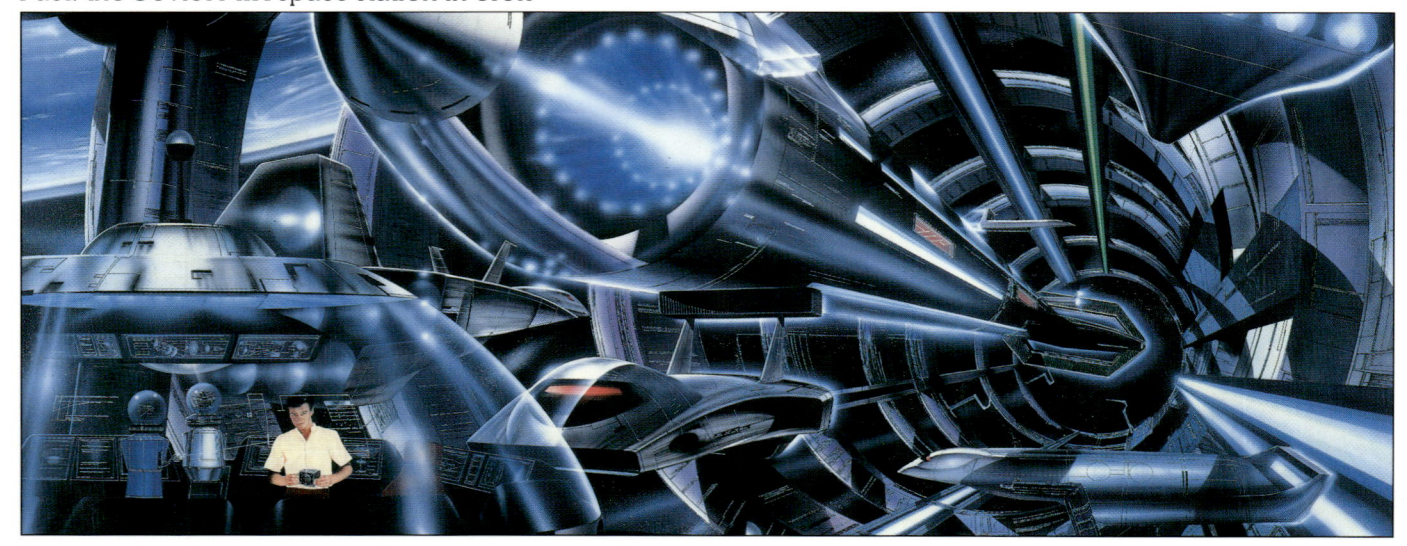

Fantasy: Artist's impression of a rotating space colony

GLOSSARY

alternative energy method of producing electrical or heat energy for homes or workplaces as an alternative to burning fossil fuels or using nuclear energy.

autocar driverless car controlled by a computer and a control track built into the road.

automation production of goods by machines that control themselves and operate without any human assistance.

biomass organic matter, mainly from plants, used as a source of energy by burning or decaying to produce an inflammable gas.

biosphere parts of the Earth (or any other planet or heavenly body) that support life – requiring air, water, and soil.

bullet train train that runs in a tunnel, and is propelled mainly by air pressure in a way similar to that in which a bullet is forced along a gun barrel.

CAT scan abbreviation of Computerized Axial Tomography. This is a method of using X-rays to take "pictures" of a section through the human body.

computer machine that solves problems by processing information according to a set of instructions called a program. Many computers solve problems relating to control of other devices and machines.

environment all of the conditions in which a plant or animal lives. It includes the atmosphere and soil, as well as the effects of other plants and animals. It often refers to the environment of all life on Earth.

fax abbreviation of facsimile transmission, a method of sending copies of a document along a telephone line to a distant receiver.

fibre-optics method of sending signals or images by passing light along glass-fibre cables.

fossil fuel material formed inside the Earth from decayed plant or animal matter, and which can be burnt to produce heat. The main fossil fuels are coal, natural gas, and petroleum.

greenhouse effect warming of the atmosphere caused by heat that has been radiated or reflected from the Earth's surface being reflected down by a layer of carbon dioxide in the atmosphere.

hologram a three-dimensional image of an object produced using lasers.

hydroponics technique for growing plants by suspending the plant with its roots hanging in a solution of nutrients.

laser device for producing a strong, narrow beam of single-colour light which can be directed very precisely.

laser surgery medical technique that involves use of lasers for operations such as welding a detached retina or destroying a tumour.

light-sensitive describing materials that have surfaces which change in some way, such as generating an electric current, when light strikes them.

microsurgery surgery in which special instruments are used under a microscope or similar device.

pollution change in the biosphere caused by the release of poisonous or harmful substances, so making the environment unsafe or destroying it.

recycling reusing materials, such as paper or glass, by collecting them after they have been used, and processing them to help to make new paper or glass.

resource anything which is in limited supply, such as fuels for energy or iron, and which can be used to make or move something.

robot machine that can sense, pick up, and move objects, and that can perform other operations on them. Robots can control themselves, following a pattern set by a computer.

service industry business that provides a service rather than goods. Examples are tourism and retailing.

short take-off and landing (STOL) aircraft aeroplane that needs only a short runway for take-off and landing.

simulator computer-controlled machine that creates sensory impressions, for example, of flying an aircraft.

technology application of science to produce a solution to a practical or industrial problem.

vertical take-off and landing (VTOL) aircraft aeroplane that can take off with no runway.

videophone type of telephone that transmits moving video pictures of users, in addition to speech.

voice synthesizer device that uses a computer to artificially produce the sounds of human speech.

INDEX

All entries in bold are found in the Glossary

acid rain 28
airports 21, 24
airships 24
alternative energy 4, **35**
ambulances 17
artificial intelligence 19
asteroids 31
atmosphere 29, 32
autocars 23, **35**
automation 14, 18, 22, **35**
autotaxis 20

banks 6, 9
bar codes 9
biomass 35
biosphere 32, **35**
biotechnology 10
bomb disposal 16
bullet trains 22, **35**

calculators 6
caravans 13
carbon dioxide 26, 29, 33
cars 23-26
CAT scan 11, **35**
catalytic converters 26
cinema 13
cities 8, 9, 19-21, 24, 27
coal 28
communications 4, 15, 17, 19-25, 34
communities 8, 9
computer games 12, 13
computers 5, 6, 9, 10, 14, 15, 18, 19, 34, **35**
concrete jungles 27
conferencing 25
criminals 17

dangerous jobs 16
deforestation 29
design 14
driverless trains 22
drugs 10

electric cars 26
electricity 26, 28, 32
electronic mail 14
electronic tagging 17, 18

emergency services 17
energy 5, 26, 28, 32, 33
environment 35
exercise 10

factories 5, 7, 14, 23, 26, 27
farming 18, 26, 27, 29
fax 25, **35**
feedback 14
fibre optics 21, **35**
fire services 17
flight simulators 13
floating cities 19
food 18, 26, 27, 32
fossil fuels 28, **35**
fuel 5, 24, 26, 28

gas 5
genetic engineering 10, 18
glass 7, 32
global warming 29
gravity 32, 33
greenhouse effect 26, **35**

health 10, 11
heating 5-7
holograms 12, **35**
home entertainment 12
home working 15
household tasks 5, 6
houses 4-8, 26-27, 34
hover transports 15
hydroponics 18, **35**

interactive video 12
irradiation 18

joysticks 34

land 26, 27, 29
land reclamation 29
laser surgery 11, **35**
lasers 11, **35**
leisure 12, 13, 26
lighting 5, 6
light-sensitive 35

management 14, 15
materials 5, 7, 14, 32

memory chips 19
metal 7, 32
methane gas 4
microsurgery 11, **35**
minerals 32
mining 16, 29, 31, 32
money 9
Moon 19, 30-32
mouse 34
multitool computers 15

NERVA 31
nerve cells 19
nuclear energy 27-28
nuclear fission 28
nuclear fusion 28
nuclear reactors 16, 30

offices 14, 15
oil 5, 28

passenger transporters 23
petrol 26
planes 20-22, 24
police 17
pollution 21, 26-30, 32, **35**
population 26, 27, 29
Prestel 34
programs 7, 9

rainforest 29
recycling 4, 7, 33, **35**
remote control 16
resources 35
robots 4-7, 14, 16, 18, 23, 34, **35**

satellites 25, 32
schools 9, 12
security 4-6
sensors 7, 14, 23
service industries 16, 17, **35**
shopping 6, 8, 9
shopping malls 9
short take-off and landing (STOL) aircraft 24, **35**
simulations 9, 12, 13, **35**
skills 9
solar energy 26, 32, 33

space 19, 30-33
space colonies 33
space shuttles 24, 33
space stations 31, 32
space transport 30, 31
space-hop aircraft 24
speech synthesizer 19
suburbs 8, 9
surgery 10, **35**

teachers 9
technology 35
telephones 6, 25, 34
theme parks 12, 13
thermal power 28
tourism 12, 13
tower blocks 8
trains 20, 22
transport 20-24, 26, 30, 32

underwater cities 19
urban planning 8

vertical take-off and landing (VTOL) aircraft 24, **35**
video 12, 25, 34
videophones 25, **35**
voice recognition 19, 34
voice synthesizers 19, **35**

walkways 21
waste 4, 7, 26, 27, 30
wave energy 28
wave power 26
wind power 26
wind turbines 28
work 14-19

Photographic Credits:
Cover and pages 6, 8 bottom, 9 left, 16 top and 33: J. Allan Cash; intro pages and pages 7, 8 top, 9 right, 10 all, 11 all, 12, 14, 16 bottom, 19 bottom, 22 middle and bottom, 23, 24 middle right, 25, 28 right, 32 top left, 33 and 34 top: Science Photo Library; pages 9 bottom, 18 right and 32 bottom left: Robert Harding Library; pages 13 top, 17, 18 bottom, 29 and 32 right: Topham Picture Library; pages 13 bottom and 27: British Film Institute; page 19 top: Solo Syndication; page 22 top: Eye Ubiquitous; page 24 left and middle left: Aviation Picture Library; page 24 bottom: British Aerospace; page 26: Times Newspaper; page 28 left: Zefa; page 34 bottom: Alex Pang.

THE taste for living WORLD COOKBOOK

Also by Beth Ginsberg and Mike Milken

The Taste for Living Cookbook:
Mike Milken's Favorite Recipes
for Fighting Cancer

Tortilla Soup, page **74**

CaP CURE — Association for the Cure of Cancer of the Prostate
1250 4th Street, Suite 360, Santa Monica, California 90401

CaP CURE Scientific and Editorial Team: Erin Pasternack, Howard R. Soule, Ph.D.
Additional research: Linda Swanson

Scientific Consultant: David Heber, M.D., Ph.D., Director, UCLA Center for Human Nutrition, Professor of Medicine, UCLA School of Medicine and Public Health

Editor: Susan Stuck
Editorial Support: Victoria Beliveau, Wendy Ruopp, Anne C. Treadwell
Art Direction/Design: Joannah Ralston, Insight Design
Illustrations: Isabelle Dervaux

Food Photographs: Bruce James, Lew Robertson, Burke/Triolo Productions
Location Photographs: Gary Moss
Photograph of Martha Stewart and Mike Milken: Todd Atkinson
Hair & Makeup: Gunn Espegard, Brenda Green for Celestine, L.A.
Food Styling: Norman Stewart, Janet Miller, Ronnda Hamilton
Prop Styling: Lorraine Triolo, Burke/Triolo Productions, Kim Jankowiak
Wardrobe: Carol Capka Jones
Assistants: Kasy Valentine, J Horton, Jeff Walls

Produced by Insight Design
384 Acorn Lane, Shelburne, VT 05482

Copyright © 1999 Association for the Cure of Cancer of the Prostate (CaP CURE)

All rights reserved. No part of this publication may be reproduced, stored in a retrieval system, or transmitted in any form or by any means, electronic, mechanical, photocopying, recording or otherwise, without the prior written permission of the copyright owner, except in the case of brief quotations embodied in critical articles and reviews.

10 9 8 7 6 5 4 3 2 1

Library of Congress Catalogue Card Number: 99-65457
Ginsberg, Beth
Milken, Mike
The Taste for Living World Cookbook
More of Mike Milken's Favorite Recipes for Fighting Cancer and Heart Disease

Includes index
ISBN 0-9673655-0-3
1. Cookbooks & Cookery. 2. Health & Fitness. 3. Medical/Nursing/Home Care

Cover Design: Joannah Ralston
Cover Photographs: Bruce James, Lew Robertson, Gary Moss
Printed in the United States

THE taste for living WORLD COOKBOOK

MORE *of* Mike Milken's Favorite Recipes for Fighting Cancer *and* Heart Disease

by Beth Ginsberg and Mike Milken

CaP CURE
ASSOCIATION FOR THE CURE OF CANCER OF THE PROSTATE

CONTENTS

World-class Breakfast 17

23 **A French Lunch**

An Italian Buffet 31

43 **Middle Eastern Mezze**

An Indian Feast 49

57 **A Chinese Banquet**

A Simple 67
Japanese Meal

Chocolate Tortilla Wraps, page **104**

Spinach and Mushroom Enchiladas, page **76**

Sukiyaki, page **71**

5 Preface
by Martha Stewart

6 Introduction
by Mike Milken

9 Building a New Pyramid
by David Heber, M.D., Ph.D.

11 Why Diet Matters
by Dean Ornish, M.D.

13 A Culinary Journey
by Beth Ginsberg

14 A Guide to Soyfoods

16 Nutritional Principles of CaP CURE

21 Start the Day with a Shake

22 Don't Forget Fiber

28 Boost Flavor — and Health — with Citrus Zests

30 Strategies for Restaurant Meals

Chinese Dumplings, page 60

73 Mexican Favorites

A Caribbean Cookout 81

87 Southern Traditions

Lunch at the U.S. Senate 95

99 A Southwest Supper

Spaghetti Bolognese, page 38

Miami Munchin' 107

111 All-American Junk Food

The Mediterranean Message	32
Viva Lycopene!	37
Lentils and Folate	50
Health Benefits from the Spice Rack	56
Learning from the Asian Diet	61
Evaluating Marketing Terms	65
Make Time for Tea	72
The Benefits of Garlic	83
Eat Your Crucifers!	90
You've Got to Move	106
Sizing It All Up	120
The Healthy World Pantry	121
Index	123
About CaP CURE	129

Chocolate Cupcakes, page 117
Glazed Cinnamon Doughnuts, page 118

ACKNOWLEDGEMENTS

I am enormously grateful to all the people who helped turn my culinary journey into a guidebook for cooks who care about their health and the health of their families.

Infinite thanks to the Vermont team of Joannah Ralston and Susan Stuck for giving shape to the idea. To Erin Pasternack at CaP CURE for her nutritional good sense. To Karen Vantrease, Jeff Moore, and Lailee Foroutan, for their tireless efforts. To Jan Strode for putting me on the map. To Frank Maranto for being everywhere we needed him to be.

A huge thank you to the food photography team at Burke/Triolo Productions: Lorraine Triolo, Jeff Burke, Lew Robertson, Bruce James, J Horton, Norman Stewart, Janet Miller and Alison Armstrong. Also to Gary Moss for bringing out the best in me.

My deepest appreciation to Gus Rivas and Akasha for their skills in the kitchen. To Ferne Milken for being our number-one booster. To Art Luna for keeping me trim, Charles Williams for keeping me fit and Anastasia Soare for raising my eyebrows. To Sue Karmel and Nancy Priddy for their unflagging courage.

And to Michael Milken, a true inspiration, a mentor and a good eater too, my thanks for making dreams come true. What a great way to visit the world.

Beth Ginsberg

This book is dedicated to my loving family: Gert, Hannah, Merle and Dottie, and to the memory of Matthew and Arthur.

PREFACE

Dear Friends,

CONGRATULATIONS on making the decision to change your diet without compromising your taste for living. I've had the pleasure of tasting many of chef Beth Ginsberg's creations, and I know you'll enjoy them. Beth has managed to do what many people thought was impossible: take traditional recipes from around the world and re-interpret them — replacing high-fat ingredients with healthy ingredients, like soy — without sacrificing taste.

Beth translates the taste for living into many culinary languages. Whether her recipe is for Japanese sukiyaki, Italian spaghetti Bolognese, or Mexican enchiladas, she never loses sight of aesthetics. Taste comes first, but Beth gives us more, by presenting the food beautifully and by creating the ambience so essential to gracious entertaining.

Although I've known Mike for many years, I received my first introduction to the *Taste for Living* approach to cooking when Mike and Beth appeared on my *Martha Stewart Living* television show. It was a visit full of revelations. I learned new ways to cook my favorite recipes without fat, the importance of adding soy protein to my diet, and how to include soy products in favorite recipes.

For many years I've admired the support the Milken Family Foundation has given to cancer research, and watched in awe the way Mike has waged his own personal war on prostate cancer. Since he founded CaP CURE in 1993, the organization has awarded more than $70 million to research scientists looking for cures and controls for prostate cancer.

I remember feeling at a loss when a close friend was diagnosed with breast cancer. One of the ways we can comfort a friend is by preparing food; serving healthy food is one of the most beautiful gestures we can make. With *The Taste for Living World Cookbook*, I'm confident that I can always offer that comfort, secure in the knowledge that the food I serve will contribute to longevity and that its taste will add to the enjoyment of every moment.

After Mike and Beth appeared on my show, I was inspired to send their first cookbook to my mother and my sisters, who became fans of the recipes for Caesar salad and spinach cannelloni. We're all grateful to Beth and Mike for sharing the *Taste for Living* and enhancing our taste for life.

Martha Stewart
Westport, Connecticut

INTRODUCTION

Mike Milken
Founder and Chairman, CaP CURE

Just the thought of a double cheeseburger with special sauce and fried onion rings at Bob's Big Boy started my mouth watering. Bob's was a Los Angeles landmark during my youth and I was one of its most loyal customers. This shouldn't surprise readers of the first *Taste for Living Cookbook* (CaP CURE, 1998) who may recall my description of a life happily spent devouring high-fat food, my abrupt conversion to healthy (but boring!) fare after a diagnosis of advanced prostate cancer, and the revelation that it was safe to return to many of my old favorite foods thanks to the work of prominent nutrition researchers and chef Beth Ginsberg.

This second book — a global tour of recipes for fighting cancer and heart disease — adheres to the principles of the first volume. First and foremost, the food must taste great. The ingredients must be readily available, low in fat and easy to prepare. Foods associated with a lower incidence of cancer, like soy protein, are incorporated wherever possible.

But there are some differences. In addition to recipes, we've organized the book so you can easily create menus for everything from casual lunches to elegant buffets. We've given recognition to the fact that many of the same ingredients that fight cancer are also part of a heart-healthy diet. And, of course, we've expanded our scope to the entire world.

The inspiration for *The Taste for Living World Cookbook* came from three sources. The overwhelmingly positive responses to the first cookbook told me that we had identified an appealing concept: don't change the foods you love; just change the ingredients. Letter after letter told how this simple concept had changed not just habits, but lives. For example, Mrs. Toby Loewy from Rockville, Maryland, wrote:

"I've tried a lot of the recipes and my husband loves them. Not only am I able to help him lose weight, but I'm protecting him from prostate problems. He's happy and proud of my cooking, your recipes, and his increasing slimness. You are probably saving lives in more ways than one. Thank you for publishing your book!"

Deborah Roach, from San Francisco, California, sent an e-mail to say: "The recipes are delicious and reproducible in the everyday kitchen. Looking forward to volume two."

The Dreiwitz family, from Hackensack, New Jersey, wrote: "The recipes are fantastic. Does Beth Ginsberg have any other healthy recipes to share with the public?"

She certainly does, and they're in this book!

A second inspiration was the memory of happy family excursions with my wife, Lori, and our three children. All five of us grew up in Los Angeles, a true microcosm of the world. Visits to southern California restaurants featuring the foods of Asia, Latin America, Europe, Africa and the Middle East are as "authentic" an experience as you'll find in the U.S.

Even in less-cosmopolitan areas than Los Angeles, however, America's changing ethnic mixture has produced an explosion of interest in the cuisines of different nations. Smaller cities that considered it exotic to have a single Chinese restaurant a generation ago now boast eateries from every continent. Supermarkets that used to relegate "foreign" foods to a tiny specialty section now overflow with everything from chipotle salsa to kimchee to garam masala. And everywhere, cooking lessons are the hottest ticket on

> These foods are intended to contribute to the taste for LIVING — and the ZEST for life.

the adult-education roster.

Also, like an increasing number of Americans, my family and I have had the good fortune to visit other countries. Despite our varied interests — one of our children loves ancient architecture, another is the family photographer, a third visits the ballet whenever possible, Lori heads for the oldest bookstore and I seek out interesting gardens — we've all shared a passion for sampling the local cuisine. In some cases, such as the wonderful scones we enjoyed in England's Lake Country, a version appears in this cookbook. But not always. We left out a dish we encountered near the Great Wall of China — grilled scorpion!

The third inspiration for this book came from the lunches and dinners Beth prepared when I entertained business guests. While she frequently served recipes from *The Taste for Living*, volume one, she would sometimes surprise us with a more exotic international meal. After enjoying several of these new dishes, I suggested that she pull them together into what has become *The Taste for Living World Cookbook*.

These recipes may help prevent cancer, limit heart disease and promote general health, which many of us need to take seriously. But cooking can be fun and healthy eating should be an enhancement of life, not a deprivation. The fact that following our guidelines may help you feel better is a bonus. These foods are intended to contribute to the taste for living — and the zest for life.

I have to laugh when I think about my old eating habits. I wasn't exactly what you would call discriminating. As a student at the University of California at Berkeley, I used to pass a doughnut shop on my way to classes. The hot doughnuts — freshly pulled from their bath of frying grease — were irresistible, especially with glazed frosting. I'd often order a baker's dozen, finishing off all 13 before dinner. (Look for a better doughnut idea on page 118.)

Even though I wasn't discriminating in my eating habits, I've always been a hopeless romantic; I decided to propose to Lori on Valentine's Day, 1968. After buying a ring, I couldn't afford to take her anyplace fancy. My plan was to pop the question at Giovanni's Italian restaurant, a beloved campus hangout. In fact, I had only enough change to buy us a medium pizza. Normally, given my voracious appetite, this would serve as a mere appetizer. As luck would have it, though, the customer at the next table had ordered an extra-large pizza with everything, and left half

Taste for Living recipes let me enjoy the foods I love

uneaten when he paid his bill. As soon as he departed, I leaned over, trying my best to appear casual, and consumed the rest of his pizza before any waiters could snatch it away. Fortunately, Lori overlooked this temporary grazing at the next table and said yes to my proposal! We were married that summer and moved on to graduate school in Philadelphia, where I developed a taste for Philly cheese steaks. (A far healthier version of this regional treat is found on page 112. And pizza lovers, see page 114.)

Soon after I finished business school, President Nixon declared war on cancer. The goal was to produce a cure within the decade, just as President Kennedy's earlier plan to put a man on the moon had been achieved in less than 10 years. We all thought it would work. After all, in our parents' generation, President Roosevelt's war on polio had produced the Salk vaccine. I knew something about polio because my father had contracted it as a child and I was among the first of the baby boomers to receive the new vaccine. What a simple concept: get a shot and wipe out a disease. Surely we could do the same with cancer.

That naïve assumption made it an even greater shock when my father was told he had malignant melanoma in 1976. At the peak of my business career, having achieved all of my career goals by age 30, I was devastated and frustrated at my inability to help. I took my father to every leading cancer center in the country and consulted with the best doctors, all to no avail. He never recovered. The one positive result from this odyssey was that it showed how the cancer research process works and how young scientists are tempted to

Sharing good food and lively conversation with young friends

abandon research for more lucrative clinical practices. And so, in the late 1970s, I began a program of research grants that helped keep bright young scientists in the laboratory. A few years later, my brother and I formalized our philanthropic efforts by establishing the Milken Family Foundation.

It has been gratifying to see researchers we supported go on to achieve great success and recognition. For example, Dennis J. Slamon, M.D., Ph.D., an eminent oncologist at UCLA, was the driving force behind the development of Herceptin, one of the only effective treatments for a particular type of breast cancer. Others, like Bert Vogelstein, M.D., Professor of Oncology and Cancer Biology at Johns Hopkins University, and Owen Witte, M.D., Professor of Microbiology and Molecular Genetics at UCLA and a member of the National Academy of Sciences, are cited often by their peers, not only for their leading-edge research contributions, but also for mentoring other physician scientists.

After nearly two decades of involvement in support of cancer research, I thought I knew quite a bit about cancer and the probability of becoming one of its victims. Still, it was a shock when I received my diagnosis in 1993. My first thought was, "Will I live to see my grandchildren?" The blunt prognosis was, "Probably not. You have 12 to 18 months to live." Six years later, I don't know for sure which treatments helped; but I know that my altered diet certainly didn't hurt. And now, thanks to the nutritional research of CaP CURE–supported scientists and Beth Ginsberg's recipes, eating is a joy, rather than "bad-tasting medicine."

The new diet was easy for me because I was especially

BUILDING A NEW PYRAMID — THE CALIFORNIA WAY

David Heber, M.D., Ph.D.
Director, U.C.L.A. Center for Human Nutrition

The U.S. government has been giving advice on how we should eat since 1916, when it issued a food guide for young children. In the 1950s, the Department of Agriculture issued the "Basic Four" food guide. It taught that you could get all the nutrition you need from four basic food groups — cereals and grains; fruits and vegetables; milk and dairy foods; and meat, beans and nuts. In 1980, a fifth group was added called "fats, sweets and alcohol." Surprisingly, spices were not included even though they enhance taste.

More was needed than simply guides that stressed "moderation and variety." The connection between health and foods was becoming clearer. In 1992, after many fits and starts, the government issued the "Food Guide Pyramid." The base of a food pyramid typically shows those foods you should eat the most of each day. At the top, it shows the foods you should eat selectively to enhance taste. Only five years later, my colleagues and I began to think about how this pyramid should be changed to accommodate the realities of the next century, to optimize health, to prevent chronic disease and to deal with the reality of overweight and obesity, which can lead to heart disease and cancer.

The result was the California Cuisine Food Pyramid, which has fruits and vegetables at the bottom, with six to 11 servings recommended. This is where you can get the unique chemicals (called phytochemicals) that protect against such diseases as cancer and heart disease. The second level is high-fiber cereals and grains. Next is the protein level. It is important to get adequate protein, but this does not mean eating red meat. You can get protein from the white meat of chicken and turkey, fish and shellfish or soy protein and measured mixtures of rice and beans. The top level of the California pyramid contains natural taste enhancers.

If you look at the USDA pyramid, you will see little dots and triangles that represent fats and sugars sprinkled through all levels of the pyramid. These hidden fats and sugars found in processed foods are used to enhance taste. In the California Cuisine Food Pyramid, we have placed at the top spices, nuts, olives, avocados, monounsaturate-rich oils (such as olive oil) and omega-3 oils (found in fish and flaxseed) to add taste. Instead of telling consumers to use this level sparingly, we have said "use as needed" to enhance taste. Taste is king and drives the rest of our pyramid. By focusing on taste, protein, fiber, fruits and vegetables, you promote variety and portion control at the same time.

There are already moves under way to change the USDA pyramid to bring it in line with some of these concepts. Until then, I hope you will think about what you eat and educate your palate. The *Taste for Living* cookbooks help you do this by translating the principles of healthy eating into the delicious reality of food that tastes terrific.

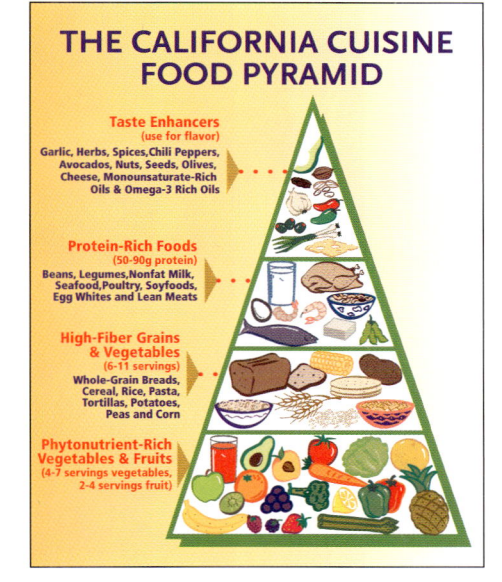

THE CALIFORNIA CUISINE FOOD PYRAMID

Taste Enhancers (use for flavor)
Garlic, Herbs, Spices, Chili Peppers, Avocados, Nuts, Seeds, Olives, Cheese, Monounsaturate-Rich Oils & Omega-3 Rich Oils

Protein-Rich Foods (50-90g protein)
Beans, Legumes, Nonfat Milk, Seafood, Poultry, Soyfoods, Egg Whites and Lean Meats

High-Fiber Grains & Vegetables (6-11 servings)
Whole-Grain Breads, Cereal, Rice, Pasta, Tortillas, Potatoes, Peas and Corn

Phytonutrient-Rich Vegetables & Fruits (4-7 servings vegetables, 2-4 servings fruit)

motivated and the food tastes great. But you don't have to change everything in your diet all at once. The recipes in this book are designed to help you make an easy transition. You may want to try one this weekend; then add a few midweek healthy snacks. It's easy — and it's up to you!

We know that some people are skeptical of, even hostile to, what they consider "health food." This calls for more creative measures. Since volume one appeared, we've had fun introducing wholesome ingredients to traditional bastions of high-fat foods.

Even skeptics are won over by the Taste for Living recipes

The venerable United States Senate dining room, for example, holds fast to its traditions. With the gracious assistance of Senators Tom Harkin and Ted Stevens, however, we breached this culinary garrison and fooled several of their colleagues, who pronounced Beth's versions of Caesar salad and three-bean chili to be delicious.

A bigger challenge was the Hart Middle School in Washington, D.C. Seventh graders, reputed to be experts on desserts, can be picky eaters. When we invited them to join us in making brownies (page 102, *The Taste for Living Cookbook*), they were a little taken aback by the substitution of silken tofu for butter. But once they tasted the results, they couldn't wait for seconds.

Okay, senators are preoccupied with affairs of state and seventh graders are, well, kids. But could we pull off the same kind of switch with sophisticated New York journalists? Our chance to find out came when Barbara Walters invited me to appear on *20/20*. Beth secured agreement from the ABC commissary staff to substitute ingredients in several dishes. With the exception of one newshound who said the boiled "hot dogs" (tofu dogs, page 42, *The Taste for Living Cookbook*) tasted different, no one was the wiser.

That was just one of dozens of media appearances Beth or I have made as *The Taste for Living* turned into a bestseller. We've had great fun talking about the book on *Charlie Rose*, *Larry King Live*, *Access Hollywood* and many others. When we cooked spinach cannelloni and made chocolate shakes on Martha Stewart's TV show, the production crew dived in as soon as the taping was over. They gave the food rave reviews.

We're not just promoting a cookbook. We're on a mission to raise awareness of the links between diet and health. Just imagine how our nation would react if a foreign enemy obtained a devastating weapon and threatened an attack that would kill half a million Americans. No price would be too high to repel such an attack. Yet, a "foreign enemy" — cancer — kills 560,000 of us every year. That's the same number of American men and women who were deployed during Operation Desert Storm. Would we be complacent if General Norman Schwarzkopf had announced that no Americans sent to the Gulf had survived?

Incredibly, however, our nation responds to this devastation with very limited cancer research funding. In testimony before a U.S. Senate subcommittee considering research appropriations in the spring of 1999, I pointed out that the U.S. cancer research budget is only about one-seventh of what Americans spend each year on beauty products!

WHY DIET MATTERS

Dean Ornish, M.D.
President and Director, Preventive Medicine Research Institute, Sausalito, California

With the *Taste for Living* cookbooks, Mike Milken and Beth Ginsberg demonstrate that a low-fat, whole-foods, plant-based diet can be both delicious and nutritious. But why take the trouble to eat this way? Because it matters. A lot. Not only are you likely to live longer, you're also likely to live better.

Many people tend to think of advances in medicine as a new drug or a new surgical technique. They have a hard time believing that simple lifestyle choices — what we eat, how we respond to stress, whether or not to smoke and how much to exercise — can make such a powerful difference in our lives, but they often do.

There is more scientific evidence than ever that when you switch from a meat-based diet to a plant-based diet, you may get a double benefit. You avoid those substances in foods that help cause heart disease, cancer, and other illnesses, and you consume literally thousands of substances that may be protective, including phytochemicals, bioflavinoids, carotenoids, retinols, isoflavones, lycopene and many others.

Over the years, I've heard so many people say, "If I change my diet, will I live longer or is it just going to seem longer? I don't care if I live a shorter life, I want to have fun." There is no reason to give up something you enjoy unless you get something back that's even better — and quickly.

I find that it is often easier to make big changes in diet and lifestyle than small ones because most people find that they feel so much better, so quickly. This reframes the reason for changing diet and lifestyle from fear of dying to joy of living.

Somehow, the things that we tend to associate with "the good life" — alcohol, high-fat foods, smoking and chronic stress — are the very ones that leave so many people feeling tired, depressed and lethargic. When you make intensive changes in your diet and lifestyle, it's not just your heart that reaps the benefits.

During the past 22 years, my colleagues and I at the Preventive Medicine Research Institute have conducted a series of clinical trials demonstrating that the progression of even severe coronary heart disease often can be reversed by making comprehensive changes in diet and lifestyle, without coronary bypass surgery, angioplasty or a lifetime of cholesterol-lowering drugs. These lifestyle changes include a very low-fat, low-cholesterol diet, stress management techniques, moderate exercise, smoking cessation and psychosocial support. This was a radical idea when we began our first study; now, it has become mainstream and is generally accepted by most cardiologists and scientists.

More recently, we found that comprehensive lifestyle changes are not only medically effective but also cost effective. At different locations around the United States, we found that many people who were eligible for bypass surgery or angioplasty were able to avoid it safely by making comprehensive lifestyle changes instead. These patients reported reductions in chest pain comparable to what can be achieved with bypass surgery or angioplasty without the costs or risks of surgery. Almost $20 billion was spent last year in the U.S. on these two operations, and billions more are spent each year on cholesterol-lowering drugs. Much of this expense could be avoided through changes in diet and lifestyle.

Unlike drugs and surgery, the only side effects of making comprehensive lifestyle changes are good ones. In the *Taste for Living*, Mike Milken and Beth Ginsberg show you how.

I believe we need to reorder our national priorities and launch a far more aggressive attack on this scourge that strikes one of every two American men and one of every three women. That's why I joined with hundreds of thousands of other concerned citizens in September 1998 for The March, a national demonstration of the constituency for increased cancer research funding. It was a tremendously moving experience, especially an evening candlelight vigil on the Mall in Washington.

Efforts like these are beginning to have an effect. Congress has increased cancer research appropriations significantly; the National Institutes of Health, the Department of Defense and other agencies are sponsoring new initiatives; and contributions to charities like CaP CURE (Association for the Cure of Cancer of the Prostate) are increasing.

CaP CURE has received more than $100 million in contributions from individuals to support its efforts against this disease. Grants from CaP CURE now support 70 human clinical trials of experimental drugs and techniques. Progress in these trials is encouraging, but the complete cure continues to elude us.

One of every six men alive today will face prostate cancer in his lifetime. Prostate cancer attacks men directly, but it affects women too. Wives, mothers, daughters, sisters, friends — they're all devastated when a loved one succumbs. Furthermore, as Donald S. Coffey, Ph.D., past president of the American Association for Cancer Research, has pointed out, there appears to be a link between the incidence of cancers of the prostate and the breast. Countries with low rates of one cancer (Japan, for example) have low rates of the other. Those with high rates of prostate cancer, like the U.S., have high rates of breast cancer. These rates vary inversely with the amount of soy protein in the diet and directly with the amount of fat. In other words, the recipes in this book could be just as protective for women as for men.

Like breast cancer, which was almost never spoken of in public a generation ago, prostate cancer has "come out of the closet." I've been joined by General Schwarzkopf, former Senator Bob Dole, golfers Arnold Palmer and Jim Colbert, baseball greats Stan Musial and Joe Torre, entertainers Harry Belafonte, Robert Goulet, Sidney Poitier and Jerry Lewis, and many others in efforts to raise awareness and money for research.

Research is vitally important. Someday, it will produce a cure. In the meantime, there are three things everyone can do to help: first, see your doctor regularly for simple cancer-screening tests; second, choose to eat more cancer-fighting foods and encourage your kids to do so; and, third, make a tax-deductible contribution to the charity of your choice that's supporting cancer research. One way you can contribute is to order more copies of this cookbook for your friends, co-workers or employees. It will increase their awareness of healthy eating and the book-sale profits will go to prostate cancer research. There's an order card in the back of the book or visit our website at www.tasteforliving.com.

Finally, I want to thank all of you who have written to me about *The Taste for Living* and who were nice enough to ask how I'm feeling. With the help of Beth Ginsberg's recipes, I'm feeling great!

P.S. I would love to hear from you. My e-mail address is mikemilken@tasteforliving.com.

Lori and I share a zest for life

A CULINARY JOURNEY

Beth Ginsberg

As I began creating the recipes for this cookbook, memories of all the cities I have lived in or traveled to or dreamed of were reawakened. I realized that I remember places not so much by their museums or monuments, but by the wonderful foods I enjoyed there.

Growing up, my family never stayed too many years in one place. I was born in Philadelphia and subsequently moved to suburban New Jersey, New York and then Miami. I have fond food memories from them all. It was a junior-year-abroad program that really opened my culinary eyes. I spent a year in Holland, which proved to be a convenient base for explorations. Two or three hours of travel in any direction let me sample vastly different styles of cooking and eating.

Cooking had always been a hobby, but I didn't consider it as a career until after college. The Culinary Institute of America in Hyde Park, New York (the other CIA), provided the training I needed to excel in professional kitchens. Food wasn't just my job, it was my creative outlet.

I started experimenting with soy in the 1980s. While I was unaware of the scientific research into its health benefits, I found that soy foods seemed to make me feel better. I had more energy and could work harder. When I opened my own restaurant in 1992, several soy-based dishes were on the menu. I became adept at using soy not only in Asian-inspired entrées but in Mexican, Italian and Middle Eastern offerings too. I ignored gastronomic borders. Soy was going global in my kitchen.

In 1994, Mike Milken introduced me to some of the country's leading nutrition researchers who were well aware of the health benefits of soy. They provided the guidelines for an overall healthful diet, stressing the need to consume 20 to 40 grams of soy protein daily, to eliminate added fats and to rely on a wide variety of fruits and vegetables. In effect, they supplied the paints and I became the painter. *The Taste for Living Cookbook* (CaP CURE, 1998) was my first canvas. And you know how painters are; they're already thinking of the next work before the paint dries on the first.

The Taste for Living World Cookbook evolved out of my culinary travels with Mike. My typical workday begins when I sit down to create the menu depending on who is dining, what's in season at the market and what I already have in the refrigerator. Before too long, tempting aromas drift down the hall from simmering soup pots and sauté pans. People stop in and ask "Where to today?" Some days it's to Italy or regional America, others it's to China, Japan or the Caribbean.

Mike and I were convinced we could bring this healthful gastronomic tour to life through *The Taste for Living World Cookbook*. Anyone interested in health and flavor could travel the culinary world with us.

The *Taste for Living* is about enjoying and celebrating life through food. It's about adding an element of health to everything you prepare by choosing healthful ingredients at the start and cooking them intelligently along the way. I hope you enjoy the journey as much as I have.

A GUIDE TO SOYFOODS

A KEY element of CaP CURE's approach to healthy eating for fighting cancer is the recommendation to consume between 20 and 40 grams of soy protein every day. The American Heart Association recognizes that soy protein can be an alternative to or helpful in conjunction with cholesterol-lowering drugs. It recommends incorporating at least 25 grams of soy protein into the diet each day. For the average American who consumes 5 grams per day, that's a huge change.

What makes soy and soy products so special?

To begin, soy protein is different from other plant-based proteins because it contains a nearly perfect set of amino acids — the building blocks of all dietary protein. Soybeans are rich in soluble fiber and B vitamins, including folate. Soy also contains phytonutrients (plant nutrients) called isoflavones that are being researched heavily for their various effects on cancer and heart disease.

Researchers have focused on two isoflavones — genistein and daidzein — and their inhibiting effect on prostate tumor cells and angiogenesis, the development of blood vessels that feed growing tumors.

In countries where soyfoods are a staple of the diet — China, Japan and other Asian countries — rates of certain cancers are lower, sometimes dramatically so. In one county in China, Qidong, the incidence of prostate cancer is 0.5 per 100,000 men. By comparison, the United States has a rate of 135.7 per 100,000, a 270-fold difference.

Substituting soy protein for animal protein in the diet has been proven to lower cholesterol levels, although it's not known exactly how it works. Soy's isoflavones may help prevent heart disease in ways other than by simply lowering cholesterol levels.

Cooks interested in flavor don't need nutrition statistics to convince them to include soy in their meals. They love its versatility — the way tofu absorbs and highlights the seasonings in a dish or how miso paste subtly enriches sauces and salad dressings or the way vibrant green edamame brightens a bean salad. If you are new to the wide array of soy products, take some time to get to know them, tasting different types and brands to find your favorite.

TOFU Also known as bean curd, tofu is sold fresh in plastic containers in the refrigerated section at the supermarket. Shelf-stable tofu is available in vacuum packages. Three main types of tofu — silken, soft and firm — are available. Ultra-smooth silken tofu is ideal for pureeing. Soft tofu works well in recipes that call for blending. Firm tofu maintains its shape for use in entrées and soups.

Fresh tofu must be refrigerated and should be used within one week of purchase. It should be covered with water for storage; change the water daily. Once opened, vacuum-packed tofu should be stored like fresh tofu.

Not all tofu tastes the same. Try different brands to find the one you like best. Tofu does contain fat, but very little of it is saturated fat. Low-fat and reduced-fat varieties are available. Pick the lowest fat version you can find.

SOY MEATS Soy has a great ability to mimic the texture of meat. As meatless meals become more popular among Americans, the quality and availability of everything from tofu hot dogs to soy burgers, soy bologna to soy sausage continue to increase. Read package labels carefully: soy deli meats may contain high amounts of sodium and some have moderate fat levels. Soy meats may not contain high levels of isoflavones, but they are still a better choice than true meat because the level of saturated fat is much lower.

MISO A basic flavoring in Japanese food, this fermented soybean paste has the consistency of peanut butter with a complex, rich flavor. It is usually made from a combination of soybeans and rice, although additional soybeans or barley may be used to replace the rice. Miso paste is usually sold in plastic tubs and can be found in large supermarkets and whole foods stores. Refrigerated, miso will keep for several months. Miso is high in sodium; use sparingly.

TEMPEH Many find this fermented soybean cake to be the meatiest of the traditional soy foods. It's chewy and full-flavored, and it holds its shape well in cooking. It's excellent marinated. Because tempeh is made from whole soybeans, it does contain more fat per ounce than firm tofu (2.2 grams versus 1.5), but it's very high in beneficial isoflavones.

EDAMAME Frozen green baby soybeans in the pod are sold under the name edamame. To prepare, see page 71. A great snack and a bright addition to salads, a ¼-cup (1½-oz/50-g) serving provides about 9 grams of soy protein.

SOY MILK Made from pressing cooked ground soybeans, soy milk is good on cereal and in smoothies, and can be used like cow's milk in most baked goods. For American tastes, it is available flavored with vanilla, strawberry, chocolate or carob, and a natural sweetener. A natural thickening agent, often carrageenan, is added to give the beverage the same texture as cow's milk. Look for soy milk in the dairy case. Shelf-stable soy milk is also available. Either is available in 2 percent, 1 percent and fat-free varieties. In *Taste for Living* recipes, we use 1 percent soy milk because it is higher in soy isoflavones than the fat-free version.

SOY CHEESES Available in a number of traditional styles including jack, cheddar, mozzarella, parmesan and American, soy cheese can be found in the dairy case. Be sure to choose a fat-free brand. If your market doesn't carry fat-free, ask the store manager to try to order it. Often they are very happy to accommodate the request. Always grate soy cheese by hand, never in the food processor.

SOY SAUCE This is one soy product that should be used sparingly. Even low-sodium varieties contain a considerable amount of sodium. Soy sauce does not contain the phytochemicals thought to protect against cancer and heart disease. Use a low-sodium tamari soy sauce for best flavor.

SOY Throughout the book, you will notice many recipes accompanied by this symbol. It indicates that the recipe provides at least 6.25 grams of soy protein per serving, one-fourth of the American Heart Association's daily recommendation.

A GUIDE TO SOYFOODS

NUTRITIONAL PRINCIPLES OF CaP CURE

To fight prostate and other cancers and to help prevent heart disease, CaP CURE (Association for the Cure of Cancer of the Prostate) recommends following the eating guidelines developed by David Heber, M.D., Ph.D., Director of the UCLA Center for Human Nutrition. Dr. Heber is one of the growing number of health professionals who are researching direct links between diet and chronic disease.

- Limit dietary fat to 15 percent of total energy intake. For instance, if you maintain your normal weight on 2,200 calories per day, consume no more than 33 grams of total fat throughout the day.
- Eat five or more servings of fruits and vegetables per day.
- Consume 25 to 35 grams of dietary fiber per day.
- Consume between 20 and 40 grams of soy protein per day.

TIPS FOR HEALTHIER EATING

There are a number of ways you can adapt your daily diet to meet the guidelines, thereby raising the overall health value of the food you eat.

Soy protein isolate powder: To ensure that you get enough soy protein every day, add soy isolate powder to shakes, baked goods, dressings, sauces and soups. You can buy a low-fat, flavored brand at most natural foods stores or order it through the mail (page 122).

Fruits and vegetables: For maximum exposure to beneficial phytochemicals, eat a wide variety of fruits and vegetables of many colors. Think of vegetables as the main course, not merely an accompaniment.

Herbs and spices: Low-fat foods get a flavor boost from a generous use of herbs and spices. There may be added health benefits too (see page 56).

Citrus zest: Add grated lemon or orange peel, also called zest, to baked goods to boost flavor and possibly enhance your health (see page 28).

Commercial salad dressings: Avoid these. Make your own salad dressings from either of the *Taste for Living* cookbooks. When dining out, ask for balsamic vinegar or lemon juice and Dijon mustard to make your own fat-free dressing.

Dairy products: Consume only nonfat dairy products, but be aware that many of these contain additives, so read labels carefully and shop in natural foods stores whenever possible. Instead of butter, use fruit spreads on waffles and toast. If you do cook with cheese, choose a reduced-fat brand: full-fat cheeses contain between 60 and 80 percent fat. Avoid sugar-rich yogurt and ice cream — they add calories and may tempt you to overindulge.

Meat: If you do eat meat, use it as a flavoring, not the focus of a meal. Limit portion size to three ounces of cooked meat, about the size of a deck of cards.

Green tea: Drink three to 10 cups daily, because it contains valuable antioxidants (see page 72). Or add green tea powder to shakes.

A WORD ABOUT INGREDIENTS AND NUTRITIONAL ANALYSIS

In recipes where a range of amounts is offered in the ingredients list, nutritional analysis is based on the lowest amount. Similarly, if a choice of ingredients is offered, the analysis is based on the first choice. Ingredients listed as optional are not included in the nutritional analysis. When a recipe's yield gives a range, the analysis is based on the higher number of servings.

All recipes include customary U.S. and metric measurements. Metric conversions have been rounded off. Actual weights may vary.

Tofu and soy cheeses differ greatly from brand to brand. For analysis purposes, we used brands with the lowest amount of fat.

World-class BREAKFAST

THE RECIPES THAT FOLLOW ARE ADAPTATIONS OF BREAKFASTS YOU CAN FIND IN EUROPE. IN Holland, for example, students and workers walk along the canals and stop for breakfast at a pannekoeken house. Unlike American pancakes, the Dutch version is cooked like an open-face omelet and filled with anything from ham and cheese to cinnamon-laced apples.

A traditional English breakfast includes eggs, bacon and tomatoes. recreating that delicious combination without the fat is now considerably easier since tasty tempeh bacon has become a regularly stocked item at the supermarket. Stick to egg whites to avoid the fat and cholesterol of the egg yolk.

- For years, moms and coaches, teachers and managers have warned us against the dangers of starting out on an empty stomach. It's true — breakfast will help you to be more alert and perform better throughout the day. It also supplies a wealth of necessary nutrients, particularly fiber, minerals and vitamins that aren't always plentiful at lunch or dinner.

SCONES

no-stick cooking spray
2¾ cups (10 oz/300 g) oat flour or cake flour
½ cup (3¼ oz/100 g) natural cane sugar
2 teaspoons baking powder
¼ teaspoon sea salt
2 ounces (60 g) low-fat silken tofu
½ cup (4 fl oz/120 ml) unsweetened applesauce
¼ cup (2 fl oz/60 ml) fat-free egg product
1 tablespoon grated orange zest
1 teaspoon pure vanilla extract
¾ cup (4 oz/120 g) currants

TOPPING

1 egg white, beaten
2 teaspoons natural cane sugar
¼ teaspoon ground cinnamon

1. Preheat oven to 400°F (200°C). Spray a baking sheet lightly with cooking spray.
2. In a large bowl, whisk together flour, sugar, baking powder and salt.
3. In a food processor, combine tofu, applesauce, egg product, orange zest and vanilla. Process until smooth. Pour over dry ingredients and stir together with a fork just until moistened. Stir in currants.
4. On a floured work surface with floured hands, knead dough briefly until it comes together. Pat dough into a circle about ¾ inch (2 cm) thick. With a biscuit cutter, cut 8 round scones. (Or, cut circle into 8 wedges.) Transfer scones to the prepared baking sheet and lightly spray with cooking spray. Brush tops with egg white. Combine sugar and cinnamon and sprinkle over scones.
5. Bake until firm to the touch, about 15 minutes.

YIELD: 8 SCONES

Per scone: 225 Calories, 2.2g Fat, 0g Saturated Fat, 0mg Cholesterol, 7g Protein, 45g Carbohydrate, 5.5g Fiber, 174mg Sodium

Nutrition Bonus: A scone from your neighborhood coffee emporium can have as much as 25 grams of fat. Ours has just over 2 grams.

OATCAKES

no-stick cooking spray
1 cup (3½ oz/110 g) oat flour
1 tablespoon natural cane sugar, plus extra for sprinkling
¼ teaspoon baking powder
⅛ teaspoon sea salt
3–4 tablespoons 1% vanilla soy milk, plus extra for brushing
1 tablespoon unsweetened applesauce
½ cup (1½ oz/45 g) old-fashioned rolled oats

1. Preheat oven to 350°F (175°C). Spray a baking sheet lightly with cooking spray.
2. In a food processor, combine oat flour, sugar, baking powder and salt. Pulse briefly. Add 3 tablespoons of the soy milk and the applesauce and pulse for 45 seconds, just until mixture forms a ball. If too dry, add a little more soy milk.
3. Place dough on a lightly floured work surface. Knead in all but 2 tablespoons of the rolled oats. Flatten into a disk and roll into a 9-inch (23-cm) circle. Brush with soy milk; sprinkle with sugar and the remaining 2 tablespoons oats. Cut into 10 wedges. Transfer to prepared baking sheet.
4. Bake until firm and lightly browned, about 15 minutes.

YIELD: 10 OATCAKES

Per oatcake: 59 Calories, 1g Fat, 0.1g Saturated Fat, 0mg Cholesterol, 2g Protein, 11g Carbohydrate, 1.6g Fiber, 38mg Sodium

Nutrition Bonus: Oats are a great source of soluble fiber, beneficial for your heart and sure to keep you satisfied for hours.

STRAWBERRY PRESERVES

over 60 minutes

Using orange juice instead of apple juice lends a tangier flavor to the preserves.

- 4 cups (1 lb/480 g) fresh strawberries, hulled and sliced
- ¾ cup (5 oz/150 g) natural cane sugar
- ¼ cup (2 fl oz/60 ml) unsweetened apple juice or orange juice
- 1½ teaspoons agar (sea gelatin) or powdered gelatin
- 1 teaspoon grated orange zest, optional
- 1 vanilla bean split lengthwise, optional

1. Combine all ingredients in a large heavy saucepan. Bring to a boil and reduce heat to medium-low.
2. Simmer for 25 minutes, stirring frequently, until preserves are thick. Remove from heat and pour into clean glass jars. (Either remove vanilla bean or keep it in preserves for added flavor.)
3. Cover and refrigerate. The preserves will keep for up to 2 weeks.

YIELD: 1½ CUPS (12 OZ/360 G) PRESERVES

Per 2-tablespoon serving: 67 Calories, 0.1g Fat, 0g Saturated Fat, 0mg Cholesterol, 0g Protein, 17g Carbohydrate, 1.1g Fiber, 1mg Sodium

WORLD-CLASS BREAKFAST

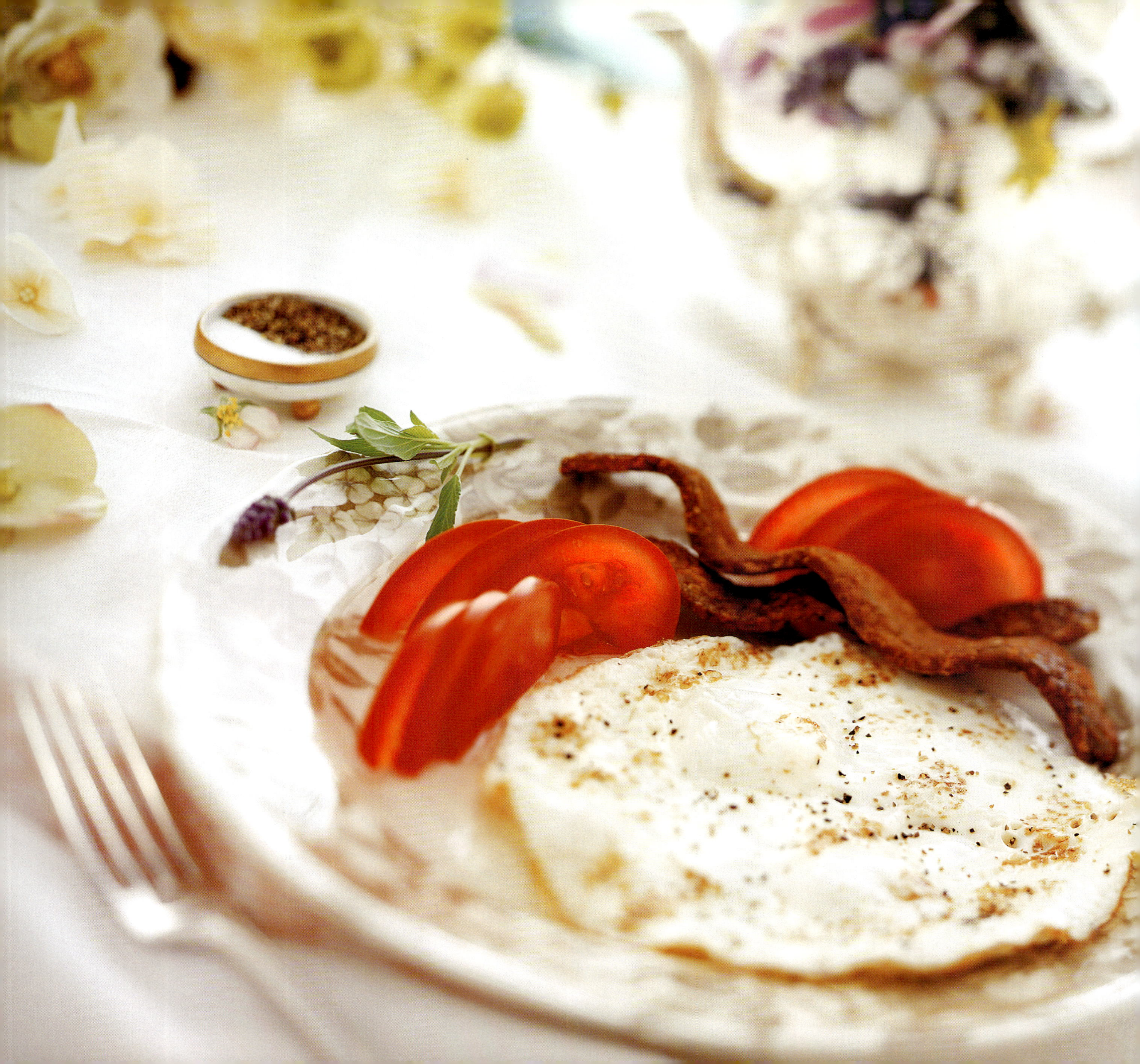

NEW ENGLISH BREAKFAST

- 4 slices vegetarian or tempeh bacon
- 1 large vine-ripened tomato
- no-stick cooking spray
- 4 egg whites
- sea salt and freshly ground black pepper to taste

1. Prepare bacon according to package directions.
2. Core tomato. Slice in half vertically. Place flat-side down and cut into thin slices. Fan slices on 2 plates.
3. Spray 2 nonstick egg pans or small skillets lightly with cooking spray and set over low heat. Add 2 egg whites to each pan. Cover and cook until eggs are firm, 2 to 4 minutes. Transfer to plates, season with salt and pepper. Serve with bacon.

YIELD: 2 SERVINGS

Per serving: 106 Calories, 0.3g Fat, 0g Saturated Fat, 0mg Cholesterol, 18g Protein, 6g Carbohydrate, 1g Fiber, 444mg Sodium

MUESLI

- 1 cup (3 oz/90 g) old-fashioned rolled oats
- 1 cup (3 oz/90 g) rolled barley or rolled triticale
- 1 cup (2 oz/60 g) fat-free corn flakes or oat flakes
- ½ cup (1 oz/30 g) wheat germ
- 2 tablespoons natural cane sugar, optional
- 1 cup (5 oz/150 g) mixed dried fruit such as raisins, cherries or blueberries
- ½ teaspoon ground cinnamon, optional

1. Mix all ingredients. Store in an airtight container.

YIELD: 4 CUPS (16 OZ/480 G)

Per ½ cup (2-oz/60-g) serving: 167 Calories, 1.7g Fat, 0.1g Saturated Fat, 0mg Cholesterol, 6g Protein, 36g Carbohydrate, 5.3g Fiber, 43mg Sodium

START THE DAY WITH A SHAKE

A very efficient way to ensure that your body gets the most beneficial components of the soybean is to add at least 20 to 40 grams of soy protein isolate powder to your daily diet. The flavorful shake below contains more than 20 grams of soy protein and 20 milligrams of isoflavones rich in tumor-suppressing genistein. It is also packed with two other potential cancer fighters — limonene from the citrus zests (see page 28) and EGCG from the green tea (see page 72).

BLUEBERRY BANANA SHAKE

Have fun experimenting with different berries or other fruits.

- ½ cup (4 fl oz/120 ml) unsweetened apple juice or orange juice
- ½ cup (4 fl oz/120 ml) brewed organic green tea or unsweetened apple juice
- ¼ cup (1 oz/30 g) frozen blueberries, preferably Maine wild blueberries
- 1 banana
- 1 teaspoon grated lemon zest
- 1 teaspoon grated orange zest
- ½ cup (1½ oz/45 g) vanilla soy protein isolate powder
- 3 capsules green tea powder (open capsules and use powder only), optional

1. Place all ingredients in a blender and puree until smooth.

YIELD: 1 SHAKE

Per shake: 265 Calories, 1.7g Fat, 0.2g Saturated Fat, 0mg Cholesterol, 22g Protein, 42g Carbohydrate, 3.3g Fiber, 207mg Sodium

WORLD-CLASS BREAKFAST

PANNEKOEKEN

DUTCH PANCAKE

- no-stick cooking spray
- ½ cup (2 oz/60 g) oat flour, whole-wheat pastry flour or all-purpose flour
- 2 tablespoons natural cane sugar
- ½ teaspoon baking powder
- ½ cup (4 fl oz/120 ml) fat-free egg product
- ½ cup (4 fl oz/120 ml) 1% vanilla soy milk
- 2 tablespoons unsweetened applesauce
- 1 teaspoon pure vanilla extract

SAUTÉED APPLES

- 2 large apples, cored, peeled and thinly sliced
- 3 tablespoons pure maple syrup
- ¼ teaspoon ground cinnamon
- 1 vanilla bean, split lengthwise

TO MAKE DUTCH PANCAKE

1. Preheat oven to 375°F (190°C). Spray a 10-inch (25-cm) nonstick ovenproof skillet once with cooking spray.
2. In a bowl, whisk together flour, sugar and baking powder.
3. In a separate bowl, beat egg product with an electric mixer until fluffy. Beat in soy milk, applesauce and vanilla. Gently fold in dry ingredients.
4. Pour batter into prepared skillet. Bake in the oven until pancake is golden and fluffy, about 20 minutes.

TO MAKE SAUTÉED APPLES

1. While pancake is baking, combine apples, maple syrup, cinnamon and vanilla bean in a medium sauté pan. Cover and cook over low heat until apples are soft, about 10 minutes. Remove vanilla bean.
2. Serve pancake warm with sautéed apples and additional maple syrup, if desired, or dust with confectioners' sugar.

YIELD: 1 PANNEKOEKEN, 4 SERVINGS

Per serving: 176 Calories, 1.2g Fat, 0g Saturated Fat, 0mg Cholesterol, 5g Protein, 37g Carbohydrate, 2.9g Fiber, 77mg Sodium

DON'T FORGET FIBER

Most Americans eat far too little dietary fiber, about 10 grams per day. That's less than half the recommended amount of 25 to 35 grams per day.

When your health professional says "eat more fiber," she's really talking about two types of dietary fiber. Soluble fiber will lower blood cholesterol levels; insoluble fiber (also known as roughage) is needed for intestinal health. As long as you eat a variety of fruits, vegetables, legumes and grains, you'll get both soluble and insoluble fiber.

The best way to jump-start a high-fiber diet is to begin each day with a bowl of hot cereal (oatmeal is terrific) or a high-fiber cold cereal (such as All-Bran, bran flakes, raisin bran or shredded wheat) and garnish it with a high-fiber fruit. This delicious habit will provide a critical seven to 15 grams of fiber. Throughout the rest of the day, eat at least five servings of fruits and vegetables and go for whole grains at every opportunity. Include legumes in your diet two or three times a week too.

If you are not used to a lot of fiber, ease into it gradually to avoid gastrointestinal distress. And don't forget to drink lots of water every day.

FIBER-RICH FOODS: Apples, Artichokes, Beans (all types), Berries (all types), Broccoli, Brussels Sprouts, Cherries, Figs, Guava, Kiwi, Leafy Vegetables (turnip tops, beet tops, collards, etc.), Mangoes, Oranges, Pears, Peas, Peppers, Potatoes (with skin), Prunes, Salad Greens, Squash, Whole Grains

A French LUNCH

- France is one of the world's leading producers of leeks. More nutritious than their onion cousins, leeks are widely used to flavor soups, stocks and stews.

- Food is an important part of the culture in France, where meals are savored and appreciated. Families make a point of eating together, sharing the day's events over the course of a leisurely supper.

- The average American is three times more likely to develop heart disease than the average Frenchman, yet the French diet is hardly a model for healthy eating. A recent study suggests that the enormous variety of foods consumed by the French contributes to their relative good health.

- Mustard has been used as a flavoring in foods for more than 3,000 years. France's Dijon mustard accounts for more than half of the world's production. The mellowed sharpness of Dijon mustard is a welcome — and fat-free — addition to salad dressings and sauces.

BETH'S FORMAL CULINARY EDUCATION BEGAN AT THE CULINARY INSTITUTE OF AMERICA, where the emphasis was on French haute cuisine, including everything from Hollandaise sauce to elaborate pâtés to butter-rich pastry confections. Yet some of the best French food is found in French homes, not in three-star restaurants. French home cooks often have a hearty leek-and-potato soup on the stovetop or a simple quiche or tart in the oven. The aromas from these welcoming kitchens inspire many of the recipes in this chapter.

Finding healthy substitutions for the cream-and-egg custards so fundamental to French cooking was a challenge at first. After repeated experiments, we've learned that a combination of low-fat silken tofu, fat-free egg product and tapioca flour or cornstarch yields a rich, creamy consistency with barely a gram of fat. You can taste the delicious results in the Quiche Lorraine on page 24 and the Crème Brûlée on page 28.

POTATO AND LEEK SOUP

30 to 60 minutes

- no-stick cooking spray
- 3 leeks, halved lengthwise, washed thoroughly and sliced (4 cups)
- 1 large onion, chopped
- 4 large baking potatoes, peeled and cut into chunks
- 3 quarts (2.8 L) Vegetable Stock (page 32)
- 1/8 teaspoon sea salt
- 1/4 teaspoon freshly ground black pepper
- 2 tablespoons snipped fresh chives

1. Spray a large soup pot once with cooking spray and set over low heat. Add leeks and onions, cover pot and cook for 10 minutes, stirring once or twice.

2. Add potatoes and stock. Bring to a boil, then reduce heat to medium-low. Simmer until potatoes are soft, about 20 minutes.

3. Puree soup in batches in a blender or food processor. Season with salt and pepper.

4. Reheat gently and serve hot. (For vichyssoise, refrigerate for at least 2 hours. Serve very cold.)

5. To serve, ladle into bowls and garnish with chives.

YIELD: 4 QUARTS (3.8 L), 10 TO 12 SERVINGS

Per serving: 65 Calories, 0.2g Fat, 0g Saturated Fat, 0mg Cholesterol, 1g Protein, 15g Carbohydrate, 1.6g Fiber, 38mg Sodium

Nutrition Bonus: Pureed potatoes lend a creamy richness to soups — without the saturated fat of cream.

QUICHE LORRAINE

over 60 minutes

- no-stick cooking spray
- 1 recipe Savory Pie Crust dough (page 26)
- 12 ounces (360 g) low-fat silken tofu
- 1 1/2 cups (12 fl oz/360 ml) fat-free egg product
- 2 tablespoons tapioca flour or cornstarch
- 1/2 teaspoon granulated onion
- 1/4 teaspoon grated nutmeg
- 1/8 teaspoon sea salt
- pinch cayenne pepper
- 5 ounces (150 g) fat-free soy cheese, grated by hand (1 1/4 cups)
- 6 ounces (360 g) soy deli meat, such as fat-free ham, Canadian bacon or tempeh bacon, cut into small dice

1. Preheat oven to 350°F (175°C). Spray a 10-inch (25-cm) quiche pan once with cooking spray.

2. Flour work surface and roll pie dough into an 11-inch (28-cm) circle. Transfer to prepared pan and gently press into corners. Bake until very lightly browned, about 10 minutes. Do not turn off oven.

3. In a blender or food processor, combine tofu, egg product, tapioca flour or cornstarch, granulated onion, nutmeg, salt and cayenne. Blend until smooth.

4. Place cheese and soy deli meat in baked crust. Pour in tofu mixture.

5. Bake for 45 minutes, or until quiche is firm.

YIELD: 8 SERVINGS

Per serving: 181 Calories, 1g Fat, 0.1g Saturated Fat, 0mg Cholesterol, 20g Protein, 22g Carbohydrate, 2g Fiber, 581mg Sodium

Nutrition Bonus: A classic quiche Lorraine contains upward of 35 grams of fat per slice. The *Taste for Living* version has only 1 gram.

Ratatouille and Quiche Lorraine

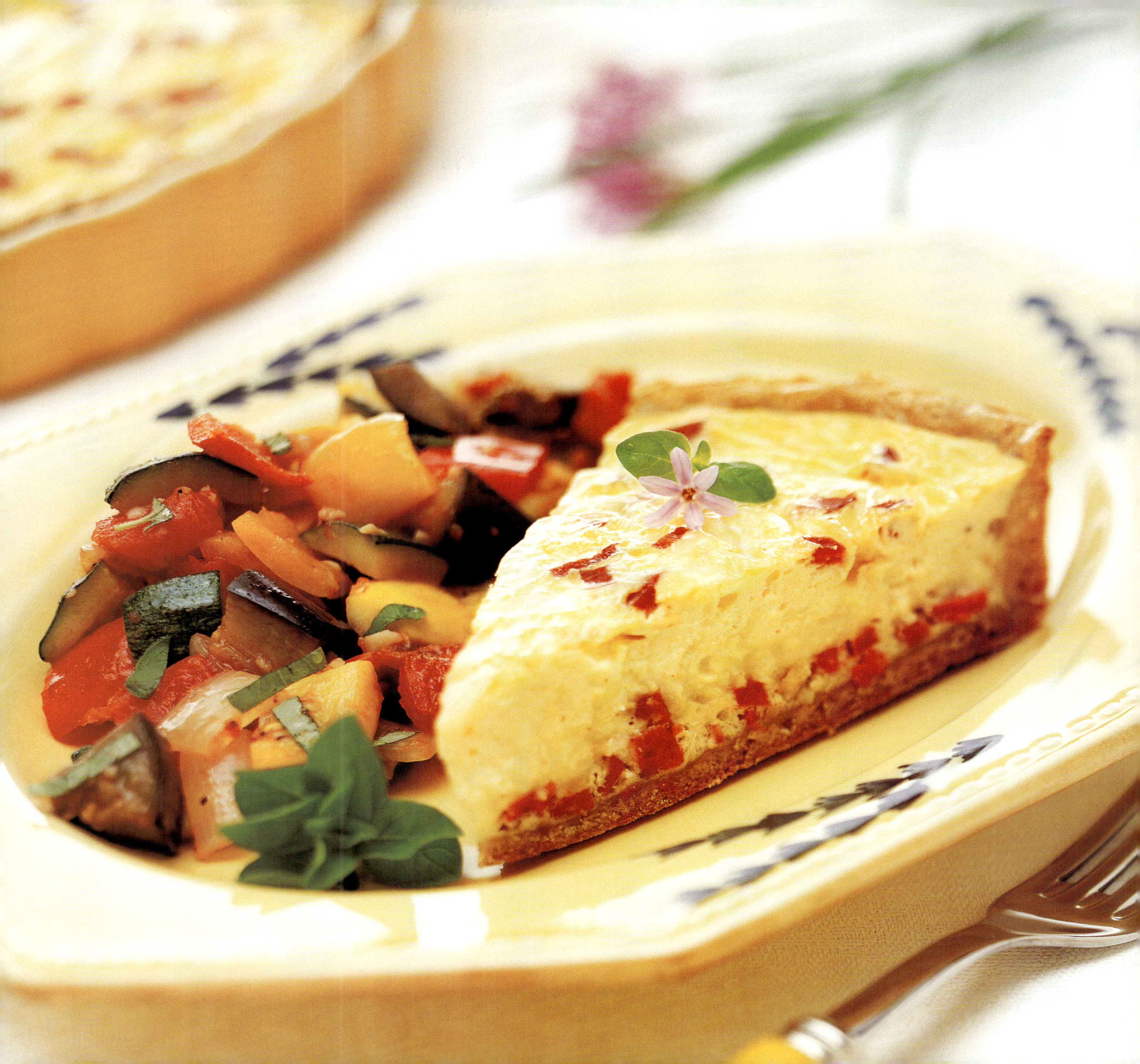

SAVORY PIE CRUST *under 30 minutes*

- ¾ cup (3½ oz/105 g) all-purpose flour
- ¾ cup (3½ oz/105 g) whole-wheat pastry flour
- ½ teaspoon baking powder
- ½ teaspoon baking soda
- pinch sea salt
- ½ cup (4 fl oz/120 ml) 1% plain soy milk

1. Combine dry ingredients in a food processor fitted with a pastry blade. With the machine running, add soy milk. Process until mixture has a granular texture.
2. Flatten dough into a disk, wrap in plastic wrap and chill for about 30 minutes.

YIELD: MAKES ONE PIE SHELL

RATATOUILLE *30–60 minutes*

- no-stick cooking spray
- 1 medium roasted onion (page 40), cut into medium dice
- 1 small eggplant, peeled (optional) and cut into large dice
- 1 red bell pepper, cut into large dice
- 1 yellow bell pepper, cut into large dice
- 2 medium zucchini, cut into large dice
- 1 tablespoon chopped fresh garlic
- 1 tablespoon dried oregano
- 1 28-ounce (840-g) can low-sodium Italian plum tomatoes with juices, chopped
- sea salt and freshly ground black pepper to taste

1. Spray a large sauté pan once with cooking spray and set it over medium-low heat. Add onions and cook briefly. Add eggplant and bell peppers and cook, stirring often, until they begin to soften, about 10 minutes. Add zucchini, garlic and oregano and cook, stirring, for 5 minutes.
2. Add tomatoes and cook, stirring, until thick and aromatic, about 15 minutes. Season with salt and pepper.

YIELD: ABOUT 10 CUPS (80 OZ/2.4 K), 10 SERVINGS

Per 1-cup (8-oz/240-g) serving: 37 Calories, 0.3g Fat, 0g Saturated Fat, 0mg Cholesterol, 2g Protein, 8g Carbohydrate, 2.3g Fiber, 10mg Sodium

LEMON TARTLETS *over 60 minutes*

CRUST

- no-stick cooking spray
- 1½ cups (6½ oz/200 g) all-purpose flour or 1⅔ cups (6½ oz/200 g) oat flour
- ½ cup (3½ oz/100 g) natural cane sugar
- ¼ teaspoon baking powder
- ¼ teaspoon baking soda
- ½ cup (4 fl oz/120 ml) 1% vanilla soy milk
- 1 tablespoon fat-free egg product, optional
- 1 teaspoon grated lemon zest

FILLING

- ½ cup (4 fl oz/120 ml) fat-free egg product
- 2 tablespoons low-fat silken tofu
- 1½ cups (12 fl oz/360 ml) water
- 1¼ cups (8½ oz/250 g) natural cane sugar
- ½ cup (4 fl oz/120 ml) fresh lemon juice, strained
- ¼ cup (1 oz/30 g) cornstarch
- 1 tablespoon grated lemon zest
- 1 teaspoon pure lemon extract
- 1 vanilla bean (optional), split lengthwise

TO MAKE CRUST

1. Preheat oven to 350°F (175°C). Spray eight 3-inch (7.5-cm) tartlet pans or one 10-inch (25-cm) tart pan lightly with cooking spray.

2. In a food processor, combine flour, sugar, baking powder and baking soda. Blend for 15 seconds. Combine soy milk, egg product and lemon zest in a cup. With the motor running, add soy milk mixture to dry ingredients. Process until dough forms a ball, about 20 seconds.

3. Transfer dough to a lightly floured surface. Knead until dough just comes together. For tartlets, divide dough into 8 equal pieces.

4. With floured hands, press dough into prepared tart pans. Cut circles of parchment paper and place in shells. Add dried beans or pie weights. Bake until crusts are lightly browned, about 10 minutes for tartlets and 15 minutes for single tart. Remove paper and beans and bake for 3 minutes more. Let cool on a wire rack.

TO MAKE FILLING

1. In a blender, puree egg product and tofu.

2. In a saucepan, combine water, sugar, lemon juice, cornstarch, lemon zest and extract. If using vanilla bean, scrape seeds from pod; add seeds and bean to mixture.

3. Cook over medium heat, stirring, until thick, about 8 minutes. Remove from heat. Stir a small amount of the lemon mixture into the egg/tofu mixture, then return mixture to saucepan. Cook over low heat, stirring, for 5 minutes. Remove vanilla bean. Spoon mixture into tart shells. Chill for 1 hour.

4. Serve with Raspberry Sauce (page 28), if desired. For a fanciful touch, garnish tartlets with crystallized violets.

YIELD: 8 SERVINGS

Per serving: 302 Calories, 0.8g Fat, 0.1g Saturated Fat, 0.2mg Cholesterol, 5g Protein, 70g Carbohydrate, 0.8g Fiber, 86mg Sodium

A FRENCH LUNCH

RASPBERRY SAUCE

- 10 ounces (300 g) frozen unsweetened raspberries, thawed
- ¾ cup (6 fl oz/180 ml) liquid fruit sweetener or apple juice concentrate
- 1 vanilla bean (optional), split lengthwise

1. In a food processor, combine raspberries and fruit sweetener or apple juice concentrate. Blend for 1 minute.

2. Transfer to a small pitcher. (If you prefer a smoother sauce, strain the puree into a pitcher.) Add vanilla bean, if using, and chill. Remove bean before serving.

YIELD: 2 CUPS (16 FL OZ/480 ML)

Per 2-tablespoon serving: 29 Calories, 0g Fat, 0g Saturated Fat, 0mg Cholesterol, 0g Protein, 7g Carbohydrate, 0.3g Fiber, 3mg Sodium

CRÈME BRÛLÉE

- 2 cups (16 fl oz/480 ml) 1% vanilla soy milk
- 1 vanilla bean
- ¾ cup (6 fl oz/180 ml) fat-free egg product
- 4 ounces (120 g) low-fat silken tofu
- ½ cup (3½ oz/100 g) plus 6 tablespoons (3 oz/100g) natural cane sugar
- 1 tablespoon tapioca flour or cornstarch
- 1 teaspoon pure vanilla extract

1. Preheat oven to 325°F (165°C).

2. Pour soy milk into a heavy saucepan. Split vanilla bean lengthwise, scrape out seeds and add to saucepan along with bean. Warm gently for 3 minutes. Remove bean.

3. In blender or food processor, combine egg product, tofu, ½ cup (3½ oz/100 g) of the sugar, the tapioca flour or cornstarch, and vanilla extract. Puree until smooth. Add warm soy milk.

4. Pour into 6 ramekins or custard cups. Set cups in a large baking dish with handles and add enough warm water to fill dish 1 inch (2.5 cm) deep.

5. Bake for 50 to 60 minutes, or until custard is just firm at the edges and slightly shaky in the center. Remove cups from water bath and chill for at least 4 hours.

6. When ready to serve, sprinkle about 1 tablespoon sugar on top of each custard and place under hot broiler for 3 minutes, or until sugar melts.

YIELD: 6 SERVINGS

Per serving: 190 Calories, 1.9g Fat, 0.2g Saturated Fat, 0.3mg Cholesterol, 6g Protein, 38g Carbohydrate, 0.1g Fiber, 105mg Sodium

Nutrition Bonus: Restaurant-style crème brûlée is usually made with heavy cream and egg yolks. The result is very high in fat — about 49 grams of fat (29 grams saturated) per serving.

BOOST FLAVOR — AND HEALTH — WITH CITRUS ZESTS

The next time you squeeze an orange or lemon, don't just toss the rind away. There are compounds in the peel — limonene and geraniol are two important ones — that may help lower cholesterol and prevent some cancers. While the research is still preliminary, there's no doubt that a little grated lemon or orange zest (the outermost layer, not the white pith) will add flavor to low-fat muffins, marinades, salad dressings and fruit salads. Be sure to scrub the fruit well with warm water and a drop of soap before grating.

Very small amounts of limonene are also found in orange juice.

CRÊPES SUZETTE

CRÊPES

- 1 cup plus 2 tablespoons (9 fl oz/270 ml) 1% vanilla soy milk
- 2/3 cup (3 oz/90 g) all-purpose flour or 2/3 cup plus 1 tablespoon (3 oz/90 g) oat flour
- 1/2 cup plus 2 tablespoons (5 fl oz/150 ml) fat-free egg product
- 2 tablespoons plus 1 teaspoon unsweetened applesauce
- 1 1/2 teaspoons natural cane sugar
- 1/2 teaspoon pure vanilla extract
- no-stick cooking spray

SAUCE

- 1/2 cup (4 fl oz/120 ml) fresh orange juice, strained
- 1 1/2 tablespoons grated orange zest
- 1/4 cup (2 fl oz/60 ml) honey, apple juice concentrate, rice syrup or liquid fruit sweetener
- 1/4 teaspoon pure vanilla extract
- 1 1/2 teaspoons cornstarch
- 1 vanilla bean (optional), split lengthwise

TO MAKE CRÊPES

1. Place soy milk, flour, egg product, applesauce, sugar and vanilla extract in a blender or food processor and mix until smooth.
2. Pour batter into a bowl and let rest for 20 minutes.
3. Spray a 6-inch (15-cm) nonstick omelet pan or griddle once with cooking spray. Heat pan over low heat. Ladle 2 tablespoons batter into pan. Tilt pan to coat bottom.
4. Cook over very low heat until batter thickens and browns around the edge. Flip crêpe with a small metal spatula and cook on other side for 2 to 3 minutes.
5. Transfer crêpe to a plate. Repeat process until all batter is used, stacking cooked crêpes one on top of the other. If the pan gets too hot, crêpes will be difficult to cook: remove pan from heat to let it cool down.
6. Crêpes can be made in advance and stored, wrapped in plastic wrap, for 1 or 2 days in the refrigerator. Or, freeze crêpes for up to 2 months.

TO MAKE SAUCE

1. In a wide saucepan, combine orange juice, orange zest, honey or other sweetener, vanilla extract and cornstarch. Whisk to blend thoroughly. Add vanilla bean, if using.
2. Heat over low heat, stirring constantly, until sauce thickens, about 8 minutes. Remove vanilla bean.
3. Dip each crêpe in warm sauce, then fold into a triangle. Place 2 crêpes on each dessert plate. Spoon remaining sauce on top.

YIELD: 6 TO 8 SERVINGS (12 TO 16 CRÊPES)

Per serving: 109 Calories, 0.4g Fat, 0g Saturated Fat, 0mg Cholesterol, 4g Protein, 23g Carbohydrate, 0.5g Fiber, 42mg Sodium

Nutrition Bonus: Classic crêpes Suzette not only have butter in the batter and the sauce, they're cooked in butter as well. All that butter adds about 23 grams of fat per serving. It's unnecessary, as this recipe so deliciously proves.

STRATEGIES FOR RESTAURANT MEALS

Eating out has become a frequent answer to the question "What can I make for dinner tonight?" And why not? It gives the cook a break, you get to try new foods or revisit old favorites, and it's fun. But if you're looking for low-fat, nutritious meals, restaurants are rarely the place to find them.

The average American eatery serves up food as if its customers were lumberjacks or farmers, not sedentary office workers. The plate itself is often billed as a platter, and the food on it rises several inches high. The bread basket overflows with a tempting array of baked goods. The total calories for the meal often can creep well above 1,000 — and the fat content of many restaurant meals can be more than you need in a whole day.

Just as you've relearned how to eat at home, you can learn a few new strategies for healthy restaurant dining.

- Begin with the menu: Choose chicken or fish over red meat and make sure it's baked, broiled or grilled rather than fried or sautéed. Simple pasta dishes without butter or cheese also make good choices. Skip right by any foods described as scalloped, au gratin, breaded, creamy, à la king or Alfredo: they are guaranteed to be loaded with fat. Stay clear of the classic French butter sauces: beurre blanc, Béarnaise and Hollandaise.

- If it's an option, order half-size or appetizer portions. For a full-size entrée, either split it with a friend or take half home to have for lunch the next day. Despite Mom's admonitions, you don't have to finish everything on your plate.

- Start your meal with a broth or pureed vegetable soup. Studies have shown that this decreases overall food consumption. Other healthful appetizers include steamed artichokes, grilled vegetables and shrimp or seafood cocktail.

- When ordering salad, order it without dressing and ask for balsamic vinegar to sprinkle over the greens. Or bring your own dressing made from a *Taste for Living* recipe.

- Drink water with your meal, or ask for a pot of hot water to make your own green tea.

- Choose the bread that looks the most hearty (whole grain) and make a conscious decision to have just one piece.

- For dessert, stick to fresh fruit or sorbet.

- Keep in mind that the dining experience isn't just about feeding yourself. Eat slowly and savor not only the food but the surroundings, the company and the conversation.

AN Italian BUFFET

ITALIAN CUISINE HAS AN INFINITE VARIETY OF PASTA, COLORFUL VEGETABLES and forthright flavors. There is something about Italian cooking that people of all ages love — there's no generation gap. When Mike and his wife, Lori, host a dinner party that includes friends and family of different ages and varying tastes, Beth usually prepares Italian food, knowing that all will enjoy it.

If you have young children, chances are they'll enjoy cooking Italian with you. The kids are always eager to help out, whether it's stirring red sauce, rolling pizza dough or shaping ravioli. The results might not be picture perfect, but the taste is always superb.

Italian pasta and pizza were built on a foundation of vegetables and grains. But once they were integrated into the American diet, more cheese and meat were added, the average portion size doubled and the fat and calorie count shot up. By keeping portion size within reason and eliminating high-fat ingredients, you can return Italian food to its healthy roots.

- **Tomatoes are the best source of lycopene, an antioxidant thought to protect against prostate cancer. The lycopene is concentrated in cooked tomato sauce.**

THE MEDITERRANEAN MESSAGE

In the 1960s, scientists began to take note of the very low rates of heart and other chronic diseases among rural populations around the Mediterranean. Diet appeared to be the key to good health and longevity. Generally, Mediterranean meals featured a grain, usually rice or pasta, served with vegetables. Dried beans supplied protein; cheese and fish were served only when available. Meat was a flavoring; only rarely was it the main focus of a meal. Olive oil, used both for cooking and as a condiment, contributed substantial calories and fat. Wine was a common beverage.

The Mediterranean diet received a great deal of attention in the 1990s as one way to prevent heart disease among Americans. Certainly its emphasis on plant foods, particularly antioxidant-rich vegetables and fiber-loaded beans, is a sound strategy. Surprisingly, however, the amount of fat in the diet (35% calories from fat) is as high as or even higher than that in the average American diet. But aren't we supposed to cut back on fat?

Keep in mind that the Mediterranean diet was not just a set of food choices, it was part of an active, even arduous life. People could consume a lot of calories in the form of fat because they burned a lot of calories. Few desk-bound Americans have that option. When we eat the Mediterranean way, we tend to get fat.

But the Mediterranean's lessons should not be ignored. Build your diet on a foundation of grains, vegetables and legumes. If you do use oil in cooking, make sure it is olive oil instead of polyunsaturated corn, soybean or safflower oil. Be as active as possible — walk, don't drive, whenever you can. Work outside.

Perhaps the most important lesson is one that is difficult to prove scientifically: Don't rush through dinner. Enjoy it and the good conversation that goes along with it. In short, celebrate life.

MINESTRONE

To make a meal out of this soup, stir in ¼ cup cooked pasta per serving.

- 6 cups (48 fl oz/1.4 L) Vegetable Stock (recipe follows)
- 4 carrots, peeled and cut into medium dice
- 3 stalks celery, tough strings peeled, stalks cut into medium dice
- 2 large boiling potatoes, peeled and cut into medium dice
- 1 14.5-ounce (435-g) can diced low-sodium tomatoes
- ½ head green cabbage, cut into large dice (about 4 cups)
- ½ cup (4 oz/120 g) cooked kidney beans
- ½ cup (4 oz/120 g) cooked white beans
- ¼ teaspoon sea salt
- freshly ground black pepper to taste

1. Combine all ingredients in a soup pot. Bring to a boil and turn down to a simmer.
2. Cook until potatoes are tender, about 30 minutes.

YIELD: ABOUT 2½ QUARTS (2.4 L), 8 TO 10 SERVINGS

Per serving: 79 Calories, 0.3g Fat, 0g Saturated Fat, 0mg Cholesterol, 3g Protein, 17g Carbohydrate, 3.5g Fiber, 93mg Sodium

VEGETABLE STOCK

If you're in a hurry, used canned fat-free, low-sodium vegetable broth in any of the *Taste for Living* recipes.

- 4 medium carrots, peeled and cut into chunks
- 2 stalks celery, tough strings peeled, stalks cut into chunks
- 2 medium onions, roughly chopped
- 1 leek, halved lengthwise and washed thoroughly
- 2 cloves fresh garlic
- 2¼ quarts (2 L) water

1. In a large pot, combine all ingredients. Bring to a boil. Reduce heat to a simmer and cook for 25 minutes.

2. Strain stock and reserve for soups and sauces. It will keep for up to 1 week in the refrigerator or for 1 month in the freezer.

YIELD: ABOUT 7 CUPS (56 FL OZ/1.7 L)

BRUSCHETTA

    no-stick cooking spray
1   fat-free baguette
4   vine-ripened tomatoes
2   teaspoons finely chopped fresh garlic
¼   cup (½ oz/15 g) chopped fresh basil leaves
    sea salt and freshly cracked black pepper to taste

1. Preheat oven to 350°F (175°C). Spray a baking sheet once with cooking spray.

2. Slice bread on the diagonal into slices ¼ inch (0.6 cm) thick. Spread slices on baking sheet.

3. Bake 20 minutes, or until bread is golden brown. (The toasts can be stored in an airtight container for up to 1 month.)

4. Slice tomatoes in half. Squeeze out seeds and cut tomatoes into medium dice.

5. Spray a sauté pan once with cooking spray and place over medium heat. Add garlic and cook, stirring constantly with a rubber spatula, for 30 seconds.

6. Add tomatoes and cook, shaking the pan, for 2 to 3 minutes, just long enough to heat tomatoes. Stir in basil and remove from heat. Season with salt and pepper.

7. Top each toast with a generous tablespoonful of the tomato mixture.

YIELD: 36 TOASTS

Per 2 toasts: 45 Calories, 0.5g Fat, 0.1g Saturated Fat, 0mg Cholesterol, 2g Protein, 9g Carbohydrate, 0.8g Fiber, 89mg Sodium

Nutrition Bonus: Bruschetta can be made with any number of vegetable toppings. We chose tomatoes because of their beneficial lycopene.

AN ITALIAN BUFFET

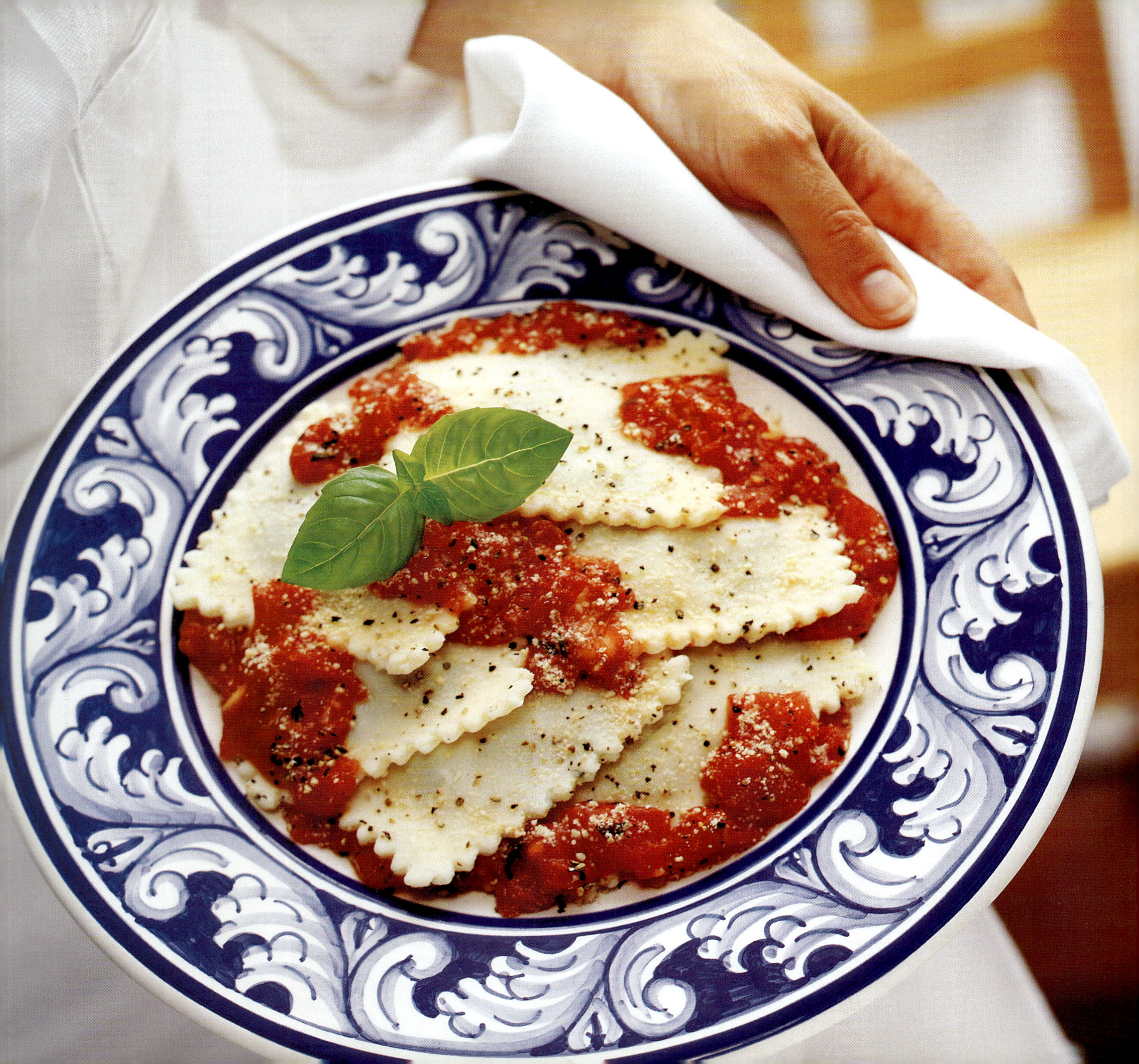

SPINACH RAVIOLI WITH FRESH TOMATO-BASIL SAUCE

Making ravioli is fun. They're easy to fill with a puree of your favorite vegetable. Serve them with a tomato sauce from either of the *Taste for Living* cookbooks.

- 7 ounces (210 g) fresh spinach, stemmed and washed, or 5 ounces (150 g) frozen spinach, thawed
- 16 ounces (480 g) low-fat soft tofu
- ¼ cup (2 fl oz/60 ml) fat-free egg product
- ½ teaspoon chopped fresh garlic
- ⅛ teaspoon sea salt
- freshly ground black pepper to taste
- 1 tablespoon chopped fresh basil or 1 teaspoon dried basil
- 1 recipe Semolina Pasta Dough (page 36), rolled into 2 sheets, or 12 ounces (360 g) store-bought fresh pasta sheets
- 1 recipe Fresh Tomato-Basil Sauce (recipe follows)

1. Bring a large saucepan of water to a boil. Stir in the fresh spinach, cook for a few seconds and drain. When cool enough to handle, squeeze out excess moisture and chop. For frozen spinach, simply squeeze out excess moisture.

2. In a food processor, puree tofu, egg product, garlic, salt and pepper until smooth. Transfer the tofu mixture to a bowl and add spinach and basil.

3. Trim the edges of the pasta sheets so they are neat and about the same length. Place one sheet on the work surface. Paint the surface lightly with water.

4. With a teaspoon, place small mounds of filling in two lines down the length of the dough, spacing them about 1½ inches (4 cm) apart.

5. Lay the second sheet of dough over the top. Gently press around each mound with your fingers to seal the layers.

Use a large knife or ravioli cutter to cut between the mounds to make individual ravioli.

6. Bring a large pot of water to a boil. Add the ravioli, stir once and cook until al dente, about 3 minutes. Ravioli are done when they float to the surface.

7. Divide ravioli evenly among shallow pasta bowls. Spoon hot Fresh Tomato-Basil Sauce on top and serve.

YIELD: 20 RAVIOLI, 5 SERVINGS

Per serving (ravioli and sauce): 449 Calories, 4.2g Fat, 0.4g Saturated Fat, 0mg Cholesterol, 24g Protein, 83g Carbohydrate, 9.4g Fiber, 353mg Sodium

FRESH TOMATO-BASIL SAUCE

- 12 large vine-ripened tomatoes (about 6½ lbs/3 K)
- no-stick cooking spray
- 2 tablespoons chopped fresh garlic
- ½ cup (4 fl oz/120 ml) Vegetable Stock (page 32)
- 1 tablespoon tomato paste
- ¼ cup (½ oz/15 g) chopped fresh basil or 4 teaspoons dried basil
- ⅛ teaspoon sea salt
- freshly cracked black pepper to taste

1. Bring a large pot of water to a boil.

2. Core tomatoes and cut an X on the bottoms with a paring knife. Place tomatoes in boiling water for 1 to 2 minutes to loosen skins. Remove to a bowl of cold water until they are cool enough to handle.

3. Peel tomatoes and squeeze gently to remove seeds. Discard seeds. Cut tomatoes into large dice.

4. Spray a large sauté pan once with cooking spray and place over low heat. Add garlic and cook, stirring, for 1 minute. If using dried basil, add it at this point.

AN ITALIAN BUFFET

5. Add chopped tomatoes, stock and tomato paste. Cover and cook gently over low heat for 20 minutes.

6. Stir in fresh basil and season with salt and pepper.

YIELD: 6 CUPS (48 FL OZ/1.4 L)

Per ½-cup (4-oz/120-g) serving: 62 Calories, 1g Fat, 0.1g Saturated Fat, 0mg Cholesterol, 2.5g Protein, 13g Carbohydrate, 2.2g Fiber, 58mg Sodium

SEMOLINA PASTA DOUGH

- 2 cups (9 oz/270 g) semolina flour
- ½ cup (4 fl oz/120 ml) fat-free egg product or 4 egg whites
- 3 tablespoons water

1. Place all ingredients in food processor and process until dough forms a ball.

2. Turn dough onto a floured surface and knead for 2 minutes. Flatten dough into a disk. Wrap in plastic wrap and chill for 30 minutes.

3. To roll pasta dough by hand, divide the dough in half. Dust a work surface with flour. Use a rolling pin to roll the dough as thin as possible. Lightly re-flour the work surface often and give the dough quarter turns to prevent sticking. Work the dough into a long rectangle about ¼ inch (0.6 cm) thick and 4 to 5 inches (10 to 12 cm) wide.

4. If you are using a pasta machine, first divide the dough in half. Roll each half into a flat rectangle with a rolling pin. Working with one half at a time, run the dough through the widest setting on the machine. Repeat 5 times, running it through progressively thinner settings. Hang the dough over a dowel or the back of a chair. Repeat these steps with the second portion of dough.

5. Cut pasta into shape as directed by chosen recipe.

YIELD: ABOUT 14 OUNCES (420 G) PASTA DOUGH

EGGPLANT PARMESAN

- ½ cup (2 oz/60 g) all-purpose flour
- ⅛ teaspoon sea salt
- ⅛ teaspoon freshly ground black pepper
- ¾ cup (6 fl oz/180 ml) fat-free egg product
- 1 cup (4 oz/120 g) fat-free Italian breadcrumbs
- 2 small or 1 large eggplant (about 1½ lbs/720 g total), cut into ¼-inch (0.6 cm) slices
- 1 recipe Marinara Sauce (page 37)
  no-stick cooking spray
- 8 ounces (240 g) fat-free mozzarella-style soy cheese, grated by hand (1 cup)
  chopped fresh parsley, for sprinkling

1. Preheat oven to 350°F (175°C).

2. In a shallow bowl, mix flour, salt and pepper. Pour egg product into a second bowl. Place breadcrumbs in a third bowl. Dip eggplant slices in flour, egg product and bread crumbs. Set on a baking sheet and let dry for 10 minutes.

3. Spread about ¾ cup (6 fl oz/180 ml) marinara sauce in a 9-by-15-inch (22-by-38-cm) baking dish.

4. Spray a sauté pan or griddle once with cooking spray and place over low heat. Working in batches, lightly brown eggplant slices on both sides.

5. Place one layer of browned eggplant slices in the prepared dish and top with ¾ to 1 cup (6 to 8 oz/180 to 240 ml) sauce. Sprinkle with soy cheese. Cover with parchment paper. Bake for 30 minutes. Let rest a few minutes, then sprinkle with parsley and slice.

YIELD: 8 SERVINGS

Per serving: 183 Calories, 0.7g Fat, 0.1g Saturated Fat, 0mg Cholesterol, 14g Protein, 32g Carbohydrate, 4.5g Fiber, 343mg Sodium

MARINARA SAUCE

Make a double batch and freeze the extra for later use.

- no-stick cooking spray
- 1 large onion, chopped
- 1½ tablespoons finely chopped fresh garlic
- 1½ teaspoons dried basil
- 1 teaspoon dried oregano
- 1 28-ounce (840-g) can low-sodium Italian plum tomatoes, drained and pureed
- 2 tablespoons tomato paste

1. Spray a large saucepan once with cooking spray and set over low heat. Add onions and cook, stirring often, until they begin to soften, about 2 minutes.

2. Add garlic, basil and oregano and stir for 15 seconds.

3. Stir in pureed tomatoes and tomato paste. Cover and cook for 25 minutes, stirring often.

YIELD: ABOUT 3 CUPS (24 FL OZ/420 ML)

Per ½-cup (4-oz/120-g) serving: 43 Calories, 0.6g Fat, 0g Saturated Fat, 0mg Cholesterol, 2g Protein, 9g Carbohydrate, 2.4g Fiber, 58mg Sodium

VIVA LYCOPENE!

It's time to extend a heartfelt thank-you to Italian-American cooks for putting red sauce on the national menu. Whether it's a lively marinara or a long-simmered ragù, tomato-based foods contain a cancer-fighting antioxidant called lycopene.

Because lycopene can be detected in the prostate, researchers have long wondered about its direct effect on prostate cells. Several studies have found strong links between the consumption of tomato products and a reduced prostate cancer risk. Still, the precise mechanism has not been established. A current theory speculates that lycopene is able to switch out-of-control, immortal prostate cancer cells back to cells with a normal life span. In a 1999 study of 10 men undergoing prostate surgery, some benefits of lycopene capsules on prostate cells were noted. Much more study is needed to confirm these findings. Nonetheless, lycopene is a potent antioxidant, and much evidence has defined an association between increased intake of lycopene and reduced risk of cancers of the lung, digestive tract, pancreas, cervix and breast.

All red tomatoes contain lycopene, but the nutrient is more concentrated and better absorbed after cooking. Tomato paste, sauce, juice and catsup provide the best sources. Lycopene is a fat-soluble antioxidant, and a little fat is needed for it to be absorbed by the body. By eating a balanced diet, you will automatically get enough fat for absorption to take place.

Processed canned tomatoes are often a source of unwanted sodium; look for low-sodium brands. Also, check the nutrition labels on jarred red sauce — the fat content varies widely.

AN ITALIAN BUFFET

ITALIAN GREENS WITH ROASTED ONION AND LEMON

under 30 minutes

- 2 bunches escarole or Swiss chard or 4 bunches spinach (about 1½ lbs/720 g total)
- 2 roasted onions (page 40), peeled and sliced
- ¼ cup (2 fl oz/60 ml) Vegetable Stock (page 32)
- juice of 1 lemon
- 1 teaspoon granulated onion
- ⅛ teaspoon sea salt
- freshly ground black pepper to taste

1. Wash greens carefully to remove all grit. Slice greens into large pieces.
2. Bring a large pot of water to a boil. Blanch greens in boiling water for 2 minutes. Drain.
3. Place greens, sliced onions and vegetable stock in a large sauté pan. Cook for 4 minutes over medium heat.
4. Stir in lemon juice and granulated onion. Season with salt and pepper.

YIELD: 6 SERVINGS

Per serving: 45 Calories, 0.3g Fat, 0g Saturated Fat, 0mg Cholesterol, 3g Protein, 10g Carbohydrate, 4g Fiber, 113mg Sodium

Nutrition Bonus: Dark leafy greens are a good source of calcium and beneficial phytonutrients.

SPAGHETTI BOLOGNESE

30–60 minutes

A very versatile sauce; try this meatless Bolognese on pizza or with any of your favorite pasta shapes.

- no-stick cooking spray
- 2 large onions, cut into small dice (about 3 cups)
- 3 tablespoons minced fresh garlic
- 2 tablespoons dried oregano
- 1 tablespoon dried basil or 3 tablespoons chopped fresh basil
- 1–3 teaspoons crushed red pepper flakes
- 12 ounces (360 g) fat-free soy sausage
- 12 ounces (360 g) fat-free soy "meat"
- 1 16-ounce (480-g) can low-sodium tomato puree
- 3 14.5-ounce (435-g) cans low-sodium diced tomatoes
- sea salt to taste
- 2 pounds (960 g) spaghetti

1. Spray a large saucepan once with cooking spray and set over low heat. Add onions and cook, stirring often, until onions are soft and barely translucent, about 5 minutes.
2. Add garlic, oregano, dried basil and red pepper flakes to taste and stir for 30 seconds. Stir in soy sausage and soy meat, breaking them apart with a wooden spoon. Add tomato puree and diced tomatoes. Cook over low heat, stirring often, for about 30 minutes, until sauce is thick. Stir in fresh basil, if using, and season with salt.
3. Meanwhile, when the sauce is nearly ready, bring a very large pot of water to a boil.
4. Add spaghetti, stir once, and cook until al dente, about 8 minutes. Drain and serve covered with sauce.

YIELD: 10 TO 12 SERVINGS

Per serving: 453 Calories, 1.8g Fat, 0.3g Saturated Fat, 0mg Cholesterol, 25g Protein, 84g Carbohydrate, 8.9g Fiber, 368mg Sodium

Nutrition Bonus: Traditional spaghetti Bolognese is often quite meaty, and the fat approaches 40 grams per serving. Our Bolognese weighs in at under 2 grams of fat per serving.

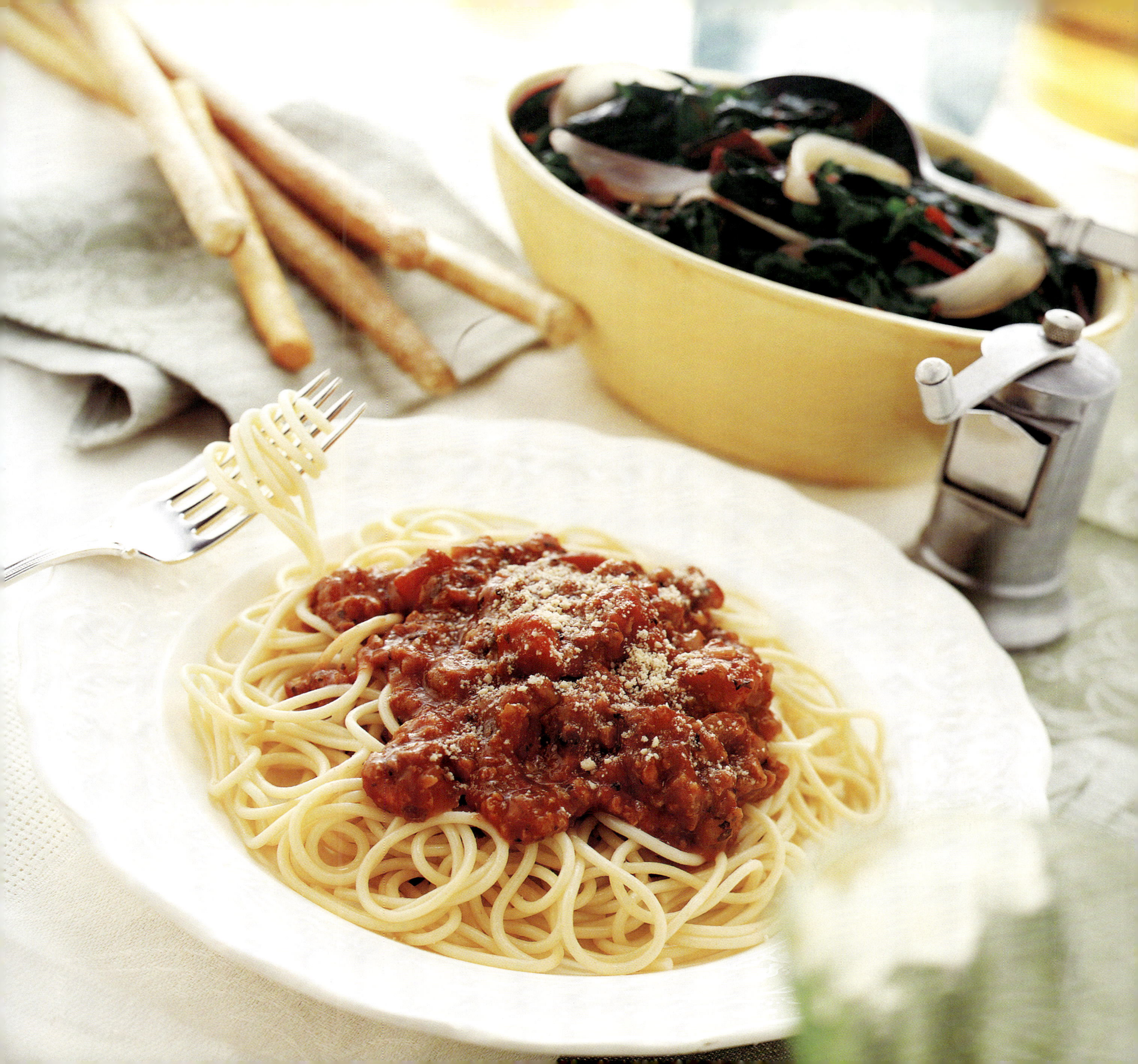

ROASTING ONIONS

Roasting is an easy, fat-free way to bring out the mellow sweetness of onions. You can use roasted onions in a range of sautés, sauces and condiments. I suggest roasting several at a time so you have them ready to use all week long. To roast, place unpeeled onions in a baking dish and bake in a 350°F (175°C) oven until soft: about 45 minutes for medium onions, 50 to 60 minutes for large onions. When cool, wrap tightly in plastic wrap. Roasted onions will keep up to 1 week in the refrigerator. One medium onion yields about ¾ cup chopped onion, one large onion yields about 1 ¼ cups chopped onion.

TOFU CACCIATORE

over 60 minutes

- 2 pounds (960 g) firm low-fat tofu, cut into ½-inch-thick (1.25-cm-thick) slices *SOY*
- no-stick cooking spray
- 1 medium onion, sliced
- 1 red bell pepper, cored and sliced
- 1 green bell pepper, cored and sliced
- 1 tablespoon finely chopped fresh garlic
- 2 teaspoons dried basil
- 2 teaspoons dried oregano
- 3 14.5-ounce (435-g) cans low-sodium chopped tomatoes, drained
- 2 tablespoons tomato paste
- ¼ cup (1 oz/30 g) all-purpose flour
- pinch sea salt
- pinch freshly ground black pepper

1. To squeeze excess moisture from tofu, place tofu slices on a baking sheet. Cover with parchment paper or plastic wrap and set a second baking sheet on top. Place weights (heavy cans or pans) on top of the baking sheet. Set aside for 15 minutes. (Or, if you want a meatier texture, spread tofu slices on a baking sheet, cover with plastic wrap and freeze until ready to use.)

2. Preheat oven to 350°F (175°C).

3. Spray a sauté pan once with cooking spray and place pan over low heat. Add onions and peppers and cook, stirring frequently, for 5 minutes.

4. Add garlic, basil and oregano and cook, stirring, for 15 seconds. Stir in tomatoes and tomato paste. Cover and simmer for 15 minutes.

5. While sauce is simmering, brown tofu: Combine flour, salt and pepper in a shallow dish. Spray a large sauté pan or griddle once with cooking spray and place pan over low heat.

6. Dredge tofu slices in seasoned flour and lightly brown on both sides. As the pieces are browned, transfer to a baking dish.

7. Cover tofu with tomato-pepper sauce. Cover baking dish with parchment paper and aluminum foil.

8. Bake for 45 to 90 minutes — the longer the cacciatore bakes, the more flavor the tofu will absorb.

YIELD: 8 SERVINGS

Per serving: 107 Calories, 1.5g Fat, 0g Saturated Fat, 0mg Cholesterol, 12g Protein, 14g Carbohydrate, 2.6g Fiber, 257mg Sodium

Nutrition Bonus: Tofu provides the tasty foundation for a low-fat entrée. Peppers, tomatoes and garlic provide a rich mix of cancer-fighting antioxidants.

TIRAMISÙ

over 60 minutes

COFFEE SYRUP

- 1 vanilla bean, optional
- 1 cup (8 fl oz/240 ml) water
- ¼ cup (2 oz/60 g) natural cane sugar
- 1 tablespoon instant decaffeinated coffee granules
- 1 tablespoon pure vanilla extract

CUSTARD FILLING

- 1 vanilla bean, optional
- 3 cups (24 fl oz/720 ml) 1% vanilla soy milk
- ¾ cup (5 oz/150 g) natural cane sugar
- ¾ cup (6 fl oz/180 ml) fat-free egg product
- ½ cup (2 oz/60 g) all-purpose flour
- 2 ounces (60 g) low-fat silken tofu, pureed
- 2 teaspoons pure vanilla extract

LADYFINGERS

- 1 package (5 oz/150 g) fat-free ladyfingers
- 2 tablespoons fat-free instant cocoa mix, for dusting
- ⅛ teaspoon ground cinnamon

TO MAKE COFFEE SYRUP

1. If using vanilla bean, split it lengthwise and scrape seeds into a small saucepan. Add water and bring to a boil. Remove from heat. Stir in sugar, instant coffee and vanilla extract. Set aside.

TO MAKE CUSTARD FILLING

1. If using vanilla bean, split it lengthwise and scrape seeds into a metal mixing bowl. Add soy milk, sugar, egg product, flour and tofu and blend with a wire whisk.

2. Place bowl over a pan of simmering water. The bowl bottom should not touch the water. Cook, stirring constantly, until mixture thickens, about 8 minutes. Stir in vanilla extract. Cover and chill.

TO ASSEMBLE

1. Line a long rectangular pâté mold with plastic wrap. (Or, use a large soufflé dish for the tiramisù. You don't have to line it.) Place a layer of ladyfingers in the bottom. You should use about half of the ladyfingers to cover the bottom. Brush ladyfingers with coffee syrup.

2. Combine instant cocoa and cinnamon in a small bowl. Spread half of the custard mixture on top of the ladyfingers and sprinkle with some of the cocoa-cinnamon mixture. Repeat with remaining ladyfingers, syrup and custard, topping the custard with a dusting of cocoa-cinnamon mixture. Chill for at least 2 hours before serving.

YIELD: 8 TO 10 SERVINGS

Per serving: 221 Calories, 0.7g Fat, 0g Saturated Fat, 0mg Cholesterol, 5g Protein, 49g Carbohydrate, 0.5g Fiber, 100mg Sodium

Nutrition Bonus: Classic tiramisù made with mascarpone cheese, cream and egg yolks has a whopping 25 grams of fat per serving.

AN ITALIAN BUFFET

BISCOTTI *over 60 minutes*

butter-flavor cooking spray
3 cups (13 oz/390 g) all-purpose flour or 3½ cups (13 oz/390 g) oat flour
¾ cup (5 oz/150 g) natural cane sugar
½ cup (4 fl oz/120 ml) unsweetened applesauce
½ cup (4 fl oz/120 ml) fat-free egg product
1 tablespoon grated orange zest
1 tablespoon pure orange extract
1 teaspoon pure vanilla extract
1½ teaspoons baking powder
⅛ teaspoon sea salt
¾ cup (4½ oz/135 g) currants or chopped raisins

GLAZE

1 egg white, beaten
1 tablespoon natural cane sugar
½ teaspoon ground cinnamon

1. Preheat oven to 325°F (165°C). Spray 2 baking sheets lightly with cooking spray.

2. Combine biscotti ingredients in a food processor fitted with a dough blade. Process for 30 seconds, or until mixture just begins to form a ball. (To mix with an electric mixer, combine dry ingredients. With the mixer running, add the remaining ingredients and mix on medium speed for 1 minute, or until dough is blended.)

3. Lightly flour a work surface. Divide dough in half and form two 12-inch (30-cm) logs. Transfer logs to one of the prepared baking sheets.

4. For glaze, lightly brush logs with beaten egg white. Combine sugar and cinnamon and sprinkle over logs.

5. Bake for 25 minutes, or until logs are firm. Let cool on the baking sheet for at least 15 minutes. Increase oven temperature to 350°F (175°C).

6. With a long serrated knife, cut logs on the diagonal into slices ¼ inch (0.6 cm) thick. Spread slices out on baking sheets and bake for 5 minutes. Turn over biscotti and bake for 5 minutes longer.

7. Biscotti will keep, stored in an airtight container, for up to 1 month.

YIELD: ABOUT 4 DOZEN BISCOTTI

Per biscotto: 52 Calories, 0.1g Fat, 0g Saturated Fat, 0mg Cholesterol, 1g Protein, 12g Carbohydrate, 0.4g Fiber, 21mg Sodium

ZABAGLIONE WITH BERRIES *under 30 minutes*

2 cups (8 oz/240 g) raspberries, strawberries or blueberries, rinsed
¾ cup (6 fl oz/180 ml) fat-free egg product
½ cup (4 fl oz/120 ml) Marsala or Madeira wine or white grape juice
¼ cup (1½ oz/45 g) natural cane sugar

1. If using strawberries, hull and slice down the center. Divide berries among 4 parfait glasses or dessert cups.

2. Place egg product, wine or grape juice and sugar in the top of a double boiler set over simmering water. With a handheld electric mixer, whip mixture until it becomes a fluffy, thickened cream, about 12 minutes.

3. Spoon zabaglione over berries and serve immediately.

YIELD: 5 SERVINGS

Per serving: 95 Calories, 0.3g Fat, 0g Saturated Fat, 0mg Cholesterol, 4g Protein, 16g Carbohydrate, 3.3g Fiber, 59mg Sodium

N Nutrition Bonus: Berries, especially raspberries, are loaded with fiber and phytonutrients shown to slow the growth of cancer cells in the laboratory.

Middle Eastern MEZZE

- In the 1960s, Crete and other parts of the eastern Mediterranean were studied for their very low rates of heart disease. Today, as populations become more urbanized, rates of heart disease and other chronic illnesses are rising. Scientists think it's caused, in part, by overnutrition — the consumption of more food than the body needs.

SIMPLY TRANSLATED, THE WORD MEZZE IS GREEK FOR APPETIZER. BUT IT'S MUCH MORE than that. It's a way of life found in Greece and throughout the eastern Mediterranean. Little tasty dishes are spread on the table and guests nibble a little of this, a little of that, over the course of an evening. The foods are casual, they're versatile and, most importantly, they can be prepared ahead.

Many Americans have enjoyed hummus and baba ghanoush at Middle Eastern restaurants where these favorites are made the authentic way, with lots of olive oil to make the dips smooth and flavorful. To cut back on the fat and calories, you can use low-fat soft or silken tofu to provide the same satiny texture. It also adds some beneficial soy protein, and the flavor is excellent.

MOUSSAKA

over 60 minutes

no-stick cooking spray

3 large eggplants (about 4 lbs/1.8 K total), peeled and cut into ½-inch (1.25-cm) slices

1 large onion, chopped

2 tablespoons chopped fresh garlic

12 ounces (360 g) ground fat-free soy "meat" — SOY

1 28-ounce (840-g) can low-sodium Italian plum tomatoes, drained and chopped

2 cups (12 oz/360 g) cooked brown rice

1 teaspoon dried oregano

¼ teaspoon ground allspice

¼ teaspoon sea salt

¼ teaspoon freshly ground black pepper

¼ cup chopped fresh parsley

¾ cup (6 fl oz/180 ml) fat-free egg product

¾ cup breadcrumbs

1. Preheat a stovetop grill pan or light an outdoor grill.

2. Spray grill lightly with cooking spray. Cook eggplant slices until browned on both sides, about 8 minutes. Set aside.

3. Preheat oven to 350°F (175°C).

4. Spray a large sauté pan once with cooking spray and heat pan over medium-low heat. Add onions and cook until soft, about 5 minutes. Stir in garlic and cook 15 seconds.

5. Add soy meat, breaking it up with a wooden spoon, and cook 3 minutes.

6. Stir in tomatoes, rice, oregano, allspice, salt, pepper and 2 tablespoons of the parsley. Cook over low heat until thick and fragrant, about 15 minutes. Remove from heat.

7. In a small bowl, combine egg product and the remaining 2 tablespoons parsley. Stir into soy meat mixture.

8. Line the bottom of a lasagne pan or other large baking dish with eggplant slices. Spread half of the soy meat mixture on top. Cover with a second layer of eggplant and meat. Sprinkle with breadcrumbs.

9. Bake until browned and bubbling, about 30 minutes.

YIELD: 10 SERVINGS

Per serving: 169 Calories, 1g Fat, 0.2g Saturated Fat, 0.4mg Cholesterol, 13g Protein, 27g Carbohydrate, 6.3g Fiber, 329mg Sodium

Nutrition Bonus: A typical moussaka recipe calls for 1 cup of olive oil to fry the eggplant. Grilling the eggplant slices uses no fat and makes for a much healthier dish.

GREEK SALAD

- 2 pounds (960 g) Yukon Gold or small white potatoes, peeled and cut into large dice
- 1 cup (4 oz/120 g) trimmed green beans
- 1 cup (6 oz/180 g) cherry tomatoes (mixed yellow and red), sliced in half
- 1 small red onion, cut in half vertically and very thinly sliced
- 1 red bell pepper, thinly sliced
- 1 green or yellow bell pepper, thinly sliced
- 4 ounces (120 g) smoked tofu, cut into medium dice
- 8 pepperoncini (Italian pickled peppers)

DRESSING

- 3 tablespoons vegetable juice, such as V8
- 3 tablespoons red wine vinegar
- 2 tablespoons liquid from pepperoncini jar
- 1 tablespoon water
- 1 teaspoon granulated garlic
- 1¼ teaspoons dried oregano
- sea salt and freshly ground black pepper to taste

1. Cook potatoes in boiling water until just tender, about 6 minutes. Drain and refresh under cold running water.
2. Cook green beans in boiling water until just tender, about 2 minutes. Drain and refresh under cold running water.
3. In a small bowl, whisk together dressing ingredients.
4. Arrange potatoes, green beans, tomatoes, onions, bell peppers, tofu and pepperoncini on a platter. Pour dressing over top.

YIELD: 8 TO 10 SERVINGS

Per serving: 97 Calories, 0.5g Fat, 0g Saturated Fat, 0mg Cholesterol, 3g Protein, 21g Carbohydrate, 2.6g Fiber, 184mg Sodium

SPANAKOPITA

- no-stick cooking spray
- 12 ounces (360 g) fresh spinach, stemmed and washed, or 10 ounces (300 g) frozen spinach, thawed
- ½ cup chopped roasted onion (page 40)
- 1 tablespoon soft low-fat tofu
- 1 tablespoon fresh lemon juice
- ⅛ teaspoon sea salt
- ½ teaspoon freshly ground black pepper
- 4 sheets phyllo dough, thawed if frozen
- 1 egg white, beaten

1. Preheat oven to 350°F (175°C). Spray a baking sheet lightly with cooking spray. Bring a large pot of water to a boil.
2. Cook fresh spinach for a few seconds in boiling water. Drain, squeezing out excess water, and chop. For frozen spinach, simply squeeze out excess water. Place in a bowl.
3. Stir in onions, tofu, lemon juice, salt and pepper.
4. Place phyllo dough on a clean work surface and cover with a clean towel. Place a damp towel on top to prevent phyllo from drying out.
5. Remove 1 sheet of phyllo from stack. Place on work surface. Cut into 4 lengthwise strips. Place 1/16 of the mixture at the bottom of one strip. Fold one corner of the strip up and over the filling, then continue to fold the strip loosely (as you would fold a flag) to form a neat triangle. Repeat with the remaining phyllo and filling. (Triangles can be frozen until ready to bake. Do not thaw before baking.)
6. Place triangles on prepared baking sheet. Brush with beaten egg white. Bake until golden, about 25 minutes.

YIELD: 16 SPINACH TRIANGLES

Per spinach triangle: 22 Calories, 0.3g Fat, 0g Saturated Fat, 0mg Cholesterol, 1g Protein, 4g Carbohydrate, 0.6g Fiber, 57mg Sodium

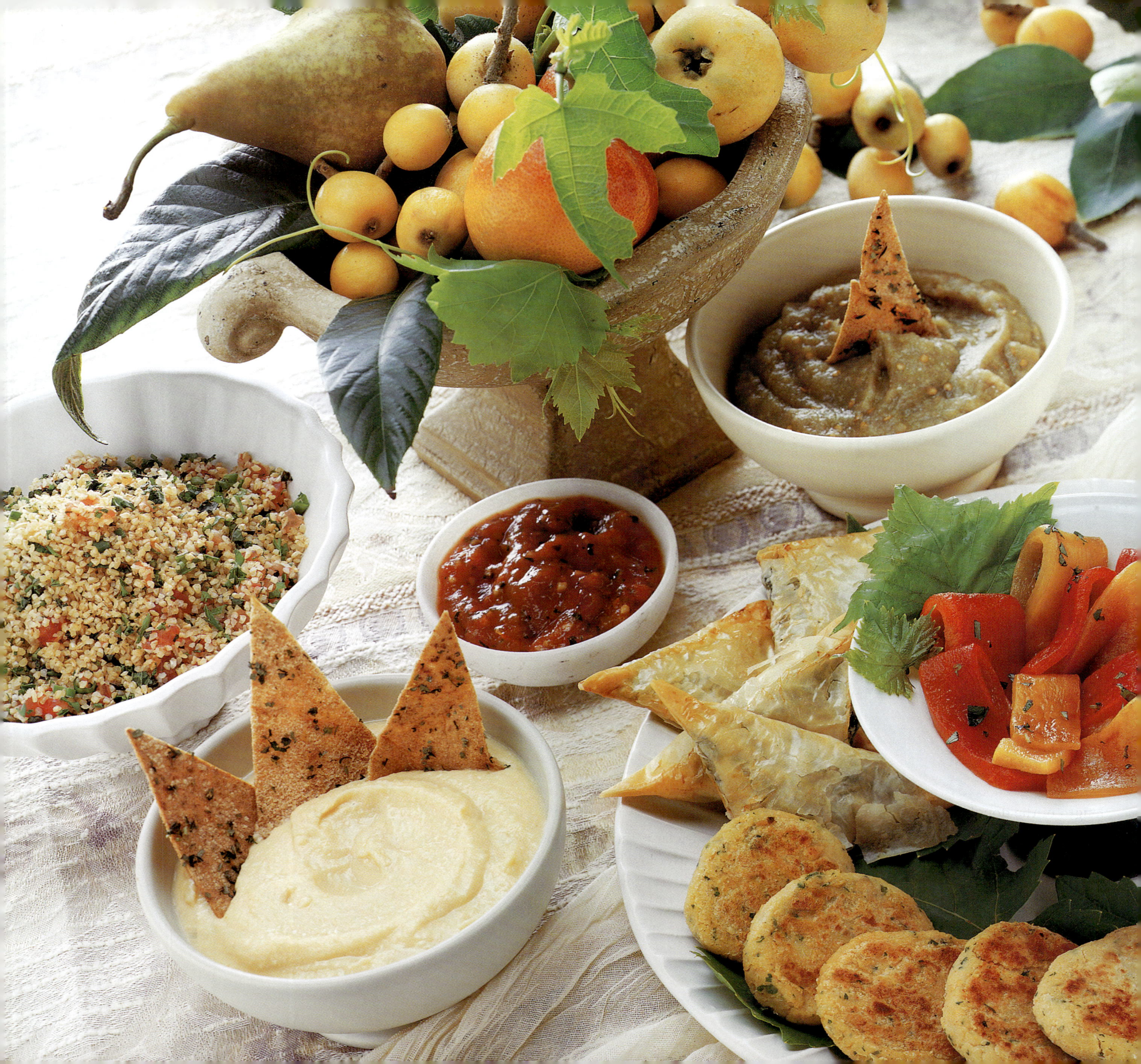

HUMMUS

over 60 minutes

- ¾ cup (5 oz/150 g) dried chickpeas (garbanzos), soaked overnight, or 2 cups (12 oz/360 g) canned chickpeas
- ¼ cup (2 fl oz/60 ml) water
- ¼ cup (2 fl oz/60 ml) fresh lemon juice
- 2 tablespoons low-fat silken tofu
- ½ teaspoon chopped fresh garlic
- ⅛ teaspoon cayenne pepper
- ⅛ teaspoon sea salt
- 1 tablespoon chopped fresh parsley

1. If using dried chickpeas, place in a saucepan, cover with water and bring to a boil. Simmer, adding more water as needed, until tender, about 1 hour 15 minutes. Drain. If using canned chickpeas, drain and rinse.
2. In a food processor, combine chickpeas, water, lemon juice, tofu, garlic, cayenne and salt. Process until smooth.
3. Transfer hummus to a bowl. Garnish with parsley.

YIELD: 2 CUPS (16 OZ/480 G), 8 SERVINGS

Per ¼-cup (2-oz/60-g) serving: 71 Calories, 1.1g Fat, 0.1g Saturated Fat, 0mg Cholesterol, 4g Protein, 12g Carbohydrate, 3.2g Fiber, 44mg Sodium

TABBOULEH

over 60 minutes

- ¾ cup (6 oz/180 g) bulgur
- 1 cup (8 fl oz/240 ml) boiling water
- 2 cups (8 oz/240 g) chopped fresh parsley
- 2 large vine-ripened tomatoes, cored, seeded and cut into small dice
- ½ cup (2 oz/60 g) sliced green onions
- 2 tablespoons tomato juice
- 1 tablespoon fresh lemon juice
- 1 tablespoon chopped fresh mint
- 1 teaspoon finely chopped fresh garlic
- ¼ teaspoon sea salt

1. Place bulgur in large bowl, add boiling water and cover with plastic wrap. Set aside for 25 minutes, then place in the refrigerator and chill for at least 30 minutes.
2. Add remaining ingredients to bowl. Toss to combine.

YIELD: ABOUT 5 CUPS (34 OZ/1 K), 10 SERVINGS

Per ½-cup (3½-oz/100-g) serving: 49 Calories, 0.3g Fat, 0.1g Saturated Fat, 0mg Cholesterol, 2g Protein, 11g Carbohydrate, 2.8g Fiber, 82mg Sodium

Nutrition Bonus: Fresh parsley is a rich source of vitamin C.

FALAFEL

over 60 minutes

- ¾ cup (5 oz/150 g) dried chickpeas (garbanzos), soaked overnight, or 2 cups (12 oz/360 g) canned chickpeas
- 2 tablespoons chopped fresh parsley
- 1 tablespoon low-fat soft tofu
- 1 tablespoon flour
- 1 teaspoon chopped fresh garlic
- ¾ teaspoon ground cumin
- ⅛–¼ teaspoon cayenne pepper
- no-stick cooking spray

1. Prepare chickpeas as described in Hummus (recipe at left).
2. In a food processor, combine chickpeas, parsley, tofu, flour, garlic, cumin and cayenne. Process 1 minute.
3. Form mixture into 20 small oval patties.
4. Spray a griddle or large sauté pan once with cooking spray. Heat pan over medium-low heat. Cook falafel for about 5 minutes on each side, until hot and light golden.

YIELD: 20 FALAFEL

Per falafel: 30 Calories, 0.5g Fat, 0g Saturated Fat, 0mg Cholesterol, 2g Protein, 5g Carbohydrate, 1.3g Fiber, 2mg Sodium

Clockwise, from upper right: Baba Ghanoush, Roasted Pepper Filets, Spanakopita, Falafel, Hummus with Pita Toast Points, Tabbouleh, Hot Sauce

MIDDLE EASTERN MEZZE

HOT SAUCE

- 5 large vine-ripened tomatoes
- 1 serrano pepper
- 1 tablespoon chopped fresh parsley
- ¼ teaspoon chopped fresh garlic
- ⅛ teaspoon sea salt

1. Preheat oven to 350°F (175°C).
2. Set tomatoes and pepper in a baking dish. Roast in oven until skins blister, about 25 minutes. Peel peppers.
3. Puree tomatoes and pepper in a food processor. Stir in parsley, garlic and salt. Serve with Falafel (page 47).

YIELD: 2 CUPS (16 OZ/480 G), 8 SERVINGS

Per ¼-cup (2-oz/60-g) serving: 19 Calories, 0.3g Fat, 0g Saturated Fat, 0mg Cholesterol, 1g Protein, 4g Carbohydrate, 1g Fiber, 44mg Sodium

BABA GHANOUSH

- 4 medium eggplants
- 2 tablespoons fresh lemon juice
- 2 teaspoons chopped fresh garlic
- 2 teaspoons low-fat silken tofu
- ¼ teaspoon sea salt

1. Preheat oven to 400°F (200°C) or light an outdoor grill.
2. Roast eggplants, turning occasionally, until skins turn reddish brown and flesh is soft, about 40 minutes. Let cool.
3. Peel eggplants and place flesh in a food processor. Add lemon juice, garlic, tofu and salt. Process until smooth. Serve with Pita Toast Points (recipe follows).

YIELD: 4 CUPS (32 OZ/960 G), 8 SERVINGS

Per ½-cup (4-oz/120-g) serving: 23 Calories, 0.2g Fat, 0g Saturated Fat, 0mg Cholesterol, 1g Protein, 5g Carbohydrate, 1.9g Fiber, 76mg Sodium

PITA TOAST POINTS

- no-stick cooking spray
- 3 no-added-fat pita breads, preferably whole-grain
- 1 tablespoon chopped fresh thyme (omit if not available)
- 1 tablespoon chopped fresh parsley

1. Preheat oven to 350°F (175°C). Spray a baking sheet lightly with cooking spray.
2. Separate top and bottom halves of pita breads. Slice each half into 8 wedges.
3. Toss pita pieces in a bowl with herbs. Spread on prepared baking sheet. Bake until crisp, about 15 minutes.

YIELD: ABOUT 4 DOZEN TOAST POINTS

Per 3-toast serving: 25 Calories, 0.2g Fat, 0g Saturated Fat, 0mg Cholesterol, 1g Protein, 5g Carbohydrate, 0.9g Fiber, 58mg Sodium

ROASTED PEPPER FILLETS

- 6 bell peppers (red and/or yellow)
- 1 teaspoon chopped fresh oregano (omit if not available)
- ⅛ teaspoon granulated garlic
- ⅛ teaspoon sea salt

1. Light an outdoor grill or preheat broiler.
2. Roast peppers, turning frequently, until skins blister and turn black. Transfer peppers to a bowl, cover with plastic wrap and set aside for 30 minutes.
3. To peel peppers, place under cool running water and peel away blistered skins. Slice open and wash out seeds.
4. Slice peppers into strips. Toss with oregano, garlic and salt.

YIELD: 8 SERVINGS

Per serving: 15 Calories, 0.1g Fat, 0g Saturated Fat, 0mg Cholesterol, 0g Protein, 4g Carbohydrate, 1g Fiber, 38mg Sodium

AN Indian FEAST

MANY EXCELLENT COOKBOOKS ON THE FOODS OF INDIA CAN BE found in the United States. But there's nothing like a visit to a good Indian specialty shop to really learn about Indian ingredients. There, you'll encounter a marvelous assortment of lentils, rice, spices, peppers and fruits. It can all be a bit overwhelming; you might want to allow time to chat with store owners and knowledgeable customers about authentic preparations. You'll learn more in an afternoon than in days of reading cookbooks.

- **India has very low rates of heart disease and certain cancers.**

- **Sometimes called the "apples of the tropics," mangoes are very popular in India, where three-fourths of the world's mangoes are grown.**

RED LENTIL DHAL

30–60 minutes

- no-stick cooking spray
- 1 large onion, chopped (about 1½ cups)
- 2 tablespoons finely chopped fresh ginger
- 1½ tablespoons chopped fresh garlic
- 2 cups (16 oz/480 g) red lentils, rinsed and picked over
- 5–6 cups (40–44 fl oz/1.2–1.3 L) Vegetable Stock (page 32) or water
- ¼ teaspoon sea salt

1. Spray a saucepan once with cooking spray and set over low heat. Add onions and cook for 2 minutes, stirring, until they turn translucent.

2. Add ginger and garlic. Cook, stirring, for 15 seconds.

3. Add lentils and stock or water. Bring to a boil. Reduce heat to a simmer and cook, stirring frequently, until lentils are soft, 25 to 30 minutes. Stir in salt.

YIELD: 8 SERVINGS

Per serving: 156 Calories, 0.5g Fat, 0g Saturated Fat, 0mg Cholesterol, 12g Protein, 28g Carbohydrate, 10.3g Fiber, 81mg Sodium

Nutrition Bonus: One serving of red lentil dhal provides nearly half of the daily requirement for folate and a hefty dose of fiber.

LENTILS AND FOLATE

There is no one perfect food, but lentils might come close. A fine source of plant protein, lentils have an advantage over other dried beans and legumes in that they don't take hours to cook. Quite tasty on their own, lentils will provide an almost-meaty, satisfying backdrop for aromatic vegetables and lively spices.

Lentils come in a range of colors from basic brown to brilliant orange. Most European lentils have a dark brown exterior. They're easy to find in supermarkets. The green French "Puy" lentils are worth seeking out. Yellow lentils and the orange-hued red lentils are sold in East Indian markets and natural foods stores.

Nutritionally, lentils bring a number of benefits to the plate: Like other legumes, they're rich in soluble fiber, which helps lower blood cholesterol. They provide some calcium, iron and other trace minerals. Lentils are also one of the best sources for folate, a B vitamin critical for preventing neural-tube birth defects. Folate, also called folic acid, may protect against some types of cancers, and new evidence strongly suggests that folate may also lower heart disease risk.

In addition to lentils, asparagus, spinach and other dark green leafy vegetables, most legumes, strawberries, orange juice and oatmeal are excellent natural sources of folate. Many bread and grain products are now enriched with folic acid. While you should try to get as much folate as you can in your diet, nearly all multivitamin supplements contain the Recommended Dietary Allowance (RDA) of 400 micrograms. Taking a supplement each day is a way to ensure that you are getting the folic acid you need.

Clockwise, from upper left: Basmati Rice with Peas, Mango Chutney, Spicy Okra with Tomatoes, Red Lentil Dahl, Vegetable Curry

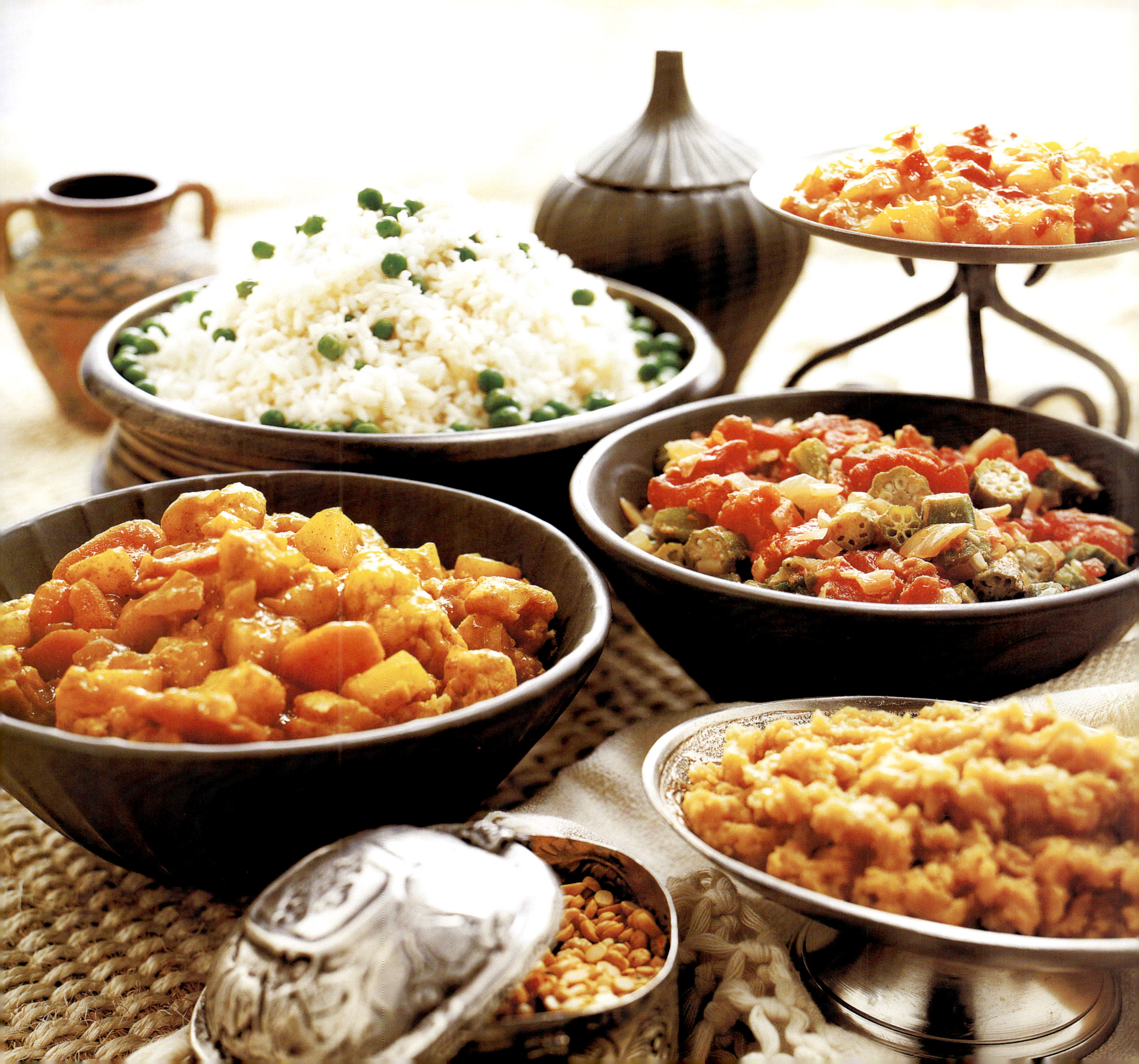

CHAPATIS *over 60 minutes*

Many supermarkets now carry whole-wheat pastry flour. You can also find it at most natural foods stores.

- 2½ cups (10 oz/300 g) whole-wheat pastry flour
- 1 teaspoon sea salt
- 1 cup (8 fl oz/250 ml) warm water
- no-stick cooking spray

1. In the bowl of a food processor fitted with a dough blade, process flour, salt and water until the mixture forms a ball.
2. Turn dough onto a floured work surface and knead for 5 minutes. Transfer to a bowl and cover tightly with plastic wrap. Let dough rest for 30 to 90 minutes.
3. Preheat oven to 200°F (95°C).
4. Divide dough into 8 equal pieces. Roll each piece into a 7-inch (18-cm) circle.
5. Spray a cast-iron griddle or skillet once with cooking spray and set over medium-low heat. Cook a chapati for 1 minute. Turn over and cook 5 minutes on second side or until chapati bubbles up. Flip back to first side and cook for 5 minutes. Then place the cooked chapati over the open flame (or on the coils) of a separate burner for a few seconds to brown, as you would a tortilla. Keep cooked chapatis warm in the oven while you cook the remaining dough.
6. If you prefer a crispy, cracker-like texture, increase oven temperature to 350°F (175°C). Bake cooked chapatis, on a pizza stone if possible, until crispy, about 10 minutes.

YIELD: 8 CHAPATIS

Per chapati: 127 Calories, 0.7g Fat, 0.1g Saturated Fat, 0mg Cholesterol, 5g Protein, 27g Carbohydrate, 4.7g Fiber, 298mg Sodium

N Nutrition Bonus: Using whole-wheat pastry flour in the dough adds fiber and produces a tender flatbread.

SAMOSAS *over 60 minutes*

- 3 medium baking potatoes, peeled and cut into large dice
- 2 carrots, peeled and cut into small dice
- ¾ cup (4 oz/120 g) fresh or frozen corn kernels
- 7 ounces (210 g) fresh spinach, stemmed and washed, or 5 ounces (150 g) frozen spinach, thawed
- 1 small roasted onion (page 40), cut into small dice
- 2 teaspoons chopped fresh cilantro
- 1½ teaspoons finely chopped fresh garlic
- ½ teaspoon chopped roasted jalapeño pepper (page 76), optional
- 1 teaspoon ground cumin
- ¼ teaspoon turmeric

- ¼ teaspoon sea salt
- no-stick cooking spray
- 4 14-by-18-inch (35-by-45-cm) sheets phyllo dough, thawed if frozen
- 2 egg whites, beaten

1. In a large saucepan, cook potatoes in boiling water until soft, about 25 minutes. Drain and mash. Transfer to a bowl.

2. Bring a large saucepan of water to a boil. Blanch carrots and corn for 2 minutes. Drain and add to mashed potatoes.

3. Bring a third pot of water to a boil. Add fresh spinach and blanch briefly. Drain and refresh under cold water. When cool enough to handle, squeeze out excess water and chop. (If using frozen spinach, simply squeeze out excess water.) Add spinach to potato mixture.

4. Stir in onions, cilantro, garlic, roasted jalapeños, cumin, turmeric and salt. Blend well.

5. Preheat oven to 350°F (175°C). Spray a baking sheet once with cooking spray.

6. Place phyllo dough on a clean, dry work surface and cover with a clean towel. Place a damp towel on top to prevent phyllo from drying out.

7. Remove 1 sheet of phyllo from stack. Place on work surface. Cut into 3 lengthwise strips. Place $\frac{1}{12}$ of the mixture at the bottom of one strip. Fold one corner of the strip up and over the filling, then continue to fold the strip loosely (as you would fold a flag) to form a neat triangle. Repeat with the remaining phyllo and filling. (Samosas can be frozen until ready to bake. Do not thaw before baking.) Transfer to prepared baking sheet and brush with egg white.

8. Bake for 25 minutes, or until just golden.

YIELD: 12 SAMOSAS

Per samosa: 80 Calories, 0.6g Fat, 0.1g Saturated Fat, 0mg Cholesterol, 3g Protein, 16g Carbohydrate, 1.8g Fiber, 108mg Sodium

MANGO CHUTNEY

over 60 minutes

Don't judge a mango's ripeness by its color. A ripe mango might have a red blush or it might be all green. It should be slightly soft, like a ripe avocado.

- 3 ripe mangoes
- 1 small onion, cut into small dice
- 1 red bell pepper, cut into small dice
- 1 tablespoon finely chopped jalapeño pepper
- 2 cups (16 fl oz/480 ml) unsweetened apple juice
- 1 tablespoon rice vinegar (brown or white)

1. To dice mangoes, stand one up and slice the skin and flesh from each side as a single piece, just clearing the long, flat seed. Deeply score the flesh diagonally in both directions through to the skin. Press the skin so the cut side pops out, looking like a hand grenade, and slice cubes of mango off the skin. Repeat with remaining mangoes.

2. Combine diced mangoes, onions, bell peppers, jalapeños, apple juice and vinegar in a large saucepan. Bring to a boil, then reduce heat to low. Simmer gently until mangoes are soft and translucent, about 30 to 40 minutes.

3. Puree half of the mixture in a blender or food processor. Transfer to a bowl and stir in the remaining mango mixture.

4. Chill before serving. The chutney will keep for 1 week in the refrigerator.

YIELD: 3 CUPS (24 OZ/720 G), 12 SERVINGS

Per ¼-cup (2-oz/60-g) serving: 59 Calories, 0.2g Fat, 0g Saturated Fat, 0mg Cholesterol, 0g Protein, 15g Carbohydrate, 1.3g Fiber, 13mg Sodium

Nutrition Bonus: Mangoes have lots of vitamins A, C and even some E, along with fiber and marvelous flavor.

SPICY OKRA WITH TOMATOES

- no-stick cooking spray
- 1 medium onion, cut into small dice
- 1 teaspoon finely chopped garlic
- 1 teaspoon finely chopped fresh ginger
- 1 pound (480 g) okra, sliced into ¼-inch-thick (0.6-cm-thick) rounds
- 1 28-ounce (840-g) can low-sodium diced tomatoes with juices
- 1 teaspoon finely chopped jalapeño or serrano pepper

1. Spray a large sauté pan once with cooking spray and set over low heat. Add onions and cook, stirring, for 2 minutes, or until translucent.
2. Add garlic and ginger and cook, stirring, for 15 seconds.
3. Add okra, tomatoes and peppers. Cook, stirring often, until okra becomes a little gooey, about 20 minutes. Serve hot.

YIELD: 8 SERVINGS

Per serving: 44 Calories, 0.2g Fat, 0g Saturated Fat, 0mg Cholesterol, 3g Protein, 9g Carbohydrate, 3.4g Fiber, 21mg Sodium

VEGETABLE CURRY

- no-stick cooking spray
- 1 small onion, cut into small dice
- 1 teaspoon finely chopped fresh garlic
- 4 teaspoons curry powder
- 1 head cauliflower, cut into florets (4 cups)
- 6 medium carrots, peeled and sliced
- 2 medium baking potatoes, peeled and diced
- 2½ cups (20 fl oz/600 ml) Vegetable Stock (page 32)
- ¼ teaspoon sea salt

1. Spray a large saucepan once with cooking spray and set over low heat. Add onions and cook, stirring, for 2 minutes, until translucent.
2. Add garlic and curry powder and cook, stirring, for 15 seconds.
3. Add cauliflower, carrots, potatoes, stock and salt. Cover and simmer until potatoes are soft, about 25 minutes.

YIELD: 8 SERVINGS

Per serving: 74 Calories, 0.4g Fat, 0g Saturated Fat, 0mg Cholesterol, 2g Protein, 17g Carbohydrate, 4g Fiber, 113mg Sodium

Nutrition Bonus: Cauliflower has the nutritional benefit of being a crucifer, and it's dense and chewy, leaving you feeling satisfied with relatively few calories.

BASMATI RICE WITH PEAS

- 2 cups (15 oz/450 g) brown or white basmati rice
- 3–4 cups (24–32 fl oz/720–960 ml) water
- ¼ teaspoon sea salt
- ½ teaspoon ground cumin
- 1 bay leaf
- 1 cup (5 oz/150 g) frozen peas

1. Place rice in a bowl. Add water to cover and let sit for 10 minutes. Drain and rinse.
2. In a large saucepan, combine rice and water (3 cups/24 fl oz/720 ml for white rice; 4 cups/32 fl oz/960 ml for brown). Stir in salt, cumin and bay leaf. Bring to a boil, reduce heat to low, cover and simmer: cook white rice for 20 minutes, brown rice for 30. Stir in peas and cook for 5 minutes longer.
3. Remove bay leaf. fluff rice with a fork and serve hot.

YIELD: 8 SERVINGS

Per serving: 186 Calories, 1.6g Fat, 0g Saturated Fat, 0mg Cholesterol, 4g Protein, 39g Carbohydrate, 2.2g Fiber, 91mg Sodium

TROPICAL FRUITS SCENTED WITH VANILLA AND CARDAMOM

under 30 minutes

- 2 ripe mangoes
- 1 vanilla bean
- 2 small ripe papayas
- ¼ teaspoon ground cardamom
- 1 ripe pineapple
- 2 ripe bananas
- 3 ripe kiwis
- 8 ripe strawberries

1. To slice a mango, stand one up and slice the skin and flesh from each side as a single piece, just clearing the long, flat seed. Remove peel with a knife and slice flesh into long strips. Place in a bowl. Repeat with the remaining mango.

2. Slice vanilla bean lengthwise, scrape out tiny seeds and add to mangoes. Toss gently. Save vanilla bean for another use.

3. Peel, seed and slice papayas. Place in a second bowl. Sprinkle with cardamom and toss gently.

4. With a long knife, cut away the pineapple peel in strips, cutting deep enough to remove the eyes with the skin. Cut into quarters lengthwise and cut away core. Slice quarters.

5. Peel and slice bananas on the diagonal.

6. Peel kiwis. Cut a decorative diamond pattern all around the outside.

7. Slice Strawberries. Arrange the fruits on a large platter.

YIELD: 8 TO 10 SERVINGS

Per serving: 108 Calories, 0.6g Fat, 0.1g Saturated Fat, 0mg Cholesterol, 1g Protein, 27g Carbohydrate, 3.7g Fiber, 4mg Sodium

Nutrition Bonus: Kiwis, papayas and mangoes have high levels of vitamins and minerals that aren't as plentiful in everyday foods.

AN INDIAN FEAST

HEALTH BENEFITS FROM THE SPICE RACK

INDIAN cuisine is known for its rich and varied use of spices, from complex curries to garam masalas containing 10 or more spices. Some researchers attribute India's low rates of cancer occurrence, at least in part, to the large amount of spice in the diet.

Even without health benefits, spices are a boon to healthful low-fat cooking, where they add flavor and even color. Here are a few you should know:

Cardamom is an ancient and exotic spice that is widely used in Middle Eastern, Indian and Scandinavian cuisines. One of its flavor components, limonene, is a compound thought to lower cholesterol and protect against some cancers.

Whole **chile peppers** and ground red pepper such as **cayenne** get their heat from capsaicin, a powerful chemical that has a number of effects on the body, including anti-cancer properties. Eating hot peppers can make you feel more relaxed — capsaicin induces your brain to release endorphins. The compound is an effective decongestant. Capsaicin is also an ingredient in some topical creams used to treat pain.

Cumin seeds are harvested from a plant related to parsley. Ground cumin is widely used as an ingredient in curry and chili powders. The spice's characteristic aroma comes from the compound curcumin, which has been found to have anti-cancer effects in cell culture.

Turmeric comes from the rhizome or underground stem of a plant in the ginger family. Also known as Indian saffron, turmeric lends vibrant yellow color to foods and is a primary ingredient in curry powder. Like cumin, it contains the beneficial compound curcumin.

Spices are sensitive to light, heat and air, which, over time, will rob them of their punch. When you put away a spice container, close the top tightly and store at room temperature in a dark place. For superior flavor, it's best to replace spices yearly.

A Chinese BANQUET

- **Fresh ginger is used in a variety of forms — chopped, grated, sliced — in Chinese cuisine. Many people find that candied ginger aids digestion and alleviates motion sickness.**

- **Rice is the most popular food in the world, and nowhere more so than in China, where annual consumption ranges from 200 to 400 pounds per person. China produces more than 90 percent of the world's rice crop.**

MOST AMERICANS HAVE LONG FEASTED ON U.S.-style Chinese food. Steaming bowls of hot-and-sour soup or plates of lo mein, sweet-and-sour pork and a stack of egg rolls are as familiar to us as hamburgers and apple pie. It's a tradition that you can now bring into your own house.

Preparing Chinese food at home is fun and allows you to control how much oil or other high-fat ingredients go into the mix. If you use a well-seasoned wok or a wide, heavy-bottomed sauté pan, you can stir-fry vegetables with almost no oil. The trick is to cook over low, not high, heat and to stir the vegetables almost constantly.

A CHINESE BANQUET 57

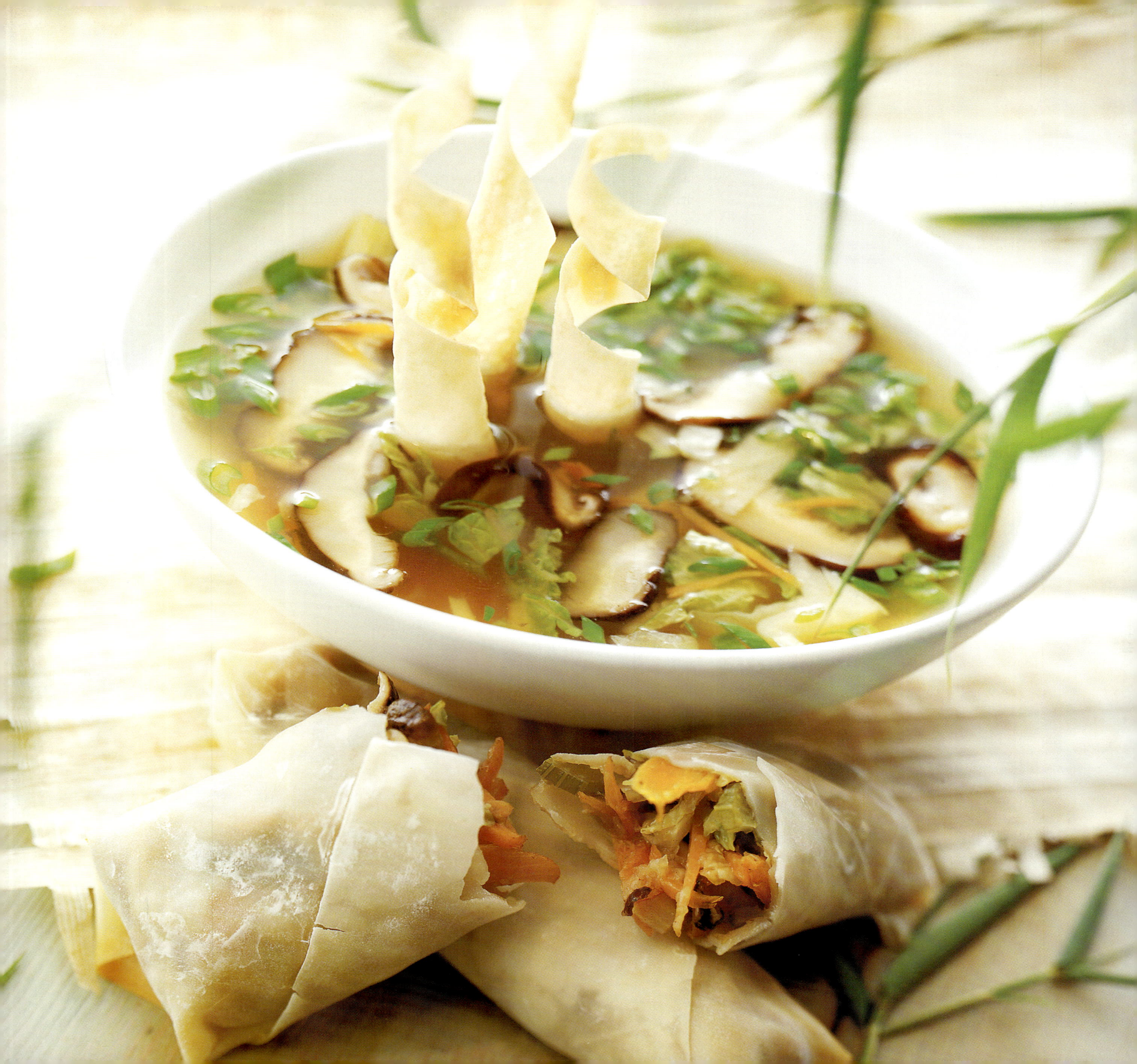

HOT AND SOUR SOUP

For an easy, pretty garnish, make wonton curls. Slice wonton wrappers into ¾-inch (2-cm) strips. Wrap strips around the handle of a wooden spoon, slip out spoon and place strips on a lightly sprayed baking sheet. Bake at 350°F (175°C) for about 10 minutes, until crisp.

8	cups (64 fl oz/1.9 L) Vegetable Stock (page 32)
½	head napa (Chinese) cabbage, cut into medium dice
5	ounces (150 g) shiitake mushrooms, stemmed and sliced
3	medium carrots, peeled and cut into julienne strips
1	5-ounce (150-g) can sliced bamboo shoots, rinsed and cut into julienne strips
3	tablespoons low-sodium tamari soy sauce
2	teaspoons grated fresh ginger
8	ounces (240 g) low-fat firm tofu, cut into small dice
2	tablespoons rice vinegar (brown or white)
⅛–¼	teaspoon cayenne pepper
3	tablespoons cornstarch
3	tablespoons water
1	bunch green onions, thinly sliced

1. In a soup pot, combine stock, cabbage, mushrooms, carrots, bamboo shoots, soy sauce and ginger. Bring to a boil, reduce heat to low and add tofu. Simmer for 15 minutes. Stir in vinegar and cayenne to taste.

2. In a small bowl, combine cornstarch and water to make a paste. Stir into soup. Heat soup gently until it thickens, about 5 minutes.

3. Ladle soup into bowls and garnish with sliced green onions and wonton curls, if desired.

YIELD: 8 SERVINGS

Per serving: 68 Calories, 0.7g Fat, 0g Saturated Fat, 0mg Cholesterol, 4g Protein, 13g Carbohydrate, 3.2g Fiber, 278mg Sodium

EGG ROLLS

Serve with duck sauce or fiery Chinese mustard.

	no-stick cooking spray
2	tablespoons cornstarch
½	cup (4 fl oz/120 ml) water
1	tablespoon grated fresh ginger
3	cups shredded napa (Chinese) or green cabbage
2	medium carrots, peeled and shredded
4	ounces (120 g) shiitake mushrooms, stemmed and cut into small dice (about 1½ cups)
1	celery stalk, tough strings peeled, cut into small dice
2	tablespoons low-sodium tamari soy sauce
2	tablespoons sliced green onions
12	fat-free egg roll wrappers

1. Preheat oven to 350°F (175°C). Spray a baking sheet once with cooking spray.

2. Dissolve 1 tablespoon of the cornstarch in ¼ cup (2 fl oz/60 ml) water. Set aside.

3. Spray a wok or large sauté pan once with cooking spray and heat pan over low heat. Add ginger and cook, stirring, for 15 seconds.

4. Add cabbage, carrots, mushrooms and celery and cook for 5 to 7 minutes, until vegetables begin to wilt. Stir in cornstarch mixture and soy sauce. Cook for 1 minute, or until sauce thickens.

5. Remove pan from heat and stir in green onions.

6. Dissolve the remaining 1 tablespoon cornstarch in ¼ cup (2 fl oz/60 ml) water. Place an egg roll wrapper on the work surface and spoon 1/12 of the mixture diagonally across the wrapper. Fold up like an envelope, brushing edges with cornstarch mixture to seal. Repeat with remaining wrappers and filling.

7. Place egg rolls on prepared baking sheet. Bake for 15 minutes, or until light brown.

YIELD: 12 EGG ROLLS

Per egg roll: 43 Calories, 0.2g Fat, 0g Saturated Fat, 0.7mg Cholesterol, 2g Protein, 9g Carbohydrate, 2.2g Fiber, 157mg Sodium

N Nutrition Bonus: Egg rolls become deliciously crispy in the oven. Why triple the calories and add 6 or more grams of fat by deep frying?

CHINESE DUMPLINGS

no-stick cooking spray
4 teaspoons grated fresh ginger
2 teaspoons finely chopped fresh garlic
8 ounces (240 g) ground fat-free soy "meat"
2/3 cup (2 oz/60 g) diced green cabbage
1 tablespoon low-sodium tamari soy sauce
3 green onions, thinly sliced, plus 30 julienne strips of green onion tops for tying dumplings
4 teaspoons cornstarch
3 tablespoons water
30 wonton wrappers

1. Spray a wok or large sauté pan once with cooking spray. Place pan over medium-low heat, add ginger and garlic and cook, stirring, for 30 seconds.

2. Add soy meat and cabbage and cook, stirring frequently, for 2 minutes. Add soy sauce and cook for 15 seconds. Transfer mixture to bowl and stir in sliced green onions.

3. Combine cornstarch and water in a small bowl.

4. Set a wonton wrapper on a clean work surface. Place 1 teaspoonful of filling in the center of wrapper. Moisten edge of wrapper with cornstarch mixture. Bring edges together and twist into a little pouch. Secure with a strip of green onion. Repeat with remaining wrappers, filling and green onion strips.

5. **For steamed dumplings:** Place dumplings in a bamboo steamer set over a pot of boiling water. Cover and steam for 10 minutes.
   For crispy dumplings: Spray a mini-muffin pan lightly with cooking spray. Set dumplings in muffin cups. Spray dumplings lightly with cooking spray. Bake at 350°F (175°C) for 15 minutes.

6. Serve dumplings with Orange-Ginger Dipping Sauce.

LEARNING FROM THE ASIAN DIET

In recent years, the Asian diet has received a great deal of attention as a healthy model for Americans — and with good reason. On the whole, Asians have dramatically lower rates of many diet-related diseases, such as heart disease and some forms of cancer, including prostate and breast cancer.

Despite different flavorings and variations in regional cuisines, eating habits throughout Asia share many characteristics nutritionally. Everywhere, the diet is plant-based — rich in complex carbohydrates, such as rice, noodles and beans, vegetables and fruits. Soy foods are eaten on a daily basis. Green tea (see Make Time for Tea, page 72) is the most common beverage. In addition, the lifestyle is quite active: many people bike or walk for transportation.

There are striking contrasts between the typical American and typical Asian diet that might explain the Asians' relative good health. The American diet contains, on average, 34% calories from fat; in Asia it's between 5% and 24%. Americans consume 10 times the amount of meat Asians do. Asian intake of dietary fiber is three times the U.S. level. It is interesting to note that the protection against disease fades when Asians emigrate to this country and adopt a higher-fat, more sedentary lifestyle.

In both of the *Taste for Living* cookbooks, we draw from the beneficial properties of the Asian diet, as confirmed by nutrition scientists, in our nutrition guidelines. We emphasize a reliance on soy foods, consuming a wide array of vegetables and natural spices, and keeping animal protein to a minimum. We also find inspiration in the Asian way of eating. Portion sizes are small, and meals are eaten at a relaxed pace, not wolfed down before moving on to the next activity. Food preparation, particularly in Japan, focuses not only on flavor but on presentation. Color, texture and the artful arrangement of the foods on the plate make eating an aesthetic experience, not just a way of feeding a hunger.

YIELD: 30 DUMPLINGS, 10 SERVINGS

Per 3-dumpling serving: 103 Calories, 0.4g Fat, 0.1g Saturated Fat, 2.2mg Cholesterol, 8g Protein, 17g Carbohydrate, 1.9g Fiber, 302mg Sodium

ORANGE-GINGER DIPPING SAUCE

under 30 minutes

¾ cup (6 fl oz/180 ml) fresh orange juice

¼ cup (2 fl oz/60 ml) low-sodium tamari soy sauce

1 tablespoon grated orange zest

1 teaspoon grated fresh ginger

1. In a blender, puree ingredients. Strain into a small bowl.

YIELD: 1 CUP (8 FL OZ/ 240 ML)

Per 1-tablespoon serving: 8 Calories, 0g Fat, 0g Saturated Fat, 0mg Cholesterol, 0g Protein, 2g Carbohydrate, 0.1g Fiber, 150mg Sodium

A CHINESE BANQUET

KUNG PAO TOFU

over 60 minutes

- 1½ cups (12 fl oz/360 ml) Vegetable Stock (page 32) or fat-free mushroom broth
- 6 tablespoons MSG-free hoisin sauce
- 2 tablespoons chopped peeled fresh ginger
- 2 tablespoons Chinese chili paste
- ¼ cup (1 oz/30 g) cornstarch
- 2 pounds (960 g) low-fat extra-firm tofu, cubed — SOY
- no-stick cooking spray
- 4 bell peppers (red, green and/or yellow), diced
- 2–3 small dried hot red peppers (optional), soaked for 15 minutes in water
- ⅔ cup (4 oz/120 g) dry-roasted soy nuts, optional
- 6 green onions, split lengthwise and thinly sliced

1. Combine stock or broth, hoisin sauce, ginger, chili paste and cornstarch in a medium bowl. Add tofu cubes and toss to coat. Let marinate for 30 minutes.
2. Preheat oven to 350°F (175°C).
3. Place marinated tofu on a large baking sheet with sides and bake for 20 minutes or until sauce thickens.
4. While the tofu is baking, cook the vegetables: Spray a wok or large sauté pan once with cooking spray and heat over low heat. Add bell peppers and cook, stirring, for 3 minutes. Drain soaked hot peppers, if using, add to the pan and cook a few seconds.
5. When the tofu is cooked, stir in cooked peppers and soy nuts, if using. Sprinkle with green onions before serving.

YIELD: 8 SERVINGS

Per serving: 127 Calories, 1.8g Fat, 0g Saturated Fat, 0mg Cholesterol, 8g Protein, 20g Carbohydrate, 2g Fiber, 545mg Sodium

Nutrition Bonus: A typical restaurant serving of kung pao chicken has more than 70 grams of fat! Roasted soy nuts are much lower in fat than peanuts or cashews and have the added benefit of soy isoflavones.

BUDDHA'S FEAST

under 30 minutes

- ½ cup (4 fl oz/120 ml) Vegetable Stock (page 32) or fat-free mushroom broth
- 3 tablespoons low-sodium tamari soy sauce
- 2 tablespoons cornstarch
- 1 tablespoon mirin (Japanese seasoning wine)
- 1 teaspoon Chinese chili paste, optional
- 4 heads baby bok choy or ½ head regular bok choy
- 12 ounces (360 g) broccoli florets
- no-stick cooking spray
- 4 carrots, peeled and thinly sliced on the diagonal
- 8 ounces (240 g) small shiitake or white button mushrooms, stemmed and rinsed
- 1 8-ounce (240-g) can sliced water chestnuts, drained
- 1 14-ounce (420-g) can baby corn, drained
- 1 tablespoon chopped fresh garlic

1. In a bowl, whisk together stock or broth, soy sauce, cornstarch, mirin and chili paste, if using. Set aside.
2. Bring a pot of water to a boil. If using baby bok choy, cut into quarters lengthwise; for regular bok choy cut into 1-inch (2.5-cm) dice. Cook for 2 minutes in boiling water; remove with a slotted spoon. In the same pot, cook broccoli florets for 1 minute. Drain. Set aside.
3. Spray a wok or large sauté pan once with cooking spray. Heat pan over medium heat; add carrots and mushrooms. Sauté for 3 minutes, stirring often.
4. Add bok choy, broccoli, water chestnuts, baby corn and garlic: cook for 1 to 2 minutes to heat. Add reserved sauce and cook, stirring, until it thickens, about 2 minutes.

YIELD: 8 SERVINGS

Per serving: 111 Calories, 0.8g Fat, 0g Saturated Fat, 0mg Cholesterol, 5g Protein, 25g Carbohydrate, 5.9g Fiber, 408mg Sodium

Front to back: Buddha's Feast, Kung Pao Tofu, Fried Rice

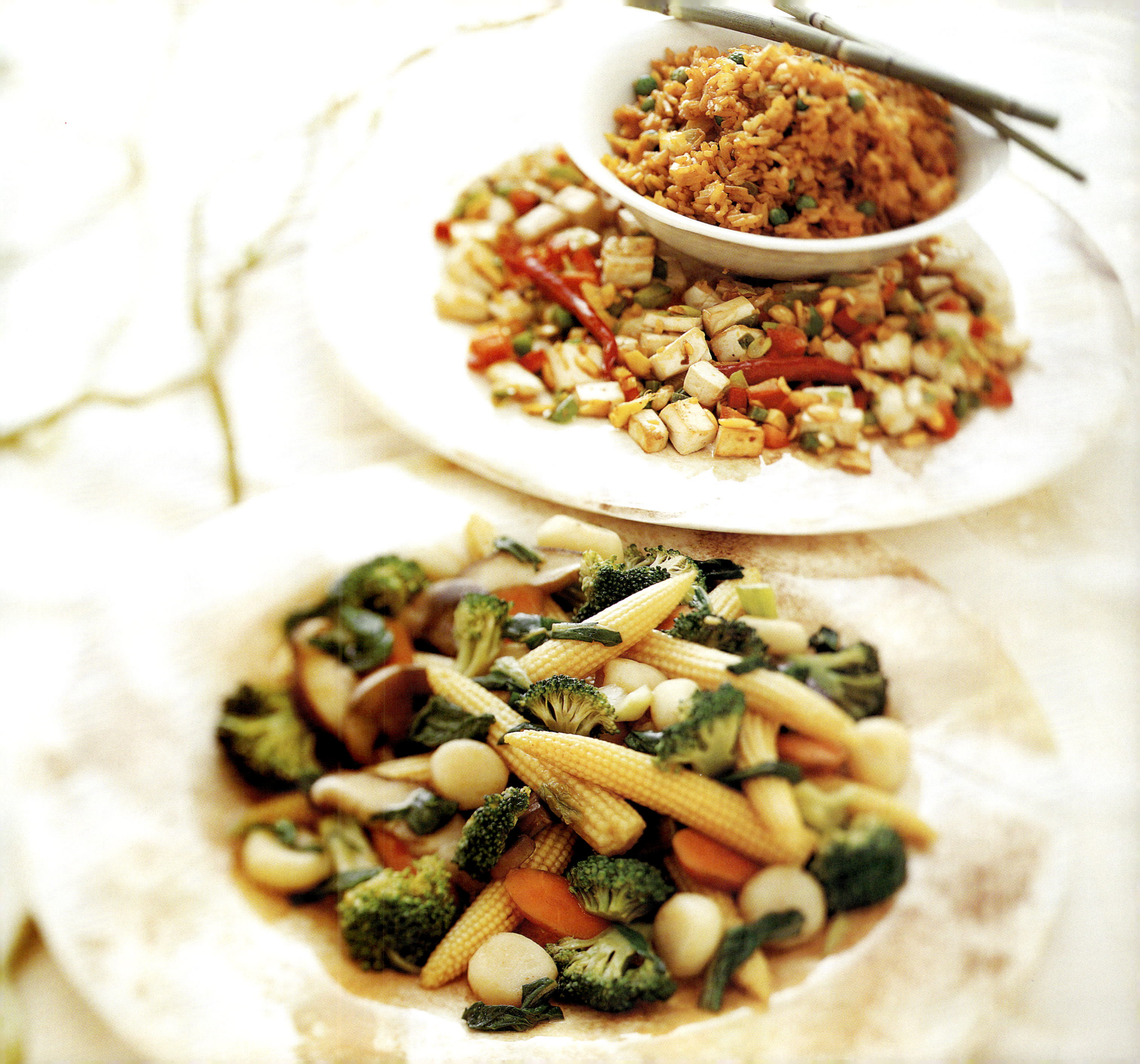

VEGETABLE LO MEIN

- 12 ounces (360 g) fresh lo mein noodles (no-added-fat)
- ½ cup (4 fl oz/120 ml) Vegetable Stock (page 32)
- 3 tablespoons MSG-free black bean sauce
- 2 tablespoons low-sodium tamari soy sauce
- 1 tablespoon mirin (Japanese seasoning wine) or 1 teaspoon natural cane sugar
- 1 tablespoon cornstarch
- no-stick cooking spray
- 1 teaspoon finely chopped fresh garlic
- ½ head napa (Chinese) cabbage, sliced into 3-inch (7.5-cm) pieces (3 cups)
- 5 ounces (150 g) shiitake mushrooms, stemmed and thinly sliced (2 cups)
- 3 medium carrots, peeled and sliced into julienne strips
- 2 stalks celery, tough strings peeled, thinly sliced on the diagonal
- 8 ounces (240 g) low-fat firm tofu, diced
- 2 cups (4 oz/120 g) bean sprouts
- 1 bunch green onions, thinly sliced on the diagonal

1. Bring a large pot of water to a boil. Cook noodles until just tender, about 6 minutes. Drain and set aside.
2. In a bowl, combine stock, black bean sauce, soy sauce, mirin or sugar and cornstarch. Whisk until smooth. Set aside.
3. Spray a wok or large sauté pan once with cooking spray and heat over low heat. Add garlic and cook, stirring, for 15 seconds.
4. Add cabbage, mushrooms, carrots, celery and tofu. Cook, stirring with a spoon in each hand, for 2 minutes.
5. Add reserved noodles and stir for 30 seconds.
6. Add reserved soy sauce mixture and cook until sauce thickens, about 1 minute. Add bean spouts and green onions. Toss.

YIELD: 8 SERVINGS

Per serving: 176 Calories, 0.8g Fat, 0g Saturated Fat, 0mg Cholesterol, 8g Protein, 34g Carbohydrate, 3.7g Fiber, 440mg Sodium

Nutrition Bonus: Like all mushrooms, shiitakes contain two crucial minerals — selenium and potassium.

FRIED RICE

- no-stick cooking spray
- 1 tablespoon grated fresh ginger
- 1 teaspoon finely chopped fresh garlic
- 4 cups (24 oz/720 g) cooked brown or white rice
- ¾ cup (3 oz/90 g) frozen peas, thawed
- 2 tablespoons low-sodium tamari soy sauce
- ½ bunch green onions, thinly sliced

1. Spray a wok or large sauté pan once with cooking spray and heat over low heat. Add ginger and garlic and cook, stirring, for 15 seconds.
2. Add rice and, with a spoon in each hand, stir and toss rice until hot, about 2 minutes. Add peas and soy sauce and cook, stirring, for 3 minutes.
3. Transfer to a bowl and garnish with sliced green onions.

YIELD: 8 SERVINGS

Per serving: 124 Calories, 0.9g Fat, 0.2g Saturated Fat, 0mg Cholesterol, 4g Protein, 25g Carbohydrate, 3g Fiber, 169mg Sodium

Nutrition Bonus: Whenever possible, choose brown rice over white. It contains many nutrients that have been removed from white rice during milling.

HOT AND SPICY EGGPLANT

Look for the cream-colored or lavender Japanese eggplants at Asian markets. They are longer and thinner than their dark purple cousins.

- ¼ cup (2 fl oz/60 ml) Vegetable Stock (page 32) or fat-free mushroom broth
- 2 tablespoons rice vinegar (brown or white)
- 2 tablespoons black bean paste
- 1 tablespoon Chinese chili paste
- 1 tablespoon mirin (Japanese seasoning wine) or 1 teaspoon natural cane sugar
- 1 tablespoon low-sodium tamari soy sauce
- 1 tablespoon cornstarch
- 2 pounds (960 g) Japanese eggplant
- no-stick cooking spray
- 2 tablespoons finely chopped peeled fresh ginger
- 1 teaspoon finely chopped fresh garlic
- 2 green onions, sliced lengthwise, and thinly sliced diagonally

1. In a bowl, whisk together stock or broth, rice vinegar, black bean paste, chili paste, mirin or sugar, soy sauce and cornstarch. Set aside.

2. Trim eggplant stems. Slice eggplants in half lengthwise and in half again. Slice into 2-inch(5-cm)-thick pieces.

3. Spray a large wok or sauté pan once with cooking spray. Heat pan over low heat; add eggplant. Cook, stirring with 2 wooden spoons, until eggplant softens, about 10 minutes. Add ginger and garlic. Cook, stirring, for 2 minutes.

4. Add reserved soy sauce mixture. Cook until sauce thickens, about 2 minutes. Toss with green onions and serve.

YIELD: 6 TO 8 SERVINGS

Per serving: 48 Calories, 0.3g Fat, 0.1g Saturated Fat, 0mg Cholesterol, 1g Protein, 11g Carbohydrate, 3g Fiber, 129mg Sodium

EVALUATING MARKETING TERMS

Lite, Reduced Fat, Natural, Fat-Free. What do these terms actually mean? Not necessarily what you might think.

The popular terms that frequently appear on food labels are little more than a marketing device. Better to evaluate ingredient lists and nutrition facts than to be swayed by the manufacturer's claims on the packaging.

Here are some widely used terms:

Reduced-Fat or Less Fat: Has at least 25 percent less fat per serving than the "regular" full-fat food cited on the label. This product can still derive most of its calories from fat.

Lite or Light: Has at least 50 percent less fat or one-third fewer calories than the "regular" full-fat food. This product can still derive most of its calories from fat.

Low-Fat: Has no more than three grams of fat per serving. Keep in mind that it's the manufacturer that determines the size of a single serving, and sometimes that serving is tiny.

Fat-Free or Nonfat: Less than one-half of 1 gram of fat per serving. Therefore, six servings of a "fat-free" product can contain nearly three grams of fat.

Reduced or Less Sodium: Has at least 25 percent less sodium per serving than the "regular" food cited on the label.

All Natural or Natural: This claim can mean almost anything. For example, lard is an all-natural ingredient, but that doesn't mean it's good for you.

PINEAPPLES AND ORANGES

1 large ripe pineapple
6 navel oranges

1. Slice bottom and leafy top off pineapple. Cut pineapple into 6 sections lengthwise. Cut away skin in one piece from each section. Trim core. Slice each section into 8 or 9 pieces. Transfer to 6 dessert plates.

2. Slice ½ inch (1.25 cm) from the top and bottom of each orange. Using a thin-bladed knife, remove the orange flesh in one piece, leaving pith behind. Cut orange flesh in half and cut halves into thin slices. With a citrus stripper, cut a decorative pattern on the hollowed orange peel. Arrange on the dessert plates.

YIELD: 6 SERVINGS

Per serving: 133 Calories, 0.9g Fat, 0.1g Saturated Fat, 0mg Cholesterol, 2g Protein, 34g Carbohydrate, 5g Fiber, 1mg Sodium

Nutrition Bonus: Oranges are not only a good surce of vitamin C, they contain folate and fiber too.

A SIMPLE Japanese MEAL

- The average Japanese eats about one pound of tofu every week. Scientists have linked this and other elements of the Japanese diet to the country's very low rates of heart disease and prostate and breast cancer.

- Shiitake mushrooms contain lentinan, a substance that is being investigated for its cancer-fighting powers. They also contain eritadenine, which is thought to reduce cholesterol levels.

JAPANESE COOKS ARE MASTERS AT PREPARING AND PRESENTING soyfoods in their many forms. Small bowls of brilliant green fresh soybeans called edamame are served as a snack or appetizer. Miso-based soups are served at many meals, often with cubes of tofu and precisely sliced vegetables soaking up the flavorful broth. For people who care about their health and want to add soy to their diet, Japanese cuisine is full of possibilities. As an added advantage, many Japanese dishes are so low in fat that you don't have to substitute ingredients to reduce the fat.

VEGETABLE SUSHI

over 60 minutes

A trip to a well-stocked natural foods store or a Japanese market will provide you with all the out-of-the-ordinary ingredients you will need to make these easy sushi rolls. Mirin is a sweetened rice wine used as a seasoning for cooking; it usually comes in 10-ounce (300-ml) bottles. The paper-thin sheets of the dried seaweed called nori are sold in plastic packaging. Wasabi is the fiery green condiment served with all sushi; it is available as a paste or powder. Pickled ginger is usually sold in jars. Last but not least, you'll need a sushi mat — an indispensable tool for rolling sushi.

RICE

- 2 cups (15 oz/450 g) brown or white Japanese sushi rice
- water for cooking rice
- 1 tablespoon mirin (Japanese seasoning wine)
- 1 tablespoon natural cane sugar
- 2 teaspoons rice vinegar (brown or white)

SUSHI

- 2½ ounces (75 g) shiitake mushrooms, stemmed, rinsed and cut into julienne strips (1 cup)
- 1 tablespoon water
- 4 ears baby corn (fresh or canned), cut in half lengthwise
- 8 green beans
- 4 sheets nori
- 1 carrot, peeled and cut into julienne strips
- ¾ cup (6 oz/180 g) pickled ginger
- 2 tablespoons wasabi paste or 4 teaspoons wasabi powder blended with 2 tablespoons water
- 1 recipe Ponzu Sauce (page 69)

TO MAKE RICE

1. Wash rice under cold running water until water runs clear. Drain in a colander for at least 15 minutes.

2. In a rice cooker or large heavy-bottomed saucepan, combine rice and water (2½ cups/20 fl oz/600 ml for white rice; 2¾ cups/22 fl oz/660 ml for brown). Bring to a boil and turn down to a simmer. Do not stir. Cook, covered, until all water is absorbed, about 15 minutes for white rice and 35 to 40 minutes for brown.

3. While rice is cooking, combine mirin, sugar and vinegar in a small saucepan. Warm over low heat until the sugar dissolves, about 5 minutes. Remove from heat and set aside.

4. Transfer cooked rice to a large bowl and gently fold in mirin mixture with a wooden spoon. Spread rice on a baking sheet and let cool to room temperature. Do not refrigerate.

TO MAKE FILLING

1. Place mushrooms in a sauté pan and sprinkle with 1 tablespoon water. Cook over low heat about 1 minute. Drain excess liquid and set aside.

2. If using fresh baby corn, cook in boiling water for 3 minutes. Drain and set aside.

3. Cook beans in boiling water for 1 minute. Drain, plunge into ice water and drain again. Set aside.

TO ROLL SUSHI

1. Place a piece of plastic wrap over sushi mat: this will keep the mat clean and make rolling easier. Set one nori sheet on top of plastic wrap. Spread about ¼ of the rice evenly over the nori, leaving a ½-inch (1.25-cm) strip bare along the two long sides.

2. About 1 inch (2.5 cm) from the edge of the rice nearest you, lay 2 corn halves end to end. Place 2 green beans

next to corn, followed by a row of mushrooms and a row of carrot strips.

3. Roll up the nori, first rolling the mat over away from you, and pressing to shape the roll. Roll up without catching the edge of the mat. Moisten the bare edge of nori with a little water and press against the roll to seal.

4. Repeat these steps with a second sheet of nori, rice and fillings.

5. For a contrasting look, roll the other half of the sushi with the rice on the outside: Begin by putting a nori sheet on the plastic wrap. Spread with rice. Turn over and continue with Steps 2, 3 and 4 above.

6. With a sharp, wet knife, slice each roll into 8 equal pieces. Serve with pickled ginger, wasabi and Ponzu Sauce on the side.

YIELD: 4 SERVINGS

Per serving: 230 Calories, 1.3g Fat, 0.2g Saturated Fat, 0mg Cholesterol, 6g Protein, 49g Carbohydrate, 5.5g Fiber, 275mg Sodium

PONZU SAUCE

under 30 minutes

- 3 tablespoons low-sodium tamari soy sauce
- 3 tablespoons rice vinegar (brown or white)
- 3 tablespoons mirin (Japanese seasoning wine)

1. Combine ingredients in a bowl and blend with a fork.
2. Divide sauce evenly among 4 little bowls.

YIELD: 4 SERVINGS

Per tablespoon: 17 Calories, 0g Fat, 0g Saturated Fat, 0mg Cholesterol, 0g Protein, 4g Carbohydrate, 0g Fiber, 205mg Sodium

A SIMPLE JAPANESE MEAL

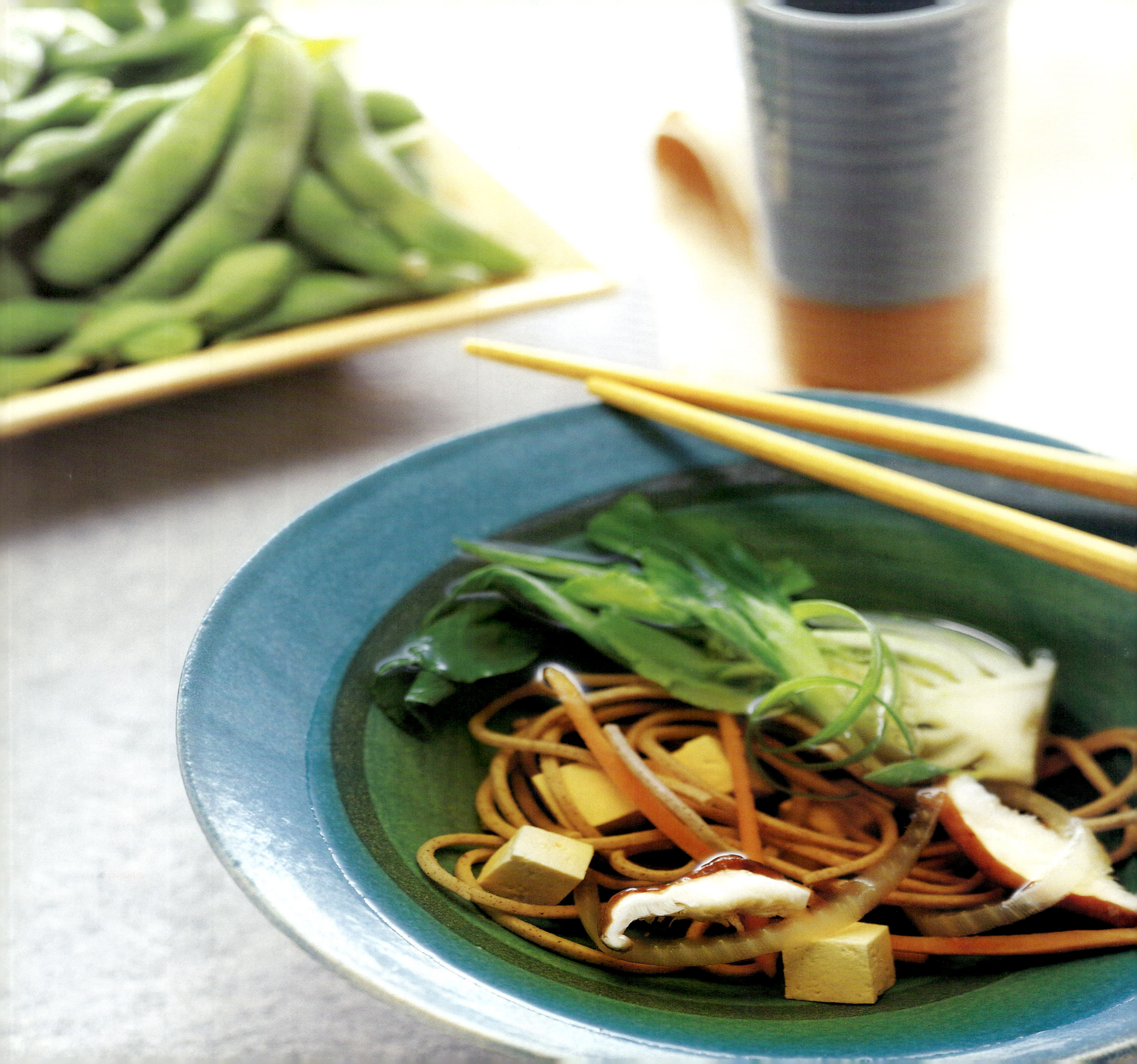

SUKIYAKI

Roasted onions give body and depth to the broth. If you do not have time to prepare them, spray a pan lightly with cooking spray and cook sliced raw onions over medium heat for 1 minute.

- 1½ pounds (720 g) low-fat firm tofu, cubed — SOY
- 1 roasted onion (page 40), cut in half and thinly sliced
- 4 ounces (120 g) shiitake mushrooms, stemmed and thinly sliced
- 6 carrots, peeled and cut into julienne strips
- 3 heads baby bok choy, sliced lengthwise down the middle, or ½ small head regular bok choy, diced
- 8 cups (64 fl oz/960 ml) fat-free mushroom broth or Vegetable Stock (page 32)
- ½ cup (4 fl oz/120 ml) low-sodium tamari soy sauce
- 3 tablespoons mirin (Japanese seasoning wine) or 1 tablespoon natural cane sugar
- 8 ounces (240 g) fresh spinach, stemmed, washed and chopped
- 8 ounces (240 g) dried clear rice vermicelli or soba noodles
- 5 green onions, split lengthwise and thinly sliced on the diagonal

1. Place tofu, onions, mushrooms, carrots, bok choy, broth or stock, soy sauce and mirin or sugar in a soup pot. Bring to a boil and reduce heat to a gentle simmer. Cook for 10 minutes.

2. Remove pot from heat and stir in spinach. Let steep for 3 minutes.

3. Meanwhile, while soup is cooking, cook rice vermicelli or soba noodles according to package directions. Drain.

4. Place the warm vermicelli or soba noodles in soup bowls and ladle hot broth and vegetables on top. Sprinkle with sliced green onions.

YIELD: 6 SERVINGS

Per serving: 274 Calories, 2.5g Fat, 0.1g Saturated Fat, 0mg Cholesterol, 17g Protein, 47g Carbohydrate, 8g Fiber, 1311mg Sodium

Nutrition Bonus: Using tofu in place of meat provides this traditional Japanese dish with even more cancer-fighting properties.

EDAMAME

- 1 pound (480 g) edamame (frozen green soybeans in the shell) — SOY

1. Cook edamame in boiling water for about 8 minutes, or until just tender. Drain.

2. When cool enough to handle, slip soybeans out of their tough pods.

3. Place in a bowl and serve.

YIELD: 1½ CUPS (10 OZ/300 G)

Per ¼-cup (1½-oz/50-g) serving: 107 Calories, 4.8g Fat, 0.6g Saturated Fat, 0mg Cholesterol, 9g Protein, 8g Carbohydrate, 3.2g Fiber, 11mg Sodium

Nutrition Bonus: Children love to shell and eat edamame. You couldn't ask for a healthier snack food.

MAKE TIME FOR TEA

Put the kettle on! A cup of tea could provide more than just a relaxing interlude in the midst of a busy day. Indications are that tea, particularly green tea, will prove to be a powerful cancer fighter. Green tea contains a rich brew of antioxidants called polyphenols, and several studies have shown a connection between drinking three to 10 cups of green tea a day and reduced rates of common forms of cancer. Recently, researchers in Sweden discovered that a particular green tea polyphenol called EGCg significantly inhibits angiogenesis — the process of blood-vessel growth that is critical for a tumor to grow or spread through the body.

Whether it is black, oolong, or green, all tea comes from the leaves of the Camellia Sinensis bush. The difference comes at processing. For black tea, the leaves are fermented first, then heated and dried. Oolong leaves are only partially fermented. Green tea, favored among Asians and health-conscious Americans, skips the fermenting process. Green tea is the best source of the polyphenols called catechins, which include EGCg.

If caffeine is a concern, green tea has only eight to 16 milligrams per six-ounce cup — one-third the caffeine of black tea and a bare fraction of what is found in coffee. If you find green tea a little bland for your taste, supermarkets now carry flavored green teas as well as green-tea capsules. Some of the green-tea-extract capsules are decaffeinated and will advertise the amount of total catechins, which should be about 160 milligrams per capsule, of which at least 100 milligrams should be EGCg.

Mexican FAVORITES

- **American-style Mexican food suffers from the same problems that Italian food does once it becomes Americanized — too many calories and way too much fat. Meat and dairy products, considered luxuries and used sparingly in rural Mexico, tend to overwhelm preparations that were originally healthful. A "light" taco platter at a Mexican franchise restaurant recently weighed in at 1060 calories and 58 grams of fat! That's half a day's worth of calories and two days' worth of fat in a single meal.**

- **The combination of either beans and rice or beans and corn provides all the amino acids your body needs to create complete protein.**

MEXICAN FOOD, WITH ITS HEALTHFUL PEPPERS, BEANS, RICE and tortillas, provides endless opportunities to create fun, nutritious meals at work and at home.

You don't need to weigh down Mexican food with regular cheese and sour cream. And it's easy to work soy into lots of Mexican dishes. The recipe on page 75 is a good example: the chimichanga filling is made with soy meat, providing about 18 grams of beneficial soy protein in one serving.

TORTILLA SOUP

Use a serrated knife to cut the kernels from the corn cobs. Freeze the stripped cobs for making vegetable broths.

- 5 cups frozen or fresh corn kernels (cut from 12 cobs)
- 1 28-ounce (840-g) can hominy, drained and rinsed
- 2 cups (16 oz/480 g) cooked or canned black beans, rinsed
- 1 14.5-ounce (435-g) can diced low-sodium tomatoes, pureed
- 3 carrots, peeled and diced (about 1 cup)
- 1 teaspoon chili powder
- 1 teaspoon chopped roasted jalapeño or serrano pepper (page 76)
- 7 cups (56 fl oz/1.6 L) Vegetable Stock (page 32)
- 1 lime, cut in half
- 2 tablespoons chopped fresh cilantro, optional

TORTILLA STRIPS

- 1 14-ounce (420-g) package no-added-fat corn or flour tortillas
- 1 teaspoon ground cumin
- 1 teaspoon chili powder
- ½ teaspoon granulated onion
- no-stick cooking spray

1. In a soup pot, combine corn, hominy, black beans, tomatoes, carrots, chili powder, roasted peppers and stock. Bring to a boil, reduce heat to medium-low and simmer until vegetables are just tender, about 25 minutes.

2. While the soup is simmering, make the tortilla strips: Preheat oven to 350°F (175°C). Slice tortillas into thin ribbons about ½ inch (1.25 cm) wide and 2 to 3 inches (5 to 7.5 cm) long. In a large bowl, toss tortilla strips with cumin, chili powder and onion. Lightly spray a baking sheet with cooking spray and spread strips on sheet. Bake for 20 minutes, until light brown.

3. Squeeze juice from lime into soup.

4. Ladle soup into bowls. Top with a mound of tortilla strips. Sprinkle with chopped cilantro, if desired.

YIELD: ABOUT 3 QUARTS (2.8 L), 8 TO 10 SERVINGS

Per serving: 255 Calories, 1.2g Fat, 0.2g Saturated Fat, 0mg Cholesterol, 10g Protein, 55g Carbohydrate, 10.3g Fiber, 386mg Sodium

CHIMICHANGAS WITH FRESH TOMATO SALSA

30–60 minutes

- no-stick cooking spray
- 1 medium onion, chopped
- 2 teaspoons finely chopped fresh garlic
- 24 ounces (720 g) fat-free ground soy "meat"
- 1 14.5-ounce (435-g) can diced low-sodium tomatoes
- 2 teaspoons chopped roasted jalapeño pepper (page 76)
- 2 teaspoons chili powder
- 1 teaspoon ground cumin
- 8 large no-added-fat flour tortillas
- 1 cup (8 oz/240 g) Fresh Tomato Salsa (recipe follows)

1. Preheat oven to 350°F (175°C). Spray a baking sheet once with cooking spray.

2. Spray a large sauté pan once with cooking spray. Place the pan over low heat, add onions and cook, stirring often, until just translucent, about 3 minutes. Stir in garlic and cook for 15 seconds.

3. Add soy meat and stir to break it up. Add tomatoes, jalapeños, chili powder and cumin. Cook, covered, for 8 minutes.

4. Warm tortillas in oven or over a flame to make them easier to roll. Place about ½ cup (4 oz/120 g) filling in the center of each tortilla. Fold outside edges in and roll up like a jelly roll.

5. Place chimichangas on prepared baking sheet and bake for 25 minutes, until browned. Serve with Fresh Tomato Salsa.

YIELD: **8 SERVINGS**

Per serving: 173 Calories, 0.4g Fat, 0g Saturated Fat, 0mg Cholesterol, 21g Protein, 26g Carbohydrate, 7.9g Fiber, 576mg Sodium

Nutrition Bonus: An oversized beef chimichanga at a restaurant can weigh in at 800 calories and 46 grams of fat — enough to feed three people!

FRESH TOMATO SALSA

under 30 minutes

- 4 medium vine-ripened tomatoes
- ½ cup (2½ oz/75 g) chopped onion
- 2 tablespoons thinly sliced green onions
- 1–2 tablespoons seeded and minced jalapeño pepper
- 1 tablespoon chopped fresh cilantro
- juice of 1 lime
- 1 tablespoon water
- ⅛ teaspoon sea salt

1. To make tomatoes easy to peel, bring a saucepan of water to a boil. Core tomatoes and cut an X on the bottom. Place in boiling water for 1 minute. Remove to a bowl of cold water.

2. When tomatoes are cool enough to handle, remove skins. Cut tomatoes in half and remove seeds.

3. Dice tomatoes.

4. In a bowl, combine diced tomatoes, onions, green onions, jalapeños, cilantro, lime juice, water and salt.

YIELD: **3½ CUPS (28 OZ/840 G)**

Per 2-tablespoon serving: 5 Calories, 0.1g Fat, 0g Saturated Fat, 0mg Cholesterol, 0g Protein, 1g Carbohydrate, 0.3g Fiber, 12mg Sodium

SPINACH AND MUSHROOM ENCHILADAS IN RED CHILI SAUCE

over 60 minutes

RED CHILI SAUCE

- 1 28-ounce (840-g) can low-sodium tomato puree
- 2 cups (16 fl oz/480 ml) Vegetable Stock (page 32)
- ¼ cup (1 oz/30 g) chili powder
- ½ teaspoon granulated garlic
- ½ teaspoon ground cumin
- ¼ teaspoon dried oregano
- ⅛ teaspoon sea salt

ENCHILADAS

- 1¾ pounds (1.6 K) fresh spinach, stemmed and washed, or 20 ounces (600 g) frozen spinach, thawed
- no-stick cooking spray
- 1 medium onion, chopped (1 cup)
- 1 pound (500 g) mushrooms, trimmed, washed and sliced
- 2 ounces (60 g) low-fat soft tofu
- 2 ounces (60 g) fat-free jack-style soy cheese, grated by hand (½ cup)
- ⅛ teaspoon sea salt
- 16 no-added-fat corn tortillas

TO MAKE RED CHILI SAUCE

1. In a large saucepan, whisk all ingredients until smooth.
2. Cook over low heat, stirring frequently, for 25 minutes. Set aside.

TO MAKE ENCHILADAS

1. Preheat oven to 350°F (175°C).
2. If using fresh spinach, bring a large pot of water to a boil. Plunge spinach into water and cook several seconds. Drain, squeeze out excess water and chop. Place in a bowl. (If using frozen spinach, simply squeeze out excess water and place in a bowl.)
3. Spray a large sauté pan once with cooking spray and set over low heat. Add onions and cook 2 minutes. Add mushrooms and cook 5 minutes more. Remove pan from heat and pour off excess liquid.
4. Stir together tofu and spinach/mushroom mixture until blended. Stir in soy cheese and salt.
5. Spread ½ cup (4 fl oz/120 ml) Red Chili Sauce in a large baking dish. Pour the remaining sauce into a shallow bowl.
6. Dip a tortilla in sauce, place on a plate and spoon 3 tablespoons filling onto center. Roll up and place in baking dish. Repeat with remaining tortillas and filling.
7. Pour any remaining sauce over enchiladas. Cover top with parchment paper or aluminum foil.
8. Bake until sauce is bubbly, about 25 minutes.

YIELD: 8 SERVINGS

Per serving: 219 Calories, 2.8g Fat, 0.4g Saturated Fat, 0mg Cholesterol, 11g Protein, 43g Carbohydrate, 9.4g Fiber, 346mg Sodium

Nutrition Bonus: Mom and Popeye were right. Spinach provides fiber and a multitude of nutrients including iron, folate, calcium and selenium.

SKILLET-ROASTING CHILES

Roasting jalapeño, serrano and other small fresh chiles softens their flesh and mellows their fire, while adding a warm roasted flavor. To roast, heat a small heavy skillet over high heat. Add the whole peppers and cook, shaking the pan, until the skins are soft and begin to char in places. Transfer peppers to a bowl to cool. When cool enough to handle, slice open and, with a small knife, scrape the flesh away from the skin. On average, one jalapeño chile yields about one tablespoon chopped.

Spinach and Mushroom Enchiladas in Red Chili Sauce, Refried Beans, Pico de Gallo, Mexican Rice, Cabbage Salad, Fresh Tomato Salsa, Sangría

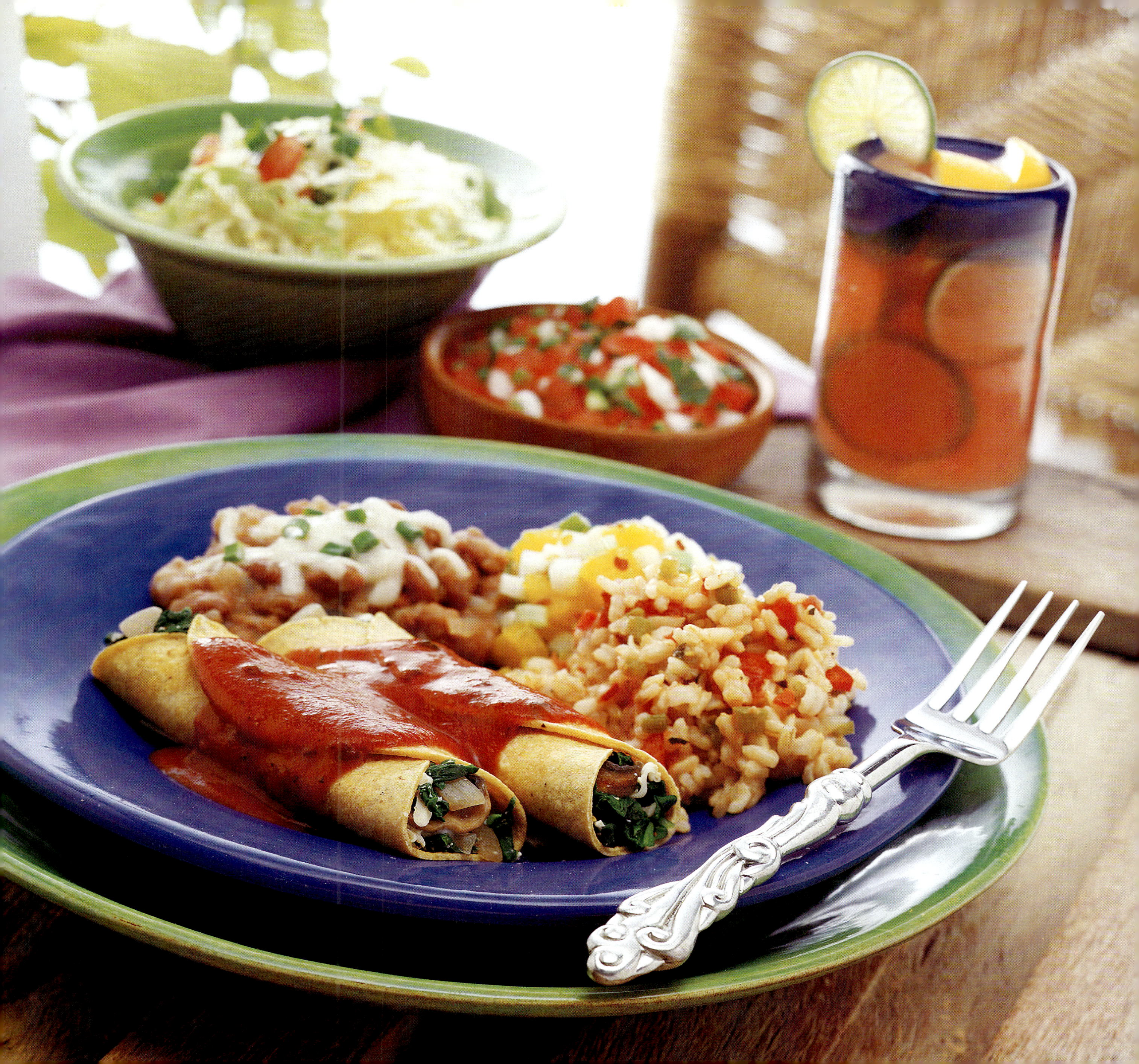

MEXICAN RICE

You can use white rice in this recipe if you prefer: simply reduce the water to 3 cups and cook for 18, not 30, minutes.

- no-stick cooking spray
- 1 medium onion, cut into small dice
- 1 small red bell pepper, cut into small dice
- 1 small green bell pepper, cut into small dice
- 1½ teaspoons finely chopped fresh garlic
- ½ teaspoon dried oregano
- 2 cups (15 oz/450 g) long-grain brown rice
- 4 cups (32 fl oz/960 ml) water
- 1 14.5-ounce (435-g) can diced low-sodium tomatoes, drained
- 1 bay leaf
- ½ teaspoon sea salt
- ¼ teaspoon ground cumin

1. Spray a large pot once with cooking spray. Place pot over low heat, add onions and peppers, and cook, stirring often, until vegetables are soft, about 5 minutes.
2. Stir in garlic and oregano. Cook for 15 seconds.
3. Add rice and stir once. Add water, tomatoes, bay leaf, salt and cumin. Bring to a boil. Turn the heat down to maintain a simmer.
4. Cover and cook for 30 minutes, or until all liquid has been absorbed. Do not stir or rice will become sticky. Remove bay leaf before serving.

YIELD: 8 SERVINGS

Per serving: 194 Calories, 1.6g Fat, 0.3g Saturated Fat, 0mg Cholesterol, 5g Protein, 41g Carbohydrate, 2.9g Fiber, 157mg Sodium

CABBAGE SALAD

- ½ head green cabbage, cored and very thinly sliced
- 1 large vine-ripened tomato, seeded and diced
- 1 roasted jalapeño pepper (page 76), peeled, seeded and chopped
- 1 tablespoon thinly sliced green onion
- 1 tablespoon chopped fresh cilantro
- juice of 1 lime
- ¼ teaspoon sea salt

1. Toss all ingredients in a large bowl. Chill for 30 minutes.

YIELD: 4 CUPS, 8 SERVINGS

Per ½-cup (4-oz/120-g) serving: 21 Calories, 0.2g Fat, 0g Saturated Fat, 0mg Cholesterol, 1g Protein, 5g Carbohydrate, 1.6g Fiber, 86mg Sodium

PICO DE GALLO

Literally "rooster's beak," this lively relish supposedly gets its name from the way diners like to peck at it.

- 2 navel oranges
- 1 jícama, peeled and cut into small dice
- ½ teaspoon crushed red pepper flakes
- juice of 1 lime
- ⅛ teaspoon sea salt

1. With a serrated knife, cut rind and pith from oranges. Cutting between the membranes, remove orange sections. Slice sections into small pieces.
2. In a bowl, mix orange pieces, jícama, red pepper flakes, lime juice and salt. Chill for 15 minutes.

YIELD: 4 CUPS (20 OZ/600 G), 8 SERVINGS

Per ½-cup (4-oz/120-g) serving: 35 Calories, 0.1g Fat, 0g Saturated Fat, 0mg Cholesterol, 1g Protein, 9g Carbohydrate, 2.8g Fiber, 40mg Sodium

REFRIED BEANS *over 60 minutes*

To save time, use canned pinto beans. You'll need three 15-ounce (450-g) cans. Rinse the beans to remove excess sodium.

- 2 cups (13 oz/390 g) raw pinto beans, rinsed and picked over
- 8½ cups (68 fl oz/2 L) water
- 1 large vine-ripened tomato, peeled, seeded and chopped
- 1 small onion, chopped
- 1 tablespoon chopped roasted jalapeño pepper (page 76)
- ¼ teaspoon sea salt
- 4 ounces (120 g) fat-free jack-style soy cheese, grated by hand (about ½ cup)
- 1 bunch green onions, split lengthwise and finely sliced

1. Place beans and 8 cups (64 fl oz/1.9 L) water in a large pot. Bring to a boil and cook until beans are tender, about 1½ hours. Drain beans.
2. In a large sauté pan over medium heat, combine cooked beans, ½ cup (4 fl oz/120 ml) water, tomatoes, onions, jalapeños and salt. Cook, stirring often, until vegetables are soft, about 20 minutes.
3. Preheat broiler.
4. Transfer half of bean mixture to a food processor and puree. Stir the pureed beans back into the beans in the pan. Reheat briefly.
5. Transfer beans to a shallow heatproof dish and sprinkle with soy cheese. Broil until cheese melts, about 5 minutes. Sprinkle with green onions and serve.

YIELD: **8 TO 10 SERVINGS**

Per serving: 155 Calories, 0.5g Fat, 0.1g Saturated Fat, 0mg Cholesterol, 11g Protein, 27g Carbohydrate, 9.8g Fiber, 162mg Sodium

Nutrition Bonus: Pinto beans are an excellent source of fiber, folate and potassium.

SANGRÍA *over 60 minutes*

- 1 lemon, scrubbed
- 1 lime, scrubbed
- 1 navel orange, scrubbed
- 1 quart (960 ml) fresh-squeezed orange juice
- 1 quart (960 ml) lemonade
- 1 cup (8 fl oz/240 ml) cranberry juice

1. For a pretty effect, with a citrus stripper (also known as a channel knife) cut lines from top to bottom all around the lemon, lime and orange. Cut fruits into very thin slices and place slices in a large pitcher.
2. Add orange juice, lemonade and cranberry juice. Chill for at least 2 hours to allow flavors to blend.

YIELD: **8 SERVINGS**

Per serving: 140 Calories, 0.4g Fat, 0g Saturated Fat, 0mg Cholesterol, 1g Protein, 35g Carbohydrate, 1.8g Fiber, 6mg Sodium

Nutrition Bonus: To cut back on calories, mix equal parts sangría and lime-flavored seltzer water.

MEXICAN FAVORITES

SUSPIROS

over 60 minutes

- 3 tablespoons fat-free cocoa powder
- ¼ teaspoon ground cinnamon
- 2 egg whites, at room temperature
- ¼ teaspoon cream of tartar
- ½ cup (3½ oz/100 g) natural cane sugar
- 1 teaspoon pure vanilla extract

1. Preheat oven to 300°F (150°C). Line a baking sheet with parchment paper.

2. Sift together cocoa powder and cinnamon onto a piece of wax paper.

3. With an electric mixer, beat egg whites and cream of tartar on high speed until foamy. Slowly add sugar, beating until soft peaks form. Reduce mixer speed to low and slowly sprinkle in cocoa-cinnamon mixture. Beat in vanilla. Increase mixer speed to high and beat until stiff peaks form.

4. Transfer mixture to a pastry bag fitted with a ½-inch (1.25-cm) star tip. Holding the pastry bag perpendicular to the prepared baking sheet, pipe 1¼-inch (3-cm) rounds, lifting the bag straight up after piping each one.

5. Bake for 20 minutes until dry and lightly colored. Turn off oven and leave cookies undisturbed for 1 hour.

6. Remove cookies from parchment. Store in an airtight container for up to 1 month.

YIELD: ABOUT 3 DOZEN LITTLE COOKIES

Per cookie: 16 Calories, 0g Fat, 0g Saturated Fat, 0mg Cholesterol, 0g Protein, 4g Carbohydrate, 0.1g Fiber, 4mg Sodium

Nutrition Bonus: Meringue-based desserts satisfy a sweet tooth without adding a single gram of fat to a meal.

A Caribbean COOKOUT

- Okra was introduced to the Caribbean from Africa, where it was called *ngombo*. This became gumbo, which now means a vegetable stew made with okra. Okra is high in fiber and folate, which are thought to play a role in the prevention of heart disease and some cancers.

- Although it's important not to get too much sun, a few minutes a day is beneficial. The body produces vitamin D from the sun shining on the skin, and vitamin D analogs are being studied for their effects in battling prostate and breast cancer.

THINK ABOUT THE CARIBBEAN, AND YOU'RE LIKELY TO THINK OF Christopher Columbus and the culinary treasures he added to today's repertoire of seasonings. He had hoped to find a shortcut to the Far East with its great stores of cloves, nutmeg and black pepper. Instead he came upon a New World filled with chile peppers, allspice and vanilla. These distinctive flavors continue to dominate Caribbean Islands cuisine. Imagine jerk marinades without the fiery heat of habanero peppers or the sultry accent of allspice, or fruit desserts without the lilting note of vanilla.

VEGETABLE GUMBO

no-stick cooking spray
1 small onion, diced
3 stalks celery, tough strings peeled, sliced
1 teaspoon chopped fresh garlic
1 14.5-ounce (435-g) can diced low-sodium tomatoes with juices
4 cups (20 oz/600 g) fresh or frozen corn kernels
3 cups (18 oz/540 g) sliced okra
2 medium boiling potatoes, peeled and cubed
7 cups (56 fl oz/1.7 L) Vegetable Stock (page 32)
sea salt and freshly ground black pepper to taste
hot sauce to taste

1. Spray a large soup pot once with cooking spray. Heat pot over low heat. Add onions and celery, cover and cook for 2 minutes. Add garlic and cook for 15 seconds.

2. Stir in tomatoes, corn, okra and potatoes. Add stock and bring to a boil. Reduce heat to a simmer. Cook until potatoes are soft and gumbo has thickened, about 30 minutes.

3. Season to taste with salt, pepper and hot sauce.

YIELD: 4 QUARTS (3.6 L), 12 SERVINGS

Per serving: 82 Calories, 0.3g Fat, 0g Saturated Fat, 0mg Cholesterol, 3g Protein, 19g Carbohydrate, 3.4g Fiber, 25mg Sodium

ROASTED PLANTAINS

Don't use green plantains in this recipe — they're too hard. Ripe plantains look blackened, like overripe bananas.

no-stick cooking spray
4 ripe plantains
1 orange, cut in half
2 teaspoons brown sugar
1 teaspoon ground cinnamon

1. Preheat oven to 350°F (175°C). Spray a large, shallow baking dish lightly with cooking spray.

2. Peel plantains and slice in half lengthwise. Cut each section at an angle into 5 slices. Keeping the pieces together, transfer to the baking dish. Repeat with the other halves.

3. Squeeze orange juice over plantains. Sprinkle with brown sugar and cinnamon.

4. Bake for 30 minutes, or until plantains are just tender.

YIELD: 8 SERVINGS

Per serving: 98 Calories, 0.2g Fat, 0g Saturated Fat, 0mg Cholesterol, 0.7g Protein, 26g Carbohydrate, 1.9g Fiber, 4mg Sodium

BLACK BEANS AND RICE

over 60 minutes

To save time, you can use canned black beans. You'll need two 28-ounce (840-g) cans. Rinse beans to remove excess salt.

BLACK BEANS

- 2½ cups (16 oz/480 g) black beans, rinsed and picked over
- 3 cloves fresh garlic
- ½ jalapeño pepper
- 2 quarts (2 L) water

RICE

- no-stick cooking spray
- 1 medium onion, chopped
- 1 celery stalk, tough strings peeled, cut into small dice
- 2 teaspoons chopped fresh garlic
- 1½ cups (10½ oz/315 g) long-grain brown or white rice
- 1 14.5-ounce (435-g) can diced low-sodium tomatoes with juices
- ⅛ teaspoon sea salt
- ⅛ teaspoon freshly ground black pepper
- 1½–2 cups (12–16 fl oz/360–480 ml) water

TO MAKE BEANS

1. Place beans, garlic, jalapeño and water in a large soup pot. Bring to a boil. Turn heat down to a simmer. Cook until beans are tender but not mushy, 1 to 1½ hours.

2. Drain beans and rinse with warm water. Pick out garlic cloves and jalapeño. Set beans aside.

TO MAKE RICE

1. Spray a large sauté pan once with cooking spray. Add onions and celery and cook, stirring, over low heat for 2 minutes. Stir in garlic and cook for 15 seconds.

2. Add rice, tomatoes, salt, pepper and water (1½ cups/ 12 fl oz/360 ml for white rice; 2 cups/16 fl oz/480 ml for brown rice). Bring to a boil, reduce heat to a simmer and cook, covered, for 20 minutes for white rice, 45 minutes for brown rice. During the final 5 minutes of cooking, stir in reserved black beans.

3. Toss with a fork and serve.

YIELD: 8 TO 10 SERVINGS

Per serving: 271 Calories, 1.7g Fat, 0.3g Saturated Fat, 0mg Cholesterol, 13g Protein, 54g Carbohydrate, 8.3g Fiber, 42mg Sodium

THE BENEFITS OF GARLIC

As a flavoring, garlic has no equal. Even a single clove can transform a recipe from ordinary to delicious. It seems to be quite potent in the health department as well. Precisely why garlic affects heart disease and certain cancers is fueling the study of its beneficial properties. For example, there is new epidemiological evidence showing that people who eat just one clove of raw or cooked garlic per day have a considerably lower risk of stomach and colorectal cancers. Researchers are studying whether other allium vegetables — onions, leeks, shallots and chives — might bring similar benefits.

Roasting transforms garlic from an assertive seasoning to a sweet, mellow, almost buttery substance that makes a wonderful fat-free spread for bread. To roast, wrap garlic head in aluminum foil and bake at 400°F (200°C) for 40 minutes. Let cool and squeeze soft garlic from the cloves.

A CARIBBEAN COOKOUT

JERK KEBABS

over 60 minutes

Habanero peppers are extremely hot. Be careful when handling them to not touch your eyes or other sensitive areas.

JERK MARINADE

- ¾ cup (6 fl oz/180 ml) fresh lime juice
- ½ cup (4 fl oz/120 ml) fresh orange juice
- 1–2 habanero or other very hot peppers or 2–3 tablespoons hot chili sauce
- 2 tablespoons low-sodium tamari soy sauce
- 1 tablespoon orange marmalade
- 3 green onions, trimmed and roughly chopped
- 2 shallots, roughly chopped
- 1½ tablespoons balsamic vinegar
- 1½ tablespoons dried basil
- 1½ teaspoons tomato paste
- 1½ teaspoons mustard seed or dried mustard
- 2 teaspoons grated orange zest
- 1 teaspoon grated lime zest
- 1 teaspoon ground allspice
- ½ teaspoon cracked black pepper
- ⅛ teaspoon sea salt

KEBABS

- 1 pound (480 g) tempeh, cut into 1-inch (2.5-cm) squares
- 1 yellow bell pepper, cut into 1-inch (2.5-cm) squares
- 1 green bell pepper, cut into 1-inch (2.5-cm) squares
- 1 red bell pepper, cut into 1-inch (2.5-cm) squares
- 1 chayote squash or zucchini, cubed
- 1 large sweet potato, cubed and cooked in boiling water until just tender

TO MAKE JERK MARINADE

1. Combine marinade ingredients in a blender and puree until smooth.

TO ASSEMBLE KEBABS

1. Pour half of the marinade into a bowl, add tempeh squares and toss to coat. Cover and chill for at least 2 hours — the longer you leave the tempeh in the marinade, the more flavor it will absorb.

2. Light an outdoor grill. If you are using wooden skewers, soak them in water for 15 minutes.

3. Thread tempeh and vegetables onto 8 skewers, alternating colors. Brush vegetables with the remaining marinade.

4. Grill kebabs over a medium-low fire, turning two or three times, until vegetables are cooked through, about 10 minutes. (If you prefer, kebabs may be roasted in a 350°F/175°C oven for 25 minutes.)

YIELD: **8 SERVINGS**

Per serving: 187 Calories, 4.8g Fat, 0.7g Saturated Fat, 0mg Cholesterol, 13g Protein, 27g Carbohydrate, 2.6g Fiber, 247mg Sodium

Nutrition Bonus: Everything threaded onto these kebabs is a supernutritious food, loaded with antioxidants and other disease fighters. The jerk marinade is great on fish or chicken, too.

Front to back: Roasted Plantains, Jerk Kebabs, Black Beans and Rice

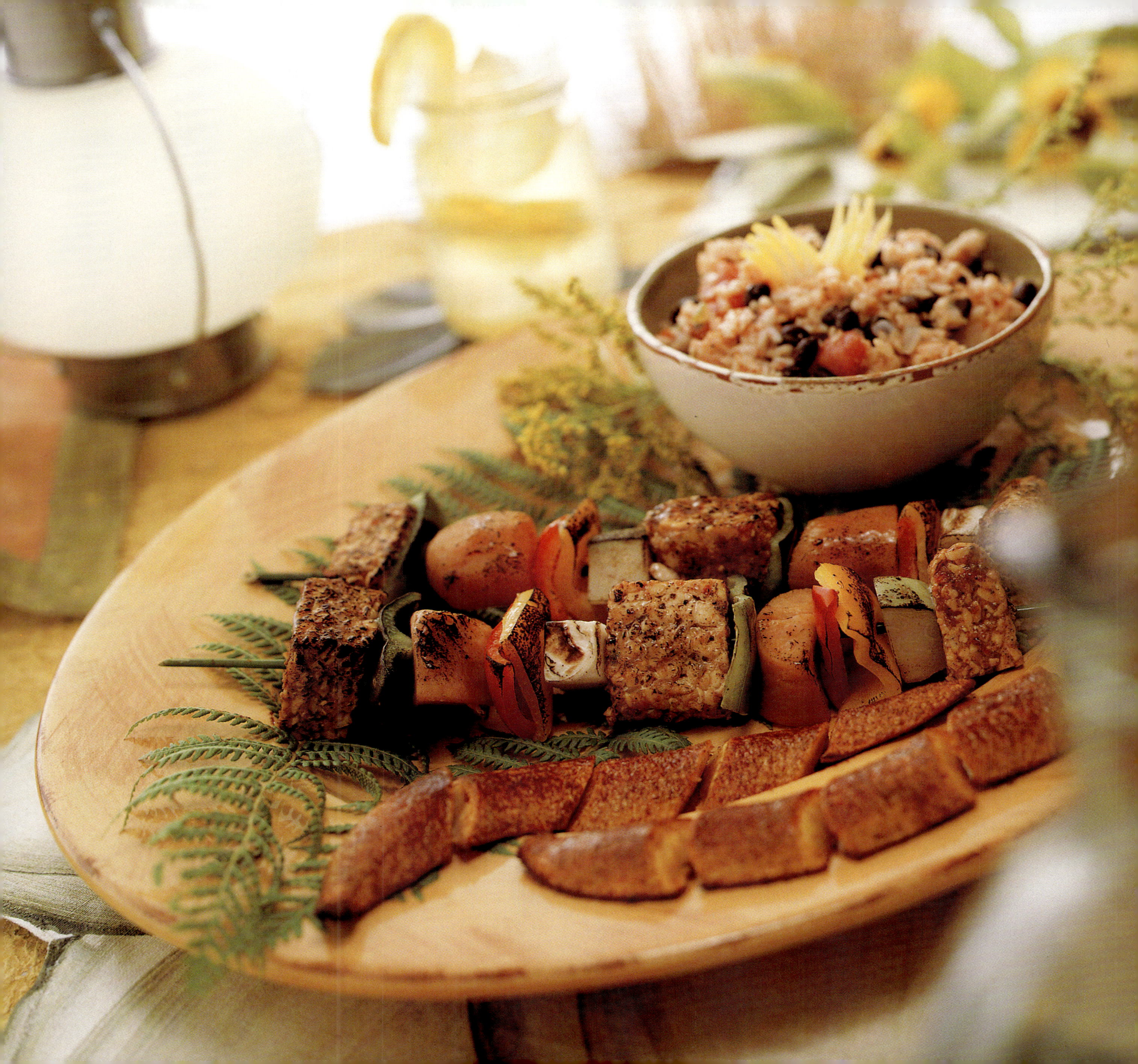

BANANA BREAD

over 60 minutes

- no-stick cooking spray
- 3 cups (13½ oz/400 g) all-purpose flour or 3½ cups (13½ oz/400 g) oat flour
- ⅔ cup (4½ oz/135 g) brown sugar or maple sugar
- ⅔ cup (4½ oz/135 g) natural cane sugar
- 1 teaspoon baking powder
- 1 teaspoon baking soda
- ¾ teaspoon ground cinnamon
- pinch sea salt
- 3 large, very ripe bananas
- ½ cup (4 fl oz/120 ml) fat-free egg product
- ⅓ cup (2½ fl oz/75 ml) 1% vanilla soy milk
- 2 tablespoons unsweetened applesauce
- 1½ teaspoons pure vanilla extract
- 1 teaspoon grated orange zest, optional
- ½ cup (2 oz/60 g) currants, optional
- ⅓ cup (2 oz/60 g) chopped dates, optional
- ⅓ cup (1½ oz/45 g) dried banana, optional

1. Preheat oven to 350°F (175°C). Spray a tube pan or large loaf pan (2-qt/2-L) lightly with cooking spray.
2. In a bowl, whisk together flour, sugars, baking powder, baking soda, cinnamon and salt. Set aside.
3. In a food processor, puree ripe bananas. Add egg product, soy milk, applesauce, vanilla and orange zest, if using, and process until mixed.
4. Add banana mixture to dry ingredients, blending with a wire whisk or a wooden spoon. Do not overmix.
5. Fold in dried fruits, if using. Transfer batter to prepared pan. Bake for 1 hour 20 minutes, or until a skewer inserted in the center comes out clean.
6. Cool on a wire rack. Serve with Caramel Sauce, if desired.

YIELD: 14 SLICES

Per slice: 213 Calories, 0.4g Fat, 0.1g Saturated Fat, 0mg Cholesterol, 4g Protein, 49g Carbohydrate, 1.6g Fiber, 131mg Sodium

CARAMEL SAUCE

under 30 minutes

- 1 cup (8 fl oz/240 ml) rice syrup
- ½ cup (4 fl oz/120 ml) 1% vanilla soy milk
- 1 teaspoon pure vanilla extract
- 1 vanilla bean, optional

1. Combine rice syrup, soy milk and vanilla extract in a heavy saucepan.
2. If using vanilla bean, split it lengthwise and scrape out seeds into soy milk mixture. Add vanilla bean as well.
3. Simmer sauce over medium-low heat until it develops a warm caramel color, about 10 minutes.
4. Remove vanilla bean. Pour sauce into a small pitcher and serve warm. The sauce will keep for up to 1 month in the refrigerator — leave vanilla bean in sauce for additional flavor. If sauce separates, blend with a whisk.

YIELD: 1¼ CUPS (10 FL OZ/300 ML)

Per 2-tablespoon serving: 75 Calories, 0.1g Fat, 0g Saturated Fat, 0mg Cholesterol, 0.2g Protein, 18g Carbohydrate, 0g Fiber, 6mg Sodium

Southern
TRADITIONS

BARBECUES AND PICNICS IN THE U.S. SOUTH CONTAIN SOME OF THE BEST — and some of the fattiest — foods you'll ever eat. Typically, platters of ribs, chicken and brisket, and pans of shepherd's pie, black-eyed peas and cornbread cover long tables. Dessert tables groan under the weight of homemade cobblers, cakes, pies, trifles and puddings.

But sacrificing high-fat meats and heavy cream does not mean giving up those flavors forever. Smoked tofu lends a smoky complexity to collard greens or black-eyed peas. Soy milk makes sweet potato pie or banana pudding just as rich as the high-fat originals.

- The traditional Southern diet actually contains some very healthy foods, including a variety of grains and nutrient-packed vegetables such as collard and mustard greens, sweet potatoes and black-eyed peas.

SOUTHERN TRADITIONS **87**

ROMAINE, TOMATO AND VIDALIA SALAD WITH CREAMY FRENCH DRESSING

- 4 large vine-ripened tomatoes, cored
- 2 medium Vidalia or other sweet onions
- 2 heads romaine lettuce, leaves separated
- 1 cup (8 oz/240 g) Creamy French Dressing (recipe follows)

1. Slice tomatoes in half vertically and then into thin slices, keeping halves together. Slice onions into very thin rings.
2. Place about 3 long romaine leaves on each of 8 salad plates. Fan a tomato half on top and sprinkle with onions. Drizzle with Creamy French Dressing.

YIELD: 8 SERVINGS

Per serving: 61 Calories, 0.7g Fat, 0.1g Saturated Fat, 0mg Cholesterol, 3g Protein, 13g Carbohydrate, 3.1g Fiber, 35mg Sodium

CREAMY FRENCH DRESSING

- 1 tablespoon chopped shallot
- 1¼ cups (10 fl oz/300 ml) low-sodium catsup
- 4 ounces (120 g) low-fat silken tofu
- 1 cup (8 fl oz/240 ml) water
- 2 tablespoons yellow mustard
- freshly ground black pepper to taste

1. Puree shallots in a food processor. Add catsup, tofu, water, mustard and pepper and process for 1 minute. The dressing will keep for 4 days in the refrigerator.

YIELD: 3 CUPS (24 OZ/720 G)

Per 2-tablespoon serving: 18 Calories, 0.2g Fat, 0g Saturated Fat, 0mg Cholesterol, 1g Protein, 4g Carbohydrate, 0.3g Fiber, 23mg Sodium

CORNBREAD

- 1 cup (6 oz/180 g) fresh or frozen corn kernels
- ¾ cup (6 fl oz/180 ml) fat-free egg product
- ½ cup (4 fl oz/120 ml) 1% vanilla soy milk
- 4 ounces (120 g) fat-free jack-style soy cheese, grated by hand (1 cup)
- 1 tablespoon chopped roasted jalapeño pepper (page 76)
- 1 tablespoon sliced green onion
- ⅓ cup (2 oz/60 g) yellow cornmeal, preferably stoneground
- ⅓ cup (1½ oz/45 g) all-purpose white flour
- ⅓ cup (1½ oz/45 g) whole-wheat pastry flour
- 2 teaspoons baking powder
- ½ teaspoon sea salt

1. Preheat oven to 350°F (175°C). Spray a 9-inch (23-cm) round cake pan lightly with cooking spray. Line pan bottom with a circle of parchment or wax paper.
2. Cook corn in boiling water for 3 minutes. Drain.
3. Puree corn in a food processor. When pureed, add egg product and soy milk and blend for 30 seconds. Stir in soy cheese, roasted jalapeños and green onions. Set aside.
4. In a mixing bowl, whisk together cornmeal, flour, pastry flour, baking powder and salt. Add corn mixture and stir until just mixed. Pour into prepared pan.
5. Bake for 45 minutes, or until a toothpick inserted in the center comes out clean.
6. If you like, serve with Pear Sauce (page 90).

YIELD: 10 SERVINGS

Per serving: 89 Calories, 0.4g Fat, 0g Saturated Fat, 0mg Cholesterol, 7g Protein, 15g Carbohydrate, 1.4g Fiber, 307mg Sodium

Clockwise, from right: Black-Eyed Peas, Shepherd's Pie, Collard and Mustard Greens, Pear Sauce, Cornbread

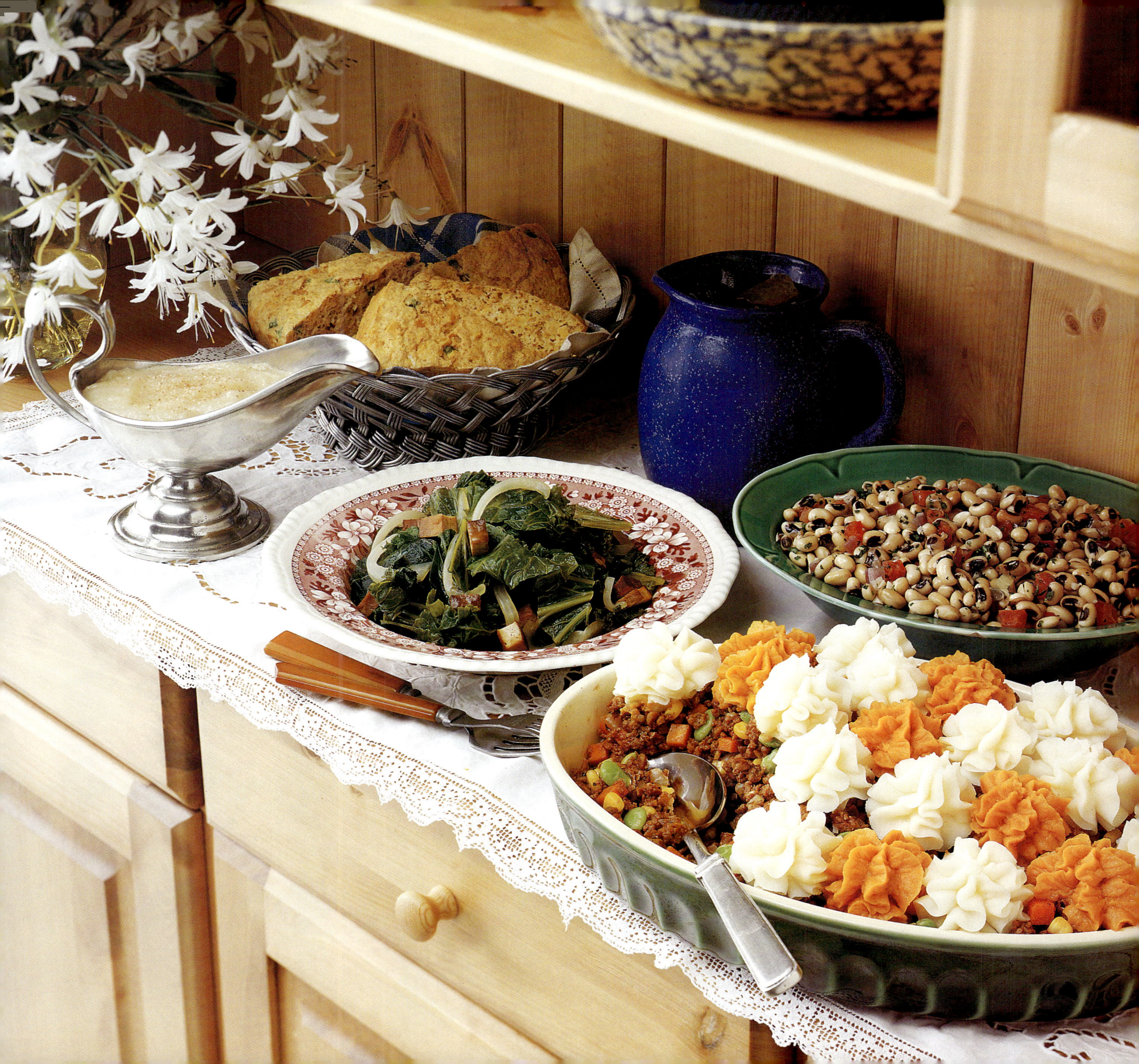

EAT YOUR CRUCIFERS!

Nutrition researchers have long observed that in regions where people eat greater amounts of vegetables belonging to the cabbage or crucifer family, rates of some cancers are lower. Rich in vitamins, minerals and dietary fiber, these vegetables also appear to be an excellent source of the cancer-fighting compounds known as phytochemicals. Scientists have identified a compound in broccoli called sulforaphane, which activates enzymes that inactivate some cancer-causing chemicals. Another compound, indole-3-carbinol, may affect sex-hormone metabolism involved with the progression of prostate cancer. Supplements made from dried crucifers have not shown the same benefits as the whole fresh vegetables.

Happily, the crucifer family offers many options. If you're not a fan of Brussels sprouts, you're certain to find vegetables you do like on the list below.

Arugula, Beet Greens, Bok Choy, Broccoli, Brussels Sprouts, Cabbage, Cauliflower, Chinese Cabbage, Collard Greens, Daikon, Horseradish, Kale, Kohlrabi, Mustard Greens, Radishes, Rutabaga, Swiss Chard, Turnips and Turnip Greens, Watercress

PEAR SAUCE

- 1 vanilla bean, optional
- 8 large pears, peeled, cored and quartered
- 2/3 cup (5½ fl oz/165 ml) water
- 1 tablespoon natural cane sugar
- ½ teaspoon pure vanilla extract
- ½ teaspoon grated nutmeg

1. If using vanilla bean, split it lengthwise and scrape seeds into a large saucepan. Add bean to the pan as well.

2. Add pears, water, sugar, vanilla extract and nutmeg to the pan. Bring to a boil and reduce heat to a simmer. Cover the pan and cook until pears are soft, about 20 minutes.

3. Remove vanilla bean. Puree sauce in a food processor or, for a chunkier sauce, mash it with a potato masher.

YIELD: 4 CUPS (ABOUT 32 OZ/1.9 K)

Per ½-cup (4-oz/120-g) serving: 93 Calories, 1g Fat, 0.1g Saturated Fat, 0mg Cholesterol, 1g Protein, 23g Carbohydrate, 3.7g Fiber, 0mg Sodium

SHEPHERD'S PIE

MASHED POTATO TOPPING

- 6 medium baking potatoes, peeled and diced
- ½ cup (4 fl oz/120 ml) Vegetable Stock (page 32)
- 1 teaspoon Dijon mustard
- ½ teaspoon sea salt
  freshly ground black pepper to taste

MASHED SWEET POTATO TOPPING

- 3 large sweet potatoes, peeled and diced
- ½ cup (4 fl oz/120 ml) Vegetable Stock (page 32)
- 1 teaspoon Dijon mustard
  freshly ground black pepper to taste

FILLING

- no-stick cooking spray
- 1 medium onion, chopped (about 1 cup)
- 1 tablespoon chopped garlic
- 1½ pounds (960 g) fat-free ground soy "meat"
- 3 carrots, peeled and diced
- ¾ cup (6 oz/180 g) fresh or frozen corn kernels
- 1 cup (8 oz/240 g) cooked fresh or frozen lima beans
- 1 14.5-ounce (435-g) can diced low-sodium tomatoes, drained
- 1 tablespoon tomato paste
- freshly cracked black pepper to taste

TO MAKE MASHED POTATO AND SWEET POTATO TOPPINGS

1. Place baking potatoes in a large saucepan, add water to cover and bring to a boil. Cook until soft, about 20 minutes. Drain and place in bowl of electric mixer. Add stock and seasonings. Beat on high speed until smooth. Set aside.

2. Repeat these same steps for sweet potatoes.

TO MAKE FILLING

1. Preheat oven to 350°F (175°C).

2. Spray a large sauté pan once with cooking spray and set pan over low heat. Add onions and cook, stirring, until soft, about 2 minutes. Add garlic and cook for 15 seconds.

3. Stir in soy meat, breaking it up with a wooden spoon. Add carrots, corn, lima beans, tomatoes and tomato paste. Cook for 10 minutes. Season with pepper.

4. Spoon mixture into a large gratin dish. Top with alternating dollops of mashed potato and sweet potato toppings. (For a pretty effect, pipe the toppings with separate pastry bags fitted with star tubes.)

5. Bake for 20 minutes, or until hot.

YIELD: **8 SERVINGS**

Per serving: 321 Calories, 0.9g Fat, 0.1g Saturated Fat, 0mg Cholesterol, 25g Protein, 56g Carbohydrate, 11.6g Fiber, 585mg Sodium

COLLARD AND MUSTARD GREENS

over 60 minutes

- 2 bunches (24 oz/720 g) collard greens
- 1 bunch (12 oz/360 g) mustard greens, stemmed
- 2 cups (16 fl oz/480 ml) Vegetable Stock (page 32)
- 1 medium onion, thinly sliced
- 2 ounces (60 g) diced smoked tofu or vegetarian Canadian bacon
- 2 tablespoons balsamic vinegar
- ⅛–¼ teaspoon sea salt
- ⅛–¼ teaspoon freshly cracked black pepper

1. Trim ends and cut out thick ribs from collard leaves. Stack collard and mustard leaves and slice into ribbons. Wash in 2 or 3 changes of water to remove all grit.

2. In a large, deep sauté pan, combine greens, stock, onions, tofu or bacon, and vinegar. Simmer over low heat for at least 1 hour, until greens are very soft. The longer they cook, the softer they become.

3. Season to taste with salt and pepper.

YIELD: **8 SERVINGS**

Per serving: 61 Calories, 0.2g Fat, 0g Saturated Fat, 0mg Cholesterol, 5g Protein, 7g Carbohydrate, 3.1g Fiber, 184mg Sodium

Nutrition Bonus: By using vegetarian deli meats and vegetable stock to give the flavoring usually provided by salt pork or country ham, you get all the benefits of the greens without an unwanted dose of saturated fat. The greens themselves are a good source of beta-carotene and other phytonutrients.

BLACK-EYED PEAS

over 60 minutes

- 2½ cups (16 oz/480 g) dried black-eyed peas, soaked overnight
- 3 quarts (3 L) water
- ½ cup (3 oz/90 g) chopped red onion
- 2 slices vegetarian Canadian bacon
- 1 tablespoon chopped fresh thyme or 1 teaspoon dried thyme leaves
- no-stick cooking spray
- 2 tablespoons chopped fresh garlic
- 2 tablespoons chopped shallot
- 2 vine-ripened tomatoes, cored and chopped
- ¼ cup (½ oz/15 g) chopped fresh parsley
- ¼ teaspoon sea salt
- ¼ teaspoon cracked black pepper
- Tabasco or other hot sauce, optional

1. Drain and rinse black-eyed peas. Place in a large soup pot and add water, half of the onions, the bacon and thyme. Bring to a boil and reduce heat to low. Simmer, stirring often, until peas are tender but not mushy, about 1 hour.

2. Remove bacon and discard. Drain excess liquid.

3. Spray a large sauté pan once with cooking spray. Add the remaining onions and cook, stirring, over low heat until translucent, about 2 minutes. Add drained black-eyed peas, garlic, shallots, tomatoes, parsley, salt and pepper. Cook until heated through. Add hot sauce to taste.

YIELD: 8 SERVINGS

Per serving: 205 Calories, 0.8g Fat, 0.2g Saturated Fat, 0mg Cholesterol, 13g Protein, 38g Carbohydrate, 12.2g Fiber, 122mg Sodium

N Nutrition Bonus: Black-eyed peas are an excellent source of folate and fiber.

BANANA PUDDING

over 60 minutes

PUDDING
- 2 cups (16 fl oz/480 ml) 1% vanilla soy milk
- ⅓ cup (1½ oz/45 g) all-purpose flour
- ⅓ cup (2½ oz/75 g) natural cane sugar
- ⅛ teaspoon sea salt
- 1 vanilla bean, optional
- ½ cup (4 fl oz/120 ml) fat-free egg product
- 1 teaspoon vanilla extract
- 1 package (about 45) fat-free vanilla wafers
- 4–5 ripe bananas, sliced on the diagonal

MERINGUE TOPPING
- 4 egg whites
- 5 tablespoons (2 oz/60 g) natural cane sugar
- pinch sea salt

TO MAKE PUDDING

1. In a saucepan, whisk together soy milk, flour, sugar and salt. If using vanilla bean, split it lengthwise and scrape out seeds into soy milk mixture. Add vanilla bean as well.

2. Place saucepan over medium heat and bring to a boil, stirring constantly. Reduce heat to low and simmer until mixture begins to thicken, about 5 minutes.

3. Remove pan from heat. Stir a small amount of the hot mixture into egg product, then return this mixture to the pan.

4. Return pan to medium-low heat. Cook, stirring constantly, for 3 minutes more, or until custard thickens to a pudding-like consistency. Remove from heat, stir in vanilla extract and remove vanilla bean.

5. Cover the bottom of a 10-inch (25-cm) pie plate with a single layer of vanilla wafers. Cover with a layer of sliced bananas. Spoon half the pudding mixture on top, spread-

ing it to the edges. Reserving 5 or 6 wafers to decorate the top, make a second layer of wafers, bananas and pudding.

TO MAKE MERINGUE

1. Preheat oven to 350°F (175°C). Put a large saucepan of water on to boil.

2. In a metal bowl that will sit securely on top of the saucepan, combine egg whites, sugar and salt. Set bowl over hot water. Stir constantly until egg whites become warm to the touch.

3. Remove bowl from heat. Beat whites with an electric mixer on high speed until stiff peaks form, about 5 minutes.

4. Spoon mounds of meringue onto the pudding, lifting the spoon to form peaks. Bake until golden, about 8 minutes. Garnish with the reserved vanilla wafers.

YIELD: 10 SERVINGS

Per serving: 215 Calories, 0.7g Fat, 0.1g Saturated Fat, 0mg Cholesterol, 5g Protein, 48g Carbohydrate, 1.5g Fiber, 155mg Sodium

SWEET POTATO PIE

over 60 minutes

- 2 large sweet potatoes (20 oz/600 g total), peeled and cut into chunks
- 1 cup (8 fl oz/240 ml) 1% vanilla soy milk
- ½ cup (3½ oz/100 g) natural cane sugar
- ⅓ cup (3 fl oz/90 ml) fat-free egg product
- 1 teaspoon pure vanilla extract
- 1 teaspoon ground cinnamon
- ¼ teaspoon grated nutmeg
- ⅛ teaspoon sea salt
- 1 9-inch (23-cm) baked pie crust (see Lemon Tartlets, page 26: add 1 teaspoon grated orange zest to dough) or baked graham cracker crust (see Key Lime Pie, page 110)

1. Cook sweet potatoes in a large saucepan of boiling water until soft, about 20 minutes.

2. Preheat oven to 400°F (200°C).

3. Drain sweet potatoes. While still hot, puree in a food processor or with an electric mixer. Add soy milk, sugar, egg product, vanilla, cinnamon, nutmeg and salt and blend until smooth.

4. Pour mixture into prebaked pie crust. Bake pie for 10 minutes. Reduce oven temperature to 350°F (175°C) and bake for 30 minutes longer, or until a toothpick inserted in the center comes out clean.

5. Cool to room temperature, then refrigerate. If you like, decorate pie slices with a small piece of Soy Nut Brittle (recipe follows).

YIELD: 10 SERVINGS

Per serving: 157 Calories, 0.7g Fat, 0.2g Saturated Fat, 0mg Cholesterol, 3g Protein, 36g Carbohydrate, 2.1g Fiber, 113mg Sodium

Nutrition Bonus: Sweet potatoes are considered to be one of nature's most nutritionally dense foods.

SOY NUT BRITTLE

- 2 cups (14 oz/420 g) natural cane sugar
- 1 cup (8 fl oz/240 ml) corn syrup
- ¾ cup (6 fl oz/180 ml) water
- no-stick cooking spray
- 2 cups (10 oz/300 g) dry-roasted soy nuts
- 2 teaspoons pure vanilla extract
- ¼ teaspoon baking soda

1. In a deep, heavy saucepan, combine sugar, syrup and water. Attach a candy thermometer to the side of the pan. Bring mixture to a boil, reduce heat to medium-low and cook until mixtures reaches 290°F (143°C). Do not stir. Do not touch syrup with your fingers.

2. While mixture is cooking, spray 2 baking sheets lightly with cooking spray. Spread soy nuts on sheets.

3. When mixture reaches 290°F (143°C), remove pan from the heat. Stir in vanilla and baking soda. Be careful: the hot sugar will sputter. Working quickly, pour mixture over soy nuts. Spread as thin as possible with a wooden spoon.

4. Cool to room temperature. Smack pans on a hard surface to break brittle into pieces. Store in a tightly covered tin.

YIELD: ABOUT 30 OUNCES (900 G)

Per 1-ounce (30-g) piece: 115 Calories, 1.7g Fat, 0.2g Saturated Fat, 0mg Cholesterol, 3g Protein, 24g Carbohydrate, 0.3g Fiber, 24mg Sodium

LUNCH AT THE U.S. Senate

- The 76 million members of the baby-boom generation — 31 percent of the U.S. population — are turning 50 at a rate of one every seven seconds. As they pass that threshold, their risk of cancer increases. But the annual U.S. cancer research budget is only about one-seventh of what Americans spend on beauty products each year.

IN THE FALL OF 1998, MORE THAN 200,000 PEOPLE WENT TO WASHINGTON, D.C. to participate in THE MARCH . . . Coming Together to Conquer Cancer, an event that brought together people who have in some way been affected by this devastating disease.

All that week, the Senate Dining Room menu featured, along with its famous bean soup, recipes from the first *Taste for Living Cookbook*. Thanks to Chef Don Perez and his crew, everything was delicious and well received by Senators and their guests. During the march itself, we provided a sampling of healthy *Taste for Living* foods to celebrities and politicians, including Vice-President Al Gore and his wife, Tipper, Cindy Crawford, Senator Bob Dole, Scott Hamilton, Jesse Jackson, Sherry Lansing and General Norman Schwarzkopf.

It was a way to send positive nutrition messages that might help many people in the future.

LUNCH AT THE U.S. SENATE

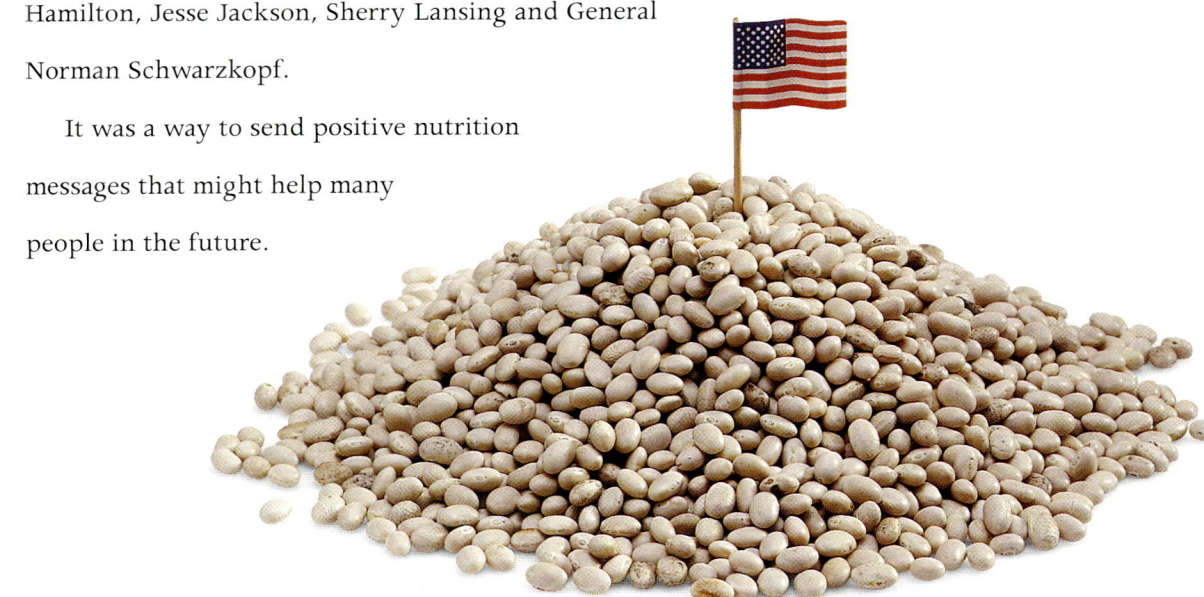

SENATE BEAN SOUP

over 60 minutes

- 2½ cups (16 oz/480 g) small navy or other white beans, soaked overnight
- 9 cups (72 fl oz/2 L) Vegetable Stock (page 32)
- 2 potatoes, peeled and cut into small dice
- 2 celery stalks, tough strings peeled, cut into small dice
- 1 large roasted onion (page 40), chopped
- 2 slices vegetarian Canadian bacon or smoked tempeh, cut into small dice
- 1 tablespoon chopped fresh garlic
- ½ teaspoon sea salt
- ¼ teaspoon freshly ground black pepper

1. Drain and rinse beans. Place in a large soup pot and add water to cover. Bring to a boil, reduce heat to a low and simmer beans for 45 minutes. (They will not be fully cooked.) Drain beans.

2. Return the beans to the soup pot. Add stock, potatoes, celery, onions, bacon or tempeh and garlic. Bring to a boil, reduce heat to low and simmer, stirring occasionally, until potatoes and beans are cooked and creamy, about 45 minutes. (Be careful not to let the soup scorch — if a bean film does form on the bottom of the pot, simply transfer soup to a clean pot and continue cooking.)

3. Season with salt and pepper and serve.

YIELD: 3 QUARTS (2.8 L), 8 TO 10 SERVINGS

Per serving: 192 Calories, 0.7g Fat, 0.2g Saturated Fat, 0mg Cholesterol, 12g Protein, 36g Carbohydrate, 12.2g Fiber, 173mg Sodium

Nutrition Bonus: You don't need ham or fat to make this soup taste great. Here smoked tempeh or vegetarian Canadian bacon provides flavor richness.

HOMEMADE POTATO CHIPS

30–60 minutes

You will need to use a French vegetable slicer called a mandoline to make these chips, or to have a very steady hand to slice the potatoes paper-thin.

- no-stick cooking spray
- 4 baking potatoes (2½ lbs/1.2 K total), scrubbed
- ⅛ teaspoon granulated onion
- pinch sea salt

1. Preheat oven to 300°F (150°C). Spray 2 baking sheets lightly with cooking spray.

2. Using a mandoline or a sharp chef's knife, slice potatoes 1/16 inch (2 mm) thick.

3. Spread potato slices on prepared baking sheets. Bake about 25 minutes, until potatoes turn golden. Check potatoes often and remove any that are done with a small metal spatula.

4. Season crispy potatoes with onion and salt (or use your favorite seasoning mixture).

5. The potato chips are best served the day they are made. If the weather is dry, the chips will keep in a plastic bag for 1 or 2 days.

YIELD: 8 SERVINGS

Per serving: 129 Calories, 0.1g Fat, 0g Saturated Fat, 0mg Cholesterol, 3g Protein, 30g Carbohydrate, 3g Fiber, 25mg Sodium

Nutrition Bonus: Full-fat commercial potato chips have about 15 grams of fat and 225 calories for a similar-size serving.

GRILLED CHEESE SANDWICHES

under 30 minutes

- 8 slices vegetarian Canadian bacon or vegetarian bacon
- 8 slices whole-grain bread
- 12 ounces (360 g) fat-free soy cheese, sliced — SOY
- 8 tomato slices
- no-stick cooking spray

1. If using vegetarian bacon, cook according to package directions.

2. Place 4 bread slices on a work surface. Top with half the soy cheese, followed by the bacon and tomato. Top with the remaining soy cheese and bread slices.

3. The sandwiches may be grilled a couple of ways: Spray a griddle once with cooking spray and brown sandwiches over medium heat for 2 minutes on each side, or until cheese is melted. Or, toast sandwiches in a sandwich iron for about 3 minutes.

YIELD: 4 SANDWICHES

Per sandwich: 287 Calories, 1.2g Fat, 0g Saturated Fat, 0mg Cholesterol, 34g Protein, 41g Carbohydrate, 6.7g Fiber, 958mg Sodium

Nutrition Bonus: A typical grilled cheese sandwich made with two slices of American cheese and browned in butter provides anywhere from 350 to 450 calories and 20 to 30 grams of fat, depending on how much butter was used in preparation.

LUNCH AT THE U.S. SENATE

HOT FUDGE SUNDAES

- 8 scoops fat-free soy ice cream or frozen yogurt
- ½ cup (4 fl oz/120 ml) Hot Fudge Sauce (recipe follows)
- ½ cup (4 fl oz/120 ml) Fat-Free Whipped Topping (recipe follows)
- 4 fresh cherries or strawberries

1. Place 2 scoops of ice cream or frozen yogurt in each of 4 sundae dishes.
2. Pour Hot Fudge Sauce on top. Garnish with Fat-Free Whipped Topping and a cherry or strawberry.

YIELD: 4 SUNDAES

Per sundae: 333 Calories, 0.6g Fat, 0.3g Saturated Fat, 0.3mg Cholesterol, 10g Protein, 74g Carbohydrate, 2g Fiber, 144mg Sodium

HOT FUDGE SAUCE

- ½ cup (2 oz/60 g) fat-free cocoa powder
- 1 tablespoon cornstarch
- ½ cup (4 fl oz/120 ml) honey, corn syrup or rice syrup
- ¼ cup (2 fl oz/60 ml) 1% chocolate soy milk
- 1 teaspoon pure vanilla extract

1. In a food processor, blend cocoa powder, cornstarch, sweetener, chocolate soy milk and vanilla.
2. Transfer sauce to a saucepan and warm over low heat.

YIELD: ABOUT 1 CUP (8 FL OZ/240 ML)

Per 2-tablespoon serving: 94 Calories, 0.6g Fat, 0.3g Saturated Fat, 0.3mg Cholesterol, 1g Protein, 22g Carbohydrate, 1.6g Fiber, 7mg Sodium

FAT-FREE WHIPPED TOPPING

- ½ cup (3½ oz/100 g) natural cane sugar
- ⅛ teaspoon cream of tartar
- 1 egg white
- 2 tablespoons water
- 1½ teaspoons pure vanilla extract

1. Place sugar, cream of tartar, egg white, water and vanilla in a metal mixing bowl set over a saucepan of simmering water. (The bottom of the bowl should not touch the water.)
2. Beat on low speed with an electric mixer for 4 minutes. Increase speed to high and beat for 4 minutes longer.
3. Remove from heat. Beat until fluffy, about 3 minutes.

YIELD: ABOUT 1 CUP (5½ OZ/165 G)

Per 2-tablespoon serving: 53 Calories, 0g Fat, 0g Saturated Fat, 0mg Cholesterol, 0g Protein, 13g Carbohydrate, 0g Fiber, 7mg Sodium

A Southwest SUPPER

- There are many healthful elements of Southwestern cooking, including a wide variety of vegetables, beans and grains. Yet Tex-Mex and other Southwestern-style restaurants tend to pour on so many calories and so much fat that diners should be careful. A typical fajita platter can have more than 1,000 calories and 60 grams of fat.

- Red, yellow or green bell peppers contain a mixture of cancer-fighting antioxidants. Capsaicin, the compound that gives chile peppers their heat, contains an anticoagulant that is thought to possibly help prevent the heart attacks and strokes caused by blood clots.

JUST WHAT IS "SOUTHWEST" CUISINE? THE CHARACTERistic sun-drenched flavors of grilled fajitas, fire-roasted chiles and garden-fresh salsas are now found everywhere from roadside diners to tony spas throughout the Southwest. It's all part of an evolving style of eating with roots in Mexican, Native American and Californian cuisines — all infused with a shot of nouvelle creativity. It's an endless source of inspiration.

It also presents some challenges. Many Southwestern dishes feature meat, particularly marinated and grilled meat. To avoid the fat, especially the saturated fat, found in meat, substitute either tempeh, a soy product, or seitan, a wheat product. Both are delicious when marinated and grilled. It's best to grill over a medium, not hot, fire, and to avoid overcooking, which causes these products to dry out.

FAJITAS

over 60 minutes

Have fun decorating the serving plates with fresh cilantro leaves, bell pepper cutouts, squiggles of mustard and heart-of-palm circles.

MARINADE

- 1 cup (8 fl oz/240 ml) fresh orange juice
- ½ cup (4 fl oz/120 ml) fresh lime juice
- ¼ cup (2 fl oz/60 ml) low-sodium tamari soy sauce
- 2 tablespoons chopped shallots
- 2 tablespoons chopped fresh cilantro, optional
- 2 teaspoons chili powder
- 2 teaspoons ground cumin
- 2 teaspoons chopped fresh garlic
- crushed red pepper flakes to taste
- 1 pound (480 g) tempeh, seitan (wheat meat) or fat-free vegetarian chicken patties, cut into ½-inch (1.25-cm) strips

SOY

VEGETABLES, TORTILLAS AND GARNISH

- 18 no-added-fat corn or flour tortillas
- no-stick cooking spray
- 1 large onion, thinly sliced
- 1 green bell pepper, cut into thin (¼-inch/0.6-cm) strips
- 1 red bell pepper, cut into thin (¼-inch/0.6-cm) strips
- 1 zucchini, cut into matchsticks
- 1 yellow squash, cut into matchsticks
- 3 green onions, sliced
- 6 ounces (180 g) fat-free jack-style soy cheese, grated by hand (1½ cups)
- 1 recipe Fresh Tomato Salsa (page 75)
- ½ recipe Lima-Mole (page 102)

TO MAKE MARINADE

1. In a food processor or blender, combine all ingredients except the tempeh, seitan or vegetarian chicken strips and blend until smooth.

2. Place tempeh, seitan or vegetarian chicken strips in a bowl. Add marinade and toss to coat. Marinate in the refrigerator for at least 1 hour.

TO PREPARE VEGETABLES AND ASSEMBLE FAJITAS

1. Preheat oven to 350°F (175°C).

2. Wrap stack of tortillas in parchment paper and place in oven. Warm for about 8 minutes.

3. Drain marinating tempeh, seitan or vegetarian chicken strips, reserving excess marinade.

4. Spray a large sauté pan or large griddle once with cooking spray and set it over medium-low heat. Add onions and peppers and cook, stirring, for about 5 minutes. Add zucchini and yellow squash, and cook, stirring, until just tender, about 7 minutes.

5. Meanwhile, if using tempeh or seitan, spray a second large sauté pan or griddle and set it over medium-low heat. Add tempeh or seitan strips and cook, stirring, for 10 minutes.

6. Add some of the reserved marinade to the vegetables and stir to loosen any browned bits. Add the vegetarian chicken strips, if using, and cook for 2 minutes. Add sliced green onions and the sautéed tempeh or seitan, if using. Toss gently.

7. Spoon onto warm tortillas, garnish with soy cheese and roll up loosely. Serve with Fresh Tomato Salsa and Lima-Mole.

YIELD: 6 TO 9 SERVINGS

Per serving: 352 Calories, 4.7g Fat, 0.7g Saturated Fat, 0mg Cholesterol, 23g Protein, 58g Carbohydrate, 9g Fiber, 883mg Sodium

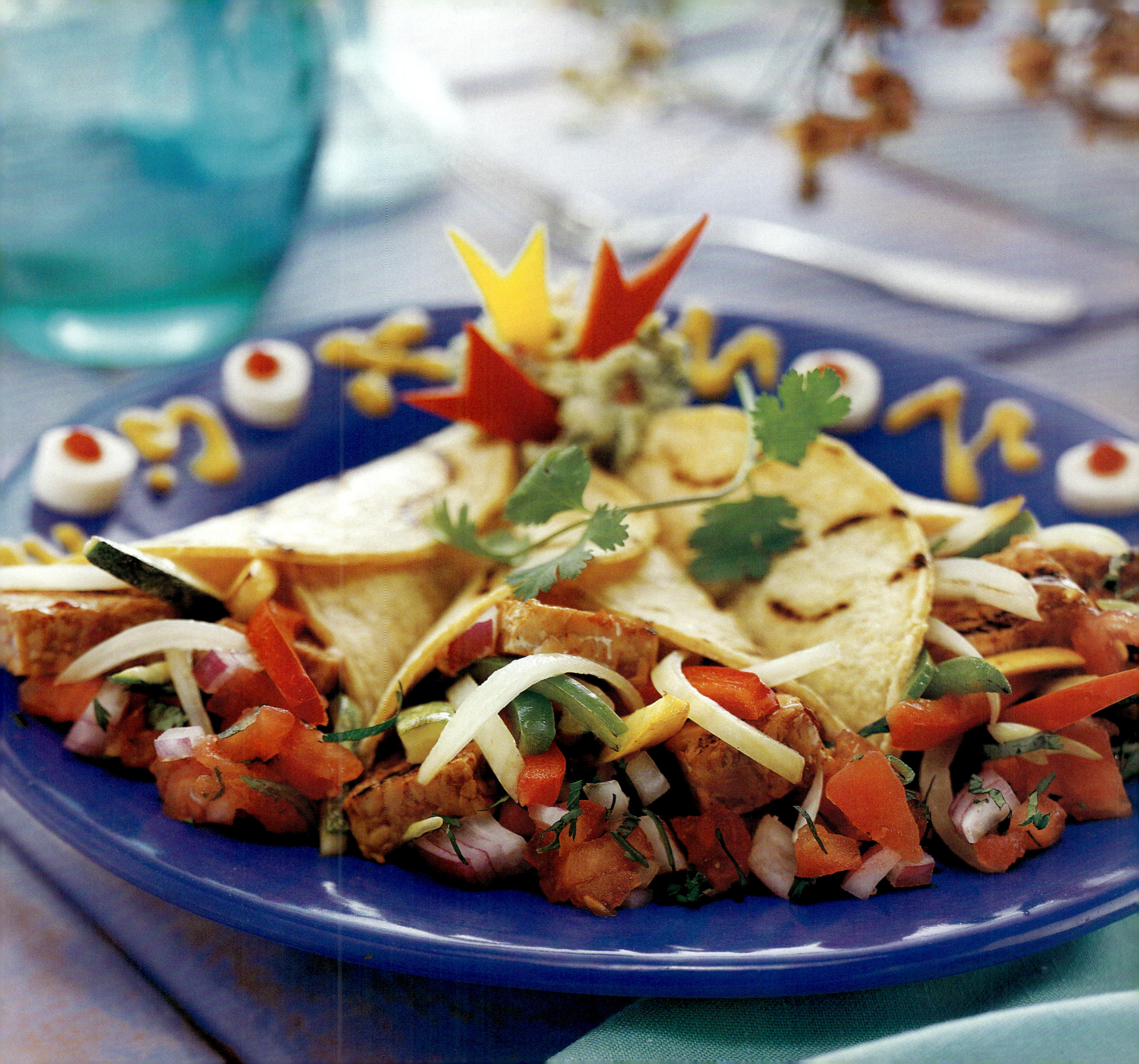

LIMA-MOLE

under 30 minutes

- 2 10-ounce (300-g) packages frozen lima beans
- juice of 2 limes
- 2 green onions, chopped
- 1 tablespoon low-fat silken tofu
- 1 tablespoon water
- 1 teaspoon minced jalapeño pepper
- ¼ teaspoon sea salt
- ¼ teaspoon ground cumin
- ½ cup diced vine-ripened tomato
- 2 tablespoons chopped fresh cilantro or parsley

1. Cook lima beans in boiling water until soft, about 10 minutes.
2. Place lima beans, lime juice, green onions, tofu, water, jalapeños, salt and cumin in a food processor and process until smooth.
3. Transfer to a bowl. Stir in tomatoes and cilantro or parsley. Serve as a garnish for any Southwestern or Mexican entrée, or serve by itself with salsa and baked tortilla chips.

YIELD: ABOUT 2½ CUPS (20 OZ/600 G)

Per 2-tablespoon serving: 47 Calories, 0.2g Fat, 0g Saturated Fat, 0mg Cholesterol, 3g Protein, 9g Carbohydrate, 2.6g Fiber, 50mg Sodium

N Nutrition Bonus: Substituting lima beans for avocados is a delicious way to save at least 4 grams of fat per serving.

SOUTHWEST CAESAR SALAD IN A FIRE-ROASTED GREEN CHILE DRESSING

30–60 minutes

For a fanciful garnish, cut tortillas into Southwest-inspired shapes — coyotes, cactus and stars are fun— and bake as directed on page 104.

- no-stick cooking spray
- 2 ears fresh corn, husked
- 1 head romaine lettuce
- 1 cup (2 oz/60 g) Tortilla Croutons (page 104)
- 1 tablespoon grated Parmesan-style soy cheese
- ½ cup (4 fl oz/120 ml) Fire-Roasted Green Chile Dressing (page 103)

1. Heat an outdoor grill. Spray grill rack with cooking spray. Place corn directly on rack and grill, turning often, until browned, about 15 minutes. Use a serrated knife to cut kernels from cobs.
2. Wash and dry lettuce leaves. Tear into bite-size pieces.
3. Place lettuce, corn, croutons and soy cheese in a salad bowl. Pour dressing on top and toss.

YIELD: 4 SERVINGS

Per serving: 118 Calories, 1.8g Fat, 0.2g Saturated Fat, 0mg Cholesterol, 6g Protein, 23g Carbohydrate, 3.7g Fiber, 152mg Sodium

N Nutrition Bonus: The standard restaurant Caesar salad, loaded with cheese, oil and fried croutons, is anything but healthful. Many contain 35 or more grams of fat per serving. Ours has all the flavor but only 2 grams of fat.

FIRE-ROASTED GREEN CHILE DRESSING

If you don't have time to roast the pepper, you can use canned roasted chiles.

- 4 ounces (120 g) low-fat silken tofu
- 1/3 cup (2 1/2 fl oz/75 ml) water
- 1/4 cup (2 fl oz/60 ml) fresh lime juice
- 2 tablespoons white miso paste
- 1 tablespoon chopped roasted pasilla pepper (page 76)
- 1 tablespoon grated Parmesan-style soy cheese
- 2 teaspoons Dijon mustard
- 1/2 teaspoon chopped fresh garlic
- 1/4 teaspoon chopped shallot
- 1/4 teaspoon chili powder
- 1/4 teaspoon Worcestershire sauce

1. Combine all ingredients in a food processor and process until smooth.
2. Dressing will keep for up to 4 days in a jar in the refrigerator. If it thickens, thin with a little water.

YIELD: 1 1/4 CUPS (10 FL OZ/300 ML)

Per 1 tablespoon: 8 Calories, 0.2g Fat, 0g Saturated Fat, 0mg Cholesterol, 1g Protein, 1g Carbohydrate, 0.1g Fiber, 39mg Sodium

TORTILLA CROUTONS

For an interesting contrast of color, use 3 yellow corn tortillas and 3 blue corn tortillas to make the croutons. Blue corn tortillas can be found in specialty shops.

    no-stick cooking spray
- 6 no-added-fat corn or flour tortillas, cut into narrow strips
- 1 teaspoon ground cumin
- ½ teaspoon chili powder
- ½ teaspoon granulated garlic

1. Preheat oven to 350°F (175°C). Spray a baking sheet lightly with cooking spray.
2. Combine tortilla strips, cumin, chili powder and garlic in a bowl. Toss well.
3. Spread strips on prepared baking sheet. Bake until crispy, about 20 minutes.

YIELD: 2 CUPS (4 OZ/120 G), 8 SERVINGS

Per serving: 88 Calories, 1.1g Fat, 0.1g Saturated Fat, 0mg Cholesterol, 2g Protein, 18g Carbohydrate, 2.3g Fiber, 65mg Sodium

CHOCOLATE TORTILLA WRAPS WITH STRAWBERRY SAUCE

CHOCOLATE TORTILLAS
- 1 cup plus 2 tablespoons (9 fl oz/270 ml) 1% chocolate soy milk
- ⅔ cup (5 fl oz/150 ml) fat-free egg product
- ⅓ cup (1½ oz/45 g) flour
- ¼ cup (1 oz/30 g) fat-free cocoa powder
- 2 tablespoons plus 1 teaspoon unsweetened applesauce
- 2 tablespoons natural cane sugar
    no-stick cooking spray

CHOCOLATE CREAM AND STRAWBERRY SAUCE
- 1 cup (8 fl oz/240 ml) 1% chocolate soy milk
- 2 ounces (60 g) low-fat silken tofu
- ¼ cup (1½ oz/45 g) natural cane sugar
- 2 tablespoons plus 2 teaspoons cornstarch
- 1 tablespoon plus 2 teaspoons fat-free cocoa powder
- ½ teaspoon pure vanilla extract
- 8 bananas
- 1 recipe Strawberry Sauce (see Raspberry Sauce, page 28, substitute frozen strawberries)

TO MAKE CHOCOLATE TORTILLAS

1. In a food processor or blender, combine soy milk, egg product, flour, cocoa, applesauce and sugar. Process until smooth. Pour batter into a bowl and set aside to rest for 20 minutes.
2. Spray a 6-inch (15-cm) nonstick crêpe pan or other small nonstick skillet once with cooking spray. Heat the pan over low heat. Ladle 2 tablespoons of batter into the pan. Swirl and tilt the pan to coat bottom. Cook over very low heat until mixture thickens and browns around the edges.

3. Flip the tortilla with a small metal spatula and cook for 2 minutes on the other side. Transfer tortilla to a plate.

4. Repeat steps 2 and 3 until batter is used up — you should have at least 8 tortillas. If tortillas begin to stick, the pan is too hot; let cool briefly.

TO MAKE CHOCOLATE CREAM AND FILL TORTILLAS

1. Puree soy milk, tofu, sugar, cornstarch, cocoa and vanilla in food processor or blender. Pour into a saucepan.

2. Cook over medium heat, stirring constantly, until mixture thickens to a creamy consistency, about 12 minutes. Transfer to a pastry bag fitted with a 3/8-inch (1-cm) plain tip.

3. Place tortillas on a work surface. Pipe some chocolate cream down the centers and spread it evenly over the tortillas with the back of a spoon. Place a banana on each tortilla and roll up. Slice each wrap into 4 sections.

4. Stand wrap sections on dessert plates. Garnish with Strawberry Sauce and little dollops of chocolate cream.

YIELD: 8 SERVINGS

Per serving: 279 Calories, 1.6g Fat, 0.4g Saturated Fat, 2.7mg Cholesterol, 6g Protein, 63g Carbohydrate, 4.5g Fiber, 74mg Sodium

YOU'VE GOT TO MOVE

EXERCISE is one of the best preventive medicines there is. It has been shown to significantly reduce the risk of heart disease and some cancers, lower blood pressure and insulin levels, and help keep off extra weight. Physical activity can be divided into three categories, and each has a special benefit for your body. Stretching keeps joints and muscles loose and limber. Strengthening builds muscles, slows bone loss and increases bone density, and lowers LDL (the "bad" cholesterol). Aerobic exercise burns fat, strengthens the heart and lungs, and raises HDL (the "good" cholesterol).

So why don't Americans get more exercise?

Some of the blame lies in the array of modern conveniences that are designed to make life easier. We sit when we used to stand or walk or lift. Tasks that once burned a few hundred calories now use next to nothing — cutting the grass with a push mower is good exercise, using a riding mower is not.

The good news is that exercise does not always have to be especially vigorous or prolonged to be beneficial, and any amount of movement is better than none. The 1996 Report on Physical Activity and Health from the Surgeon General recommends that everyone get 30 minutes of moderate physical activity every day. You don't have to join a gym to get it; there are a number of common activities — including many chores — that will qualify as exercise.

- Shop for fruits and vegetables at a farmers' market. Strolling from stall to stall burns calories and is far more satisfying than rolling your cart through the supermarket produce aisle.

- Take a vigorous walk at lunchtime — around the block, to the post office, to the store. If you're already a regular walker, increase the distance or include a steep hill. Walk and talk with friends or colleagues. For every hour you spend at your desk, get up and walk around for five minutes.

- Take the stairs, not the escalator or the elevator.

- Work in the yard or garden. Rake. Clip. Dig. Plant. Prune. Weed.

- Play golf and walk the holes.

- Give away the bread machine. Kneading dough is probably one of the most soul-satisfying activities ever invented.

- When watching TV, don't just sit there. An hour of prime-time television includes 15 minutes of commercials — plenty of time to do sit-ups, push-ups, jumping jacks or stretching exercises. Better still, pop in an exercise or yoga video and follow along.

- For long calls, use the cordless phone and walk upstairs, downstairs, around the garden — just keep moving.

- Be sure to include some form of strength training in your daily routine — even if it's lifting cans of tomatoes or sacks of dried beans.

Once physical activity becomes a part of your daily routine, you'll probably discover you really enjoy exercise and would like to join an exercise class or start working out. Before you know it, you might find yourself training for a triathlon.

Miami
MUNCHIN'

LONG BEFORE SOUTH BEACH BECAME THE PLACE TO BE IN MIAMI, THE delicious Cuban sandwiches called "medianoches" were sold by street vendors there. Beth's version of these sandwiches has become Mike Milken's favorite lunch. (Of course, maybe it's the dessert he's after — a slice of sweet and tart Key lime pie.)

The abundance of citrus and other fruits and vegetables really defines Florida eating. You can incorporate tropical fruits into savory dishes to add color, flavor and a wealth of micronutrients. For a tasty example, turn to page 108 for the Tropical Slaw, which features papaya and oranges.

- **Florida produces 70 percent of the U.S. orange crop. Ninety percent of Florida's oranges are turned into juice. Keep in mind that it's more nutritious to eat a fresh orange than to drink the juice. There's more fiber and you feel more satisfied with fewer calories.**

MEDIANOCHE SANDWICHES

A sandwich iron, similar to a waffle iron, makes these sandwiches crispy and delicious — without adding any fat!

- 4 5-inch (13-cm) pieces French bread
- 2 tablespoons mustard
- 12 slices vegetarian deli meat (ham, Canadian bacon, bologna or a mix) *SOY*
- 4 ounces (120 g) fat-free mozzarella-style soy cheese, thinly sliced
- 4 reduced-sodium dill pickle spears

1. Slice bread in half horizontally. Spread mustard on bottom halves. Top each with 2 pieces deli meat, cheese, pickle and the remaining 1 piece deli meat. Place bread on top.
2. Toast in sandwich press for 4 minutes. (Alternatively, heat a nonstick pan over medium heat. Spray once with cooking spray and place sandwich in pan. Using a small plate, flatten sandwich and weight down with a heavy can. Cook for 2 minutes, flip, flatten and weight again. Cook for 2 minutes more.)

YIELD: 4 SANDWICHES

Per sandwich: 284 Calories, 2.3g Fat, 0.4g Saturated Fat, 0mg Cholesterol, 24g Protein, 39g Carbohydrate, 2.7g Fiber, 1122mg Sodium

BLACK BEAN SOUP

- 1 pound (480 g) dried black beans, picked over, rinsed and soaked overnight
- no-stick cooking spray
- 1 large onion, finely chopped
- 3 celery stalks, tough strings peeled, finely chopped
- 1 tablespoon finely chopped fresh garlic
- 14 cups (3½ qts/3.2 L) Vegetable Stock (page 32)
- 1 jalapeño pepper, chopped
- ¼–½ teaspoon sea salt
- 1 vine-ripened tomato, seeded and cut into small dice
- 1 bunch green onions, thinly sliced

1. Spray a large soup pot once with cooking spray. Set pot over low heat and add chopped onions, celery and garlic. Cook, stirring, until vegetables are soft, about 2 minutes.
2. Drain beans and add to the pot. Add stock and jalapeños. Bring to a boil, reduce heat and simmer, stirring often, until beans are soft, about 1½ hours.
3. For a smooth soup, puree in batches in a food processor or blender. For a chunky soup, puree only half the mixture. Reheat gently and season with salt.
4. Ladle soup into bowls and garnish with tomato and green onions. Black bean soup freezes well.

YIELD: 2½ QUARTS (2.4 L), 10 SERVINGS

Per 1-cup (8-fl oz/240-ml) serving: 170 Calories, 0.7g Fat, 0.2g Saturated Fat, 0mg Cholesterol, 10g Protein, 32g Carbohydrate, 7.7g Fiber, 81mg Sodium

TROPICAL SLAW

Choose a slightly underripe papaya for this recipe.

- 2 navel oranges
- 1 medium jícama, peeled and cut into julienne strips
- 1 cup (6 oz/180 g) julienned papaya
- 1 cup (6 oz/180 g) julienned hearts of palm
- ½ red onion, cut in half vertically and very thinly sliced
- 1 teaspoon grated lime zest
- juice of 1 lime
- ¼ teaspoon crushed red pepper flakes
- ⅛ teaspoon sea salt

1. With a serrated knife, cut rind and pith from oranges. Cutting between the membranes, remove orange sections

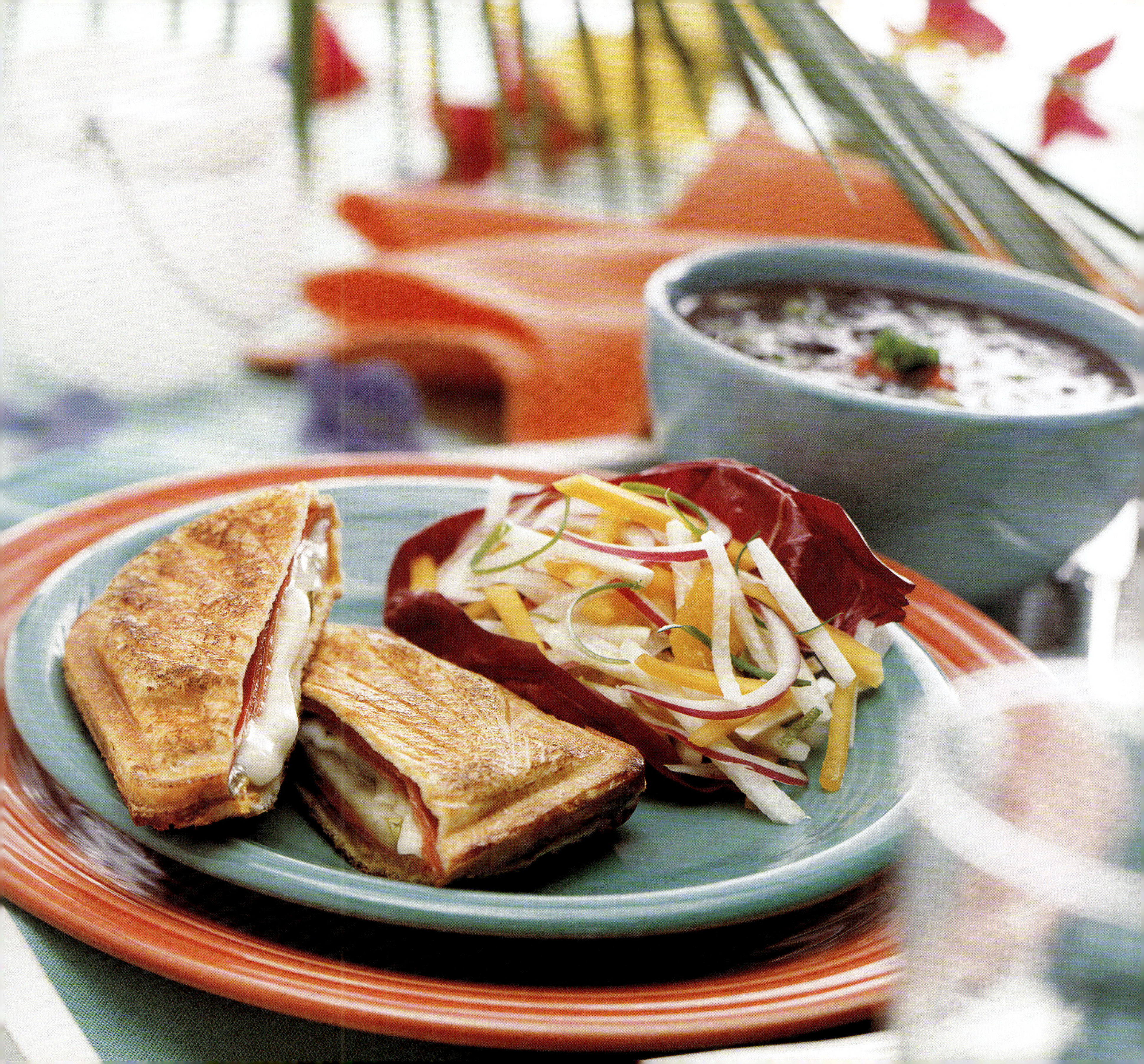

and let them drop into a bowl as you work.

2. Add remaining ingredients and toss to mix.

YIELD: ABOUT 7 CUPS (30 OZ/900 G), 8 SERVINGS

Per serving: 68 Calories, 0.2g Fat, 0g Saturated Fat, 0mg Cholesterol, 2g Protein, 17g Carbohydrate, 3.7g Fiber, 43mg Sodium

KEY LIME PIE *over 60 minutes*

The smaller, yellower Key lime has a flavor that's both less harsh and more intense than the common Persian lime.

GRAHAM CRACKER CRUST
- 24 fat-free graham cracker squares
- 2 tablespoons natural cane sugar
- 2 tablespoons 1% vanilla soy milk
- no-stick cooking spray

KEY LIME FILLING
- 1¼ cups (10 fl oz/300 ml) 1% vanilla soy milk
- ¾ cup (6 fl oz/180 ml) fat-free egg product
- 2 ounces (60 g) low-fat silken tofu
- ¾ cup (5 oz/150 g) natural cane sugar
- ½ cup (4 fl oz/120 ml) lime juice, preferably from Key limes
- 1 tablespoon grated lime zest
- 1 tablespoon tapioca flour or cornstarch
- ½ teaspoon pure vanilla extract

MERINGUE
- 4 egg whites, at room temperature
- ¼ cup (1¾ oz/50 g) natural cane sugar
- pinch sea salt

TO MAKE CRUST

1. Preheat oven to 350°F (175°C).

2. In a food processor, process graham crackers to make fine crumbs — you should have about 2 cups. Add sugar and soy milk and process for 30 seconds, or until mixture has the texture of sand.

3. Spray a 10-inch (30-cm) pie plate lightly with cooking spray. Press crumb mixture into bottom and sides.

4. Prebake crust for 5 minutes. Let cool for 10 minutes before filling. Leave oven on.

TO FILL AND BAKE PIE

1. Combine filling ingredients in a blender or food processor. Puree until smooth. If the mixture is lumpy, work it through a fine sieve. Pour filling mixture into pie crust.

2. Bake for 40 minutes, or until custard is firm. Let cool.

TO MAKE MERINGUE

1. Bring a large saucepan of water to a boil.

2. Combine egg whites, sugar and salt in a metal bowl that will sit securely on top of the pan. Place bowl over hot water. Stir constantly until egg whites are warm to the touch.

3. Remove bowl from the pan and beat with an electric mixer at high speed until stiff peaks form, about 12 minutes. Transfer meringue to a pastry bag fitted with a wide star tip.

4. Preheat broiler.

5. Pipe meringue onto pie in a lattice pattern. Broil about 5 inches (10 cm) below the heating element until meringue is firm and lightly browned.

YIELD: 10 SERVINGS

Per serving: 157 Calories, 0.8g Fat, 0.1g Saturated Fat, 0mg Cholesterol, 5g Protein, 34g Carbohydrate, 0.4g Fiber, 123mg Sodium

ALL-AMERICAN Junk Food

YOU CAN'T THINK OF AMERICA WITHOUT THINKING OF JUNK FOOD. AND WHY take it out of your diet completely? Changing your eating habits doesn't mean eating only brown rice and vegetables at every meal. It means replacing certain ingredients to create something that looks and tastes so much like the traditional version that most people can't tell the difference. That's what this chapter does. The Philly Cheese Steak (page 112) is made with tempeh and fat-free soy cheese. The Corn Dogs (page 112) have a tasty tofu dog in the center and they're baked, not fried. The Chocolate Cupcakes (page 117) get their chocolatey goodness from fat-free cocoa powder and their tender crumb from silken tofu in the batter. Please enjoy these and other classic junk foods gone 21st century!

- Americans consume an average of 21.6 pounds of snack foods per person per year. About one-third of that is potato chips.

- Americans now eat more food, more snacks and bigger portions than they did in 1970.

- The cost to American society of diet-related health conditions — heart disease, cancer, stroke and diabetes — is estimated at $250 billion annually.

CORN DOGS *over 60 minutes*

You will need 8 sturdy wooden skewers for the corn dogs.

- 1 recipe Pizza Dough (page 114)
- ½ cup (4 oz/120 g) canned creamed corn
- ¼ teaspoon turmeric
- cornmeal, preferably stoneground, for sprinkling
- 8 fat-free tofu hot dogs *SOY*
- 1 egg white, beaten
- mustard, catsup and pickle relish, optional

1. Prepare Pizza Dough as instructed on page 115, adding creamed corn and turmeric to the flour along with the yeast mixture. Let rise 1 hour.

2. Preheat oven to 425°F (215°C). Sprinkle a baking sheet with cornmeal.

3. Turn dough out onto a floured work surface and roll into a rope about 16 inches (40 cm) long. Divide the rope into 8 equal pieces. Roll each piece into a rectangle about 1 inch (2.5 cm) longer than a tofu dog. Place a dog on top, roll up and pinch edges closed. Insert a skewer in one end.

4. Brush corn dogs with beaten egg white and sprinkle generously with cornmeal. Transfer to the prepared baking sheet and place seam-side down.

5. Bake until browned, about 20 minutes. Serve with your favorite condiments.

YIELD: 8 CORN DOGS

Per corn dog: 244 Calories, 0.7g Fat, 0.1g Saturated Fat, 0mg Cholesterol, 15g Protein, 44g Carbohydrate, 2.7g Fiber, 506mg Sodium

PHILLY CHEESE STEAKS *under 30 minutes*

- no-stick cooking spray
- 1½ pounds (720 g) tempeh or seitan (wheat meat), thinly sliced *SOY*
- 1 red bell pepper, thinly sliced
- 1 green bell pepper, thinly sliced
- 1 medium onion, cut in half vertically and thinly sliced
- 2 fat-free French baguettes
- 8 ounces (240 g) fat-free mozzarella-style soy cheese, thinly sliced
- catsup or mustard to taste

1. Preheat oven to 350°F (175°C).

2. Spray a large sauté pan once with cooking spray. Heat pan over medium heat, add tempeh or seitan and cook for 1 minute on each side. Transfer slices to a plate.

3. Spray the pan once again with cooking spray. Cook peppers and onions over medium-low heat, stirring often, until soft, about 5 minutes. Set aside.

4. Cut baguettes into thirds. Slice each section in half horizontally, open and place on a baking sheet. Divide the seitan or tempeh, pepper mixture and soy cheese equally among the breads.

5. Bake until cheese melts, about 15 minutes.

6. Smear with catsup or mustard as desired and press sandwiches closed.

YIELD: 6 SANDWICHES

Per sandwich: 516 Calories, 11g Fat, 1.8g Saturated Fat, 0mg Cholesterol, 37g Protein, 69g Carbohydrate, 3.5g Fiber, 748mg Sodium

Nutrition Bonus: Although tempeh, a soy food, does contain some fat, it is rich in beneficial soy isoflavones. If you make the cheese steaks with seitan, a wheat-based product, the fat drops to 2.6 grams per sandwich. Try it both ways to see which version you like best. Either way is far healthier than a typical Philly cheese steak with its 680 calories and 35 grams of fat.

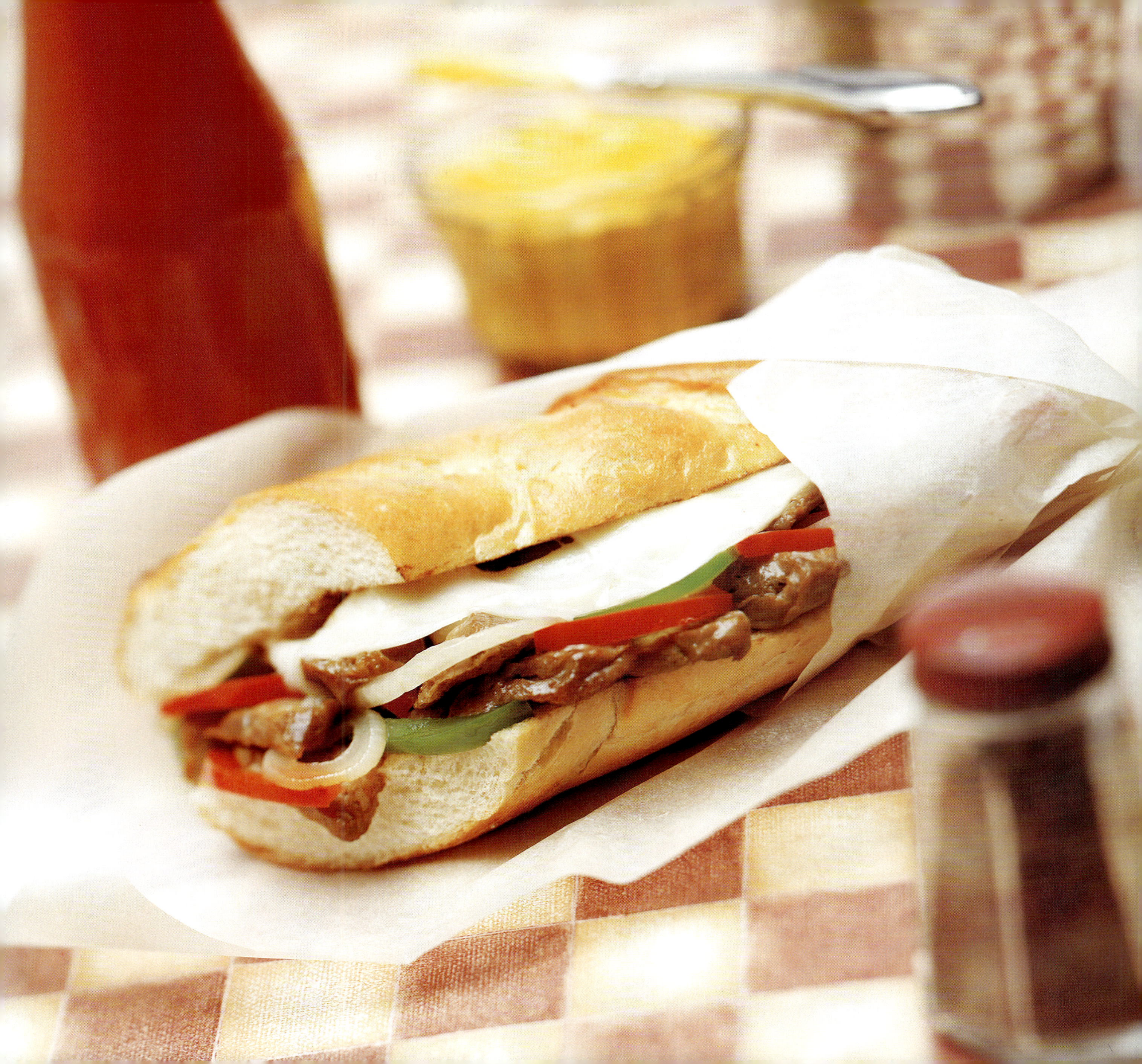

CHICAGO DEEP-DISH PIZZA

over 60 minutes

DOUGH

- 2 packages active dry yeast
- 1 cup (8 fl oz/240 ml) warm (not hot) water
- 1 teaspoon honey or natural cane sugar
- 2 cups (9 oz/270 g) semolina or all-purpose flour
- ½ cup (2½ oz/75 g) cornmeal, preferably stoneground
- ¾ teaspoon sea salt
- no-stick cooking spray

SAUCE

- no-stick cooking spray
- 3 tablespoons chopped fresh garlic
- 2 teaspoons dried oregano
- 6 tablespoons (1 oz/30 g) chopped fresh basil or 2 tablespoons dried basil
- 2 28-ounce (840-g) cans low-sodium Italian plum tomatoes, drained and coarsely chopped
- ⅛ teaspoon sea salt
- freshly cracked black pepper or crushed red pepper flakes to taste

FILLING

- 20 ounces (600 g) fresh spinach, stemmed and washed, or 15 ounces (450 g) frozen spinach, thawed
- no-stick cooking spray
- 1 small onion, chopped
- 1 teaspoon chopped fresh garlic
- 8 ounces (240 g) mushrooms, trimmed and sliced
- 12 ounces (360 g) fat-free vegetarian sausage, crumbled *SOY*
- ¼ teaspoon fennel seeds or aniseed
- ¼ teaspoon crushed red pepper flakes
- 8 ounces (240 g) fat-free mozzarella-style soy cheese, grated by hand (1 cup)

THE TASTE FOR LIVING WORLD COOKBOOK

TO MAKE PIZZA DOUGH

1. In a small bowl, soften yeast in warm water for 10 minutes. Stir in honey or sugar.
2. Fit a food processor with a dough blade. Add flour, cornmeal and salt and pour in yeast mixture. Process until dough forms a ball.
3. Transfer dough to a floured work surface and knead for 3 minutes.
4. Spray a large bowl once with cooking spray. Place dough in bowl, turning once. Cover with a clean, dry towel. Put bowl in a warm place. Let dough rise for 1 hour.

TO MAKE SAUCE

1. Spray a large sauté pan once with cooking spray. Heat pan over low heat, add garlic and cook for 15 seconds. Stir in dried oregano and dried basil, if using.
2. Add tomatoes, bring to a simmer and cook for 5 minutes. Stir in fresh basil, if using.
3. Season with salt and cracked black pepper or red pepper flakes. Set aside.

TO MAKE FILLING

1. Bring a pot of water to a boil. Add fresh spinach and cook for a few seconds. Drain, squeezing out excess liquid, and chop. For frozen spinach, squeeze out excess moisture.
2. Spray a large sauté pan with cooking spray. Set pan over low heat, add onions and cook, stirring, until translucent, about 5 minutes. Add garlic and cook for 15 seconds.
3. Add mushrooms and cook for 10 minutes. Stir in spinach, sausage, fennel or aniseed and red pepper flakes; cook until heated through. Remove from heat. Stir in half of the cheese.

TO ASSEMBLE PIZZA

1. Preheat oven to 450°F (235°C).
2. Punch down risen dough. Transfer to a 12-inch (30-cm) deep-dish pizza pan or pie plate. Flatten dough into pan, pushing it up the sides with your fingertips.
3. Spread sauce over dough. Top with the filling and sprinkle with the remaining cheese.
4. Bake on bottom oven rack until crust is firm and golden, about 25 to 30 minutes.

YIELD: **8 SERVINGS**

Per serving: 306 Calories, 1.5g Fat, 0.1g Saturated Fat, 0mg Cholesterol, 23g Protein, 52g Carbohydrate, 6.7g Fiber, 759mg Sodium

Nutrition Bonus: Tomato sauce is an excellent source of lycopene, a phytonutrient believed to help protect against many cancers, including breast and prostate cancer.

PIZZA AMERICA

Any way you slice it, Americans eat a lot of pizza. After burgers, it's the most popular food service item. The National Association of Pizza Operators reports that Americans eat about 100 acres of pizza each day, which averages out to 46 slices of pizza for every man, woman and child over the course of a year. That translates into 7.7 pounds of mozzarella per person per year.

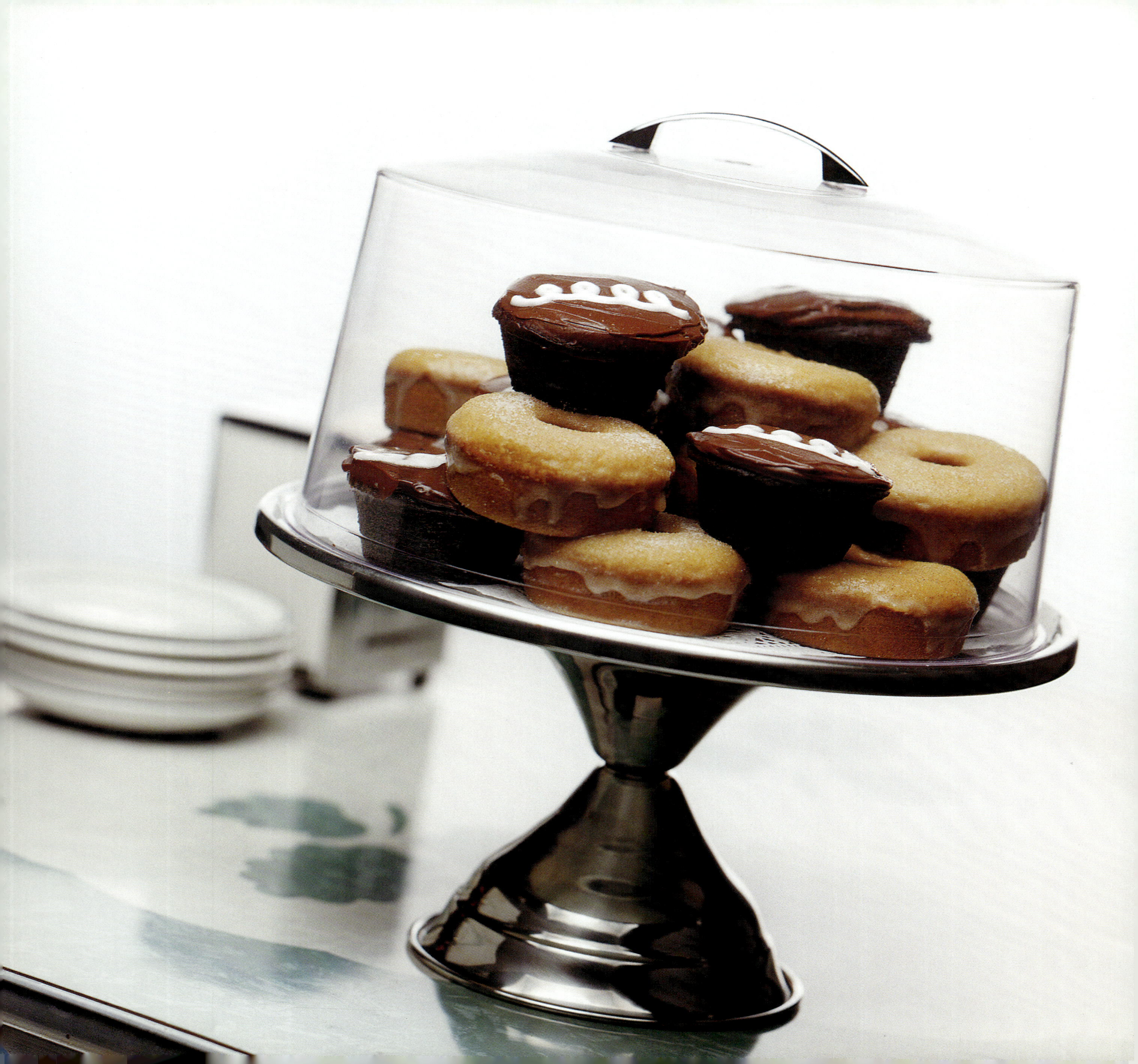

CHOCOLATE CUPCAKES

over 60 minutes

CAKE

- no-stick cooking spray
- 1½ cups (10 oz/300 g) natural cane sugar
- 1 cup (4 oz/120 g) all-purpose flour
- 1 cup (4½ oz/135 g) fat-free cocoa powder
- 1 teaspoon baking powder
- 1 teaspoon baking soda
- 2 egg whites
- 5 ounces (150 g) low-fat silken tofu
- ¾ cup plus 2 tablespoons (7 fl oz/210 ml) unsweetened applesauce
- ½ teaspoon pure vanilla extract

CUSTARD FILLING

- 1½ cups (12 fl oz/360 ml) 1% vanilla soy milk
- 1 ounce (30 g) low-fat silken tofu
- 6 tablespoons (2½ oz/75 g) natural cane sugar
- 6 tablespoons (3 fl oz/90 ml) fat-free egg product
- ¼ cup (1 oz/30 g) all-purpose flour
- 1 teaspoon pure vanilla extract

CHOCOLATE ICING

- 8 ounces (240 g) low-fat silken tofu
- ¾ cup (3½ oz/100 g) confectioners' sugar
- ½ cup (2¼ oz/70 g) fat-free cocoa powder
- 1 teaspoon pure vanilla extract
- 1 teaspoon rice syrup or light corn syrup

TO MAKE CUPCAKES

1. Preheat oven to 350°F (175°C). Spray the cups of a 12-cup muffin pan with cooking spray. (Do not use paper liners.)
2. Sift sugar, flour, cocoa, baking powder and baking soda into a large mixing bowl.
3. In a food processor, combine egg whites, tofu, applesauce and vanilla. Puree until smooth.
4. Add tofu mixture to dry ingredients. Beat with an electric mixer until smooth. Spoon batter into prepared pan.
5. Bake until a toothpick inserted in the center of a cupcake comes out clean, about 25 minutes.
6. Cool cupcakes in the pan. When cool, knock the edge of the pan on a hard surface and tilt onto the table. Cupcakes should come out easily. Repeat if some are stuck.

TO MAKE CUSTARD FILLING

1. In a metal mixing bowl, combine soy milk, tofu, sugar, egg product and flour. Whisk until smooth. Set bowl over a saucepan of simmering water. (The bowl bottom should not touch the water.) Cook, stirring, until custard thickens, about 8 minutes. Add vanilla. Chill for 30 minutes.

TO MAKE CHOCOLATE ICING

1. In a blender, combine tofu, confectioners' sugar, cocoa, vanilla and rice syrup or corn syrup. Blend until smooth. Chill for 30 minutes.

TO FILL AND ICE CUPCAKES

1. With a serrated knife, slice tops off cupcakes. Set tops aside. With a small sharp knife, working from the top, cut out a core section from the center of each cupcake, stopping about ¼ inch (0.6 cm) from the bottom.
2. Transfer custard to a pastry bag fitted with a ½-inch (1.25-cm) tip. Fill each cupcake with custard. Replace cupcake tops.
3. Frost cupcakes with chocolate icing. With remaining custard, pipe a stripe down the center of each cupcake.

YIELD: 12 CUPCAKES

Per cupcake: 285 Calories, 1.8g Fat, 0.6g Saturated Fat, 0mg Cholesterol, 8g Protein, 60g Carbohydrate, 3.9g Fiber, 194mg Sodium

Chocolate Cupcakes and Glazed Cinnamon Doughnuts

GLAZED CINNAMON DOUGHNUTS

If you don't have a doughnut pan or mini-Bundt pan, bake the batter as muffins — you'll get everything but the hole!

DOUGHNUTS

	no-stick cooking spray
2¾ cups	(11 oz/330 g) cake flour
1 cup	(6½ oz/200 g) natural cane sugar
2 teaspoons	baking powder
1 teaspoon	baking soda
¼ teaspoon	ground cinnamon
⅛ teaspoon	grated nutmeg
1 cup	(8 fl oz/240 ml) 1% vanilla soy milk
¾ cup	(6 fl oz/180 ml) unsweetened applesauce
2 ounces	(60 g) low-fat silken tofu
½ cup	(4 fl oz/120 ml) fat-free egg product
2	egg whites

GLAZE

2 cups	(10 oz/300 g) confectioners' sugar, sifted
4 ounces	(120 g) low-fat silken tofu
1 teaspoon	pure vanilla extract
2 tablespoons	natural cane sugar
¼ teaspoon	ground cinnamon

TO MAKE DOUGHNUTS

1. Preheat oven to 350°F (175°C). Spray the molds of 2 doughnut pans or mini-Bundt pans lightly with cooking spray. (If you only have 1 pan, bake the recipe in 2 batches, refrigerating second batch until ready to bake.)

2. Sift flour, sugar, baking powder, baking soda, cinnamon and nutmeg into a mixing bowl.

3. In a food processor, puree soy milk, applesauce and tofu until smooth. With the motor running, add egg product and egg whites.

4. Add tofu mixture to dry ingredients. Beat with an electric mixer until smooth.

5. Pour batter into prepared molds, smoothing the surfaces.

6. Bake for 15 to 20 minutes, or until the tops spring back when touched lightly. Loosen edges and turn doughnuts out onto a wire rack to cool. (If baking in 2 batches, cool the pan, clean it, then recoat it with cooking spray.)

TO GLAZE DOUGHNUTS

1. In a food processor, combine confectioners' sugar, tofu and vanilla extract and process until smooth. Transfer to a bowl and chill for 20 minutes.

2. In a small bowl, combine cane sugar and cinnamon.

3. Dip each cooled doughnut in glaze and sprinkle with cinnamon sugar. If not serving immediately, chill.

YIELD: 12 DOUGHNUTS

Per doughnut: 261 Calories, 0.6g Fat, 0g Saturated Fat, 0mg Cholesterol, 5g Protein, 60g Carbohydrate, 0.8g Fiber, 198mg Sodium

Nutrition Bonus: A single bakery-made cake doughnut can have between 10 and 16 grams of fat — considerably more fat than you'd find in a baker's dozen made from our recipe!

POPCORN BALLS

½ cup (4 oz/120 g) popcorn kernels
1¾ cups (14 fl oz/420 ml) light corn syrup
2 tablespoons pure maple syrup
2 teaspoons rice vinegar (white or brown)
1 teaspoon pure vanilla extract
   butter-flavored cooking spray

1. Pop popcorn in an air popper. Transfer popcorn to a large roasting pan or heatproof bowl.

2. In a heavy saucepan, combine corn syrup, maple syrup and vinegar. Attach a candy thermometer to the side of the pan and cook until mixture reaches the soft crack stage, 275°F (143°C): a small amount dropped into very cold water will separate into hard but pliable threads. Remove from heat. Stir in vanilla.

3. Pour syrup over popcorn, stirring it in gently with a long-handled wooden spoon until all the popcorn is coated. Be careful; the syrup is very hot.

4. After about 5 minutes, when popcorn is cool enough to handle, spray your hands with cooking spray and form popcorn mixture into 12 balls.

5. Wrap popcorn balls in cellophane. They will keep for 2 weeks in an airtight container or tin.

YIELD: 12 POPCORN BALLS

Per popcorn ball: 172 Calories, 0.4g Fat, 0g Saturated Fat, 0mg Cholesterol, 1g Protein, 44g Carbohydrate, 0.8 Fiber, 57mg Sodium

SIZING IT ALL UP

Have you noticed that the typical bagel has swollen to the point where the hole has all but disappeared? That your morning muffin is now as wide as a saucer? Jumbo, colossal, extra-extra large, king-size and super-size have become standard terms for describing portions.

All too often we equate size with value. But is bigger really better?

It's never a bargain for your body to consume more food than you need. The extra calories will be stored as fat, which starts you in the direction of being overweight and can lead to obesity. There is overwhelming evidence that obesity is a risk factor for heart disease, diabetes and some cancers, including prostate cancer.

Obesity is the number one health problem in the United States. Since the early 1990s, obesity has increased from an incidence of one in four Americans to the point where one in two Americans is overweight, and one in three is medically obese. It's not a coincidence that we have seen a rise in several chronic diseases, including heart disease and diabetes. In studies of more than 750,000 people, the American Cancer Society found an association between obesity and cancers of the prostate, breast, ovaries, uterus, kidney, gallbladder and pancreas.

Self-control is the obvious remedy — and it starts at the plate. A healthful serving of chicken breast, for instance, is no more than three ounces of trimmed cooked meat, about the size of a deck of cards. And that bulked-up bagel counts as three, not one, servings of bread.

CaP CURE and the *Taste for Living* cookbooks follow the U.S. Department of Agriculture's portion-size guidelines, which are listed below. They will help you eat the right foods in the right amounts.

RECOMMENDED PORTION SIZE

VEGETABLES

1 cup (3 oz/90 g) raw leafy vegetables
½ cup (3 oz/90 g) other vegetables — cooked or chopped raw
¾ cup (6 fl oz/180 ml) vegetable juice

FRUIT

1 medium apple, banana, peach or orange
½ cup (3 oz/90 g) chopped, cooked or canned fruit
¾ cup (6 fl oz/180 ml) fruit juice

BREADS, GRAINS AND PASTA

1 slice bread
1 ounce (30 g) ready-to-eat cereal
½ cup (3 oz/90 g) cooked cereal, rice or pasta

MEAT, POULTRY, FISH, DRIED BEANS, EGGS

2–3 ounces (60–90 g) cooked lean meat, poultry or fish
½ cup (3½ oz/100 g) cooked dried beans
1 egg

THE HEALTHY WORLD PANTRY

ASIAN STAPLES

You'll find these wonderful flavor boosters at Asian grocers and large supermarkets.

Black Bean Sauce: Made from fermented black soybeans; use sparingly.
Chinese Chili Paste: A lively combination of red peppers, fermented soybeans, flour and garlic used widely in Chinese cooking.
Edamame: Green soybeans. *See page 71.*
Green Tea: *See page 72.*
Hoisin Sauce: Made from soybeans, garlic, hot peppers and spices, hoisin adds salty and sweet flavors. Look for MSG-free brands.
Mirin: A Japanese sweet seasoning wine made from glutinous rice.
Miso: Also called bean paste. *See page 15.*
Nori: Paper-thin sheets of pressed dried seaweed used for wrapping sushi.
Pickled ginger: Thinly sliced ginger preserved in sweet vinegar; served with sushi.
Rice: There's so much more to rice than the ubiquitous long-grain white rice. Try aromatic **basmati** and **jasmine** varieties in pilafs and to accompany Asian dishes. **Sushi rice** is a short-grain variety whose grains stick together for making sushi. If possible, choose **brown rice** over white. It contains the entire grain with only the inedible husk removed, making it higher in fiber and nutrients.
Soy Sauce: Use Japanese low-sodium tamari soy sauce for best flavor.
Rice Vinegar: Not as acidic as distilled white vinegar, rice vinegars are great for salad dressings. Available in brown and white.
Tofu: Use low-fat tofu in *Taste for Living* recipes. Look for it in the refrigerator case at the supermarket. Also available in shelf-stable packaging. *See page 14.*
Wasabi: The Japanese version of horseradish, this fiery condiment comes in powder or paste form.

SWEETENERS

Apple Juice Concentrate and Unsweetened Applesauce: Natural sweeteners whose flavor blends well with many other seasonings and spices. The pectin in apple juice and applesauce helps keep low-fat baked goods tender.
Brown Sugar: Refined white sugar colored with molasses.
Confectioners' Sugar: A dusting gives a professional look to desserts.
Corn Syrup: Adds body to fat-free dessert sauces.
Honey: Different honeys derive their distinct flavors from the flowers the bees feed upon. **Buckwheat** honey is dark, with a bitter edge. **Tupelo, orange blossom** and **clover** honeys are light in flavor with a delicate fragrance. **French lavender** honey is particularly fine.
Liquid Fruit Sweetener: A caramel-colored to dark syrup made from fruit and sometimes grain carbohydrates. Useful as a sweetener and for reducing fat in baked goods.
Maple Sugar and Maple Syrup: It takes 40 gallons of maple sap to make one gallon of maple syrup. Read the label — and buy only pure maple syrup.
Molasses: A by-product of sugar refining, molasses is strong-flavored. Use in marinades and in spiced baked goods.
Natural Cane Sugar: Less processed than refined white sugar, natural cane sugar retains the flavor and color of natural cane juice.
Rice Syrup: A thick sweet syrup made by processing rice starch. Use in place of corn syrup.

FAT BUSTERS

Fat-Free Egg Product: Made from real egg whites, tiny amounts of xanthum gum with a little beta carotene for color, fat-free egg product does not contain the cholesterol or fat of egg yolks. Use like regular eggs.
Fat-Free Soy Cheese: Currently available in mozzarella, cheddar and jack styles. Always grate by hand. *See page 15.*
Fat-Free Soy Meat, Soy Sausage and Soy Deli Slices: Great products for adding meaty flavor and texture without the fat and cholesterol. *See page 14.*
Low-Fat Soy Milk: Choose 1% soy milk — it has half the fat of 2%. *See page 15.*
No-Stick Cooking Spray: A one-second spray of oil delivers less than 1 gram of fat.

BAKING BASICS

All-Purpose Flour: Unbleached is best.
Cake Flour: A low-protein flour that helps keep low-fat baked goods tender.
Cocoa Powder: Fat-free brands are available at many health foods stores.
Cornmeal: Stoneground is preferred.
Oat Flour: Can be substituted for all-purpose flour in most recipes: for every 1 cup all-purpose flour, substitute 1 cup plus 2 tablespoons oat flour. (Weight measurements do not need adjustment.)
Old-Fashioned Rolled Oats: Loaded with beneficial soluble fiber, oats make a tasty, healthful addition to muffins and other baked goods.
Semolina: Milled from high-protein durum wheat, semolina is used in the best pastas.
Whole-Wheat Pastry Flour: Adds dietary fiber without making baked goods tough. Store it in the freezer.

SOURCES

Harney & Sons Fine Teas

Offers a wide selection of excellent Japanese and Chinese green teas and several flavored green teas.
Telephone: 1-888-HARNEYTEA
Web: www.harney.com

Nutritious Foods

For Health Source
soy protein isolate powder.
1-800-445-3350

Penzeys Spices

The catalogue contains a wealth of information about the history and uses of spices and herbs around the world.
Telephone: 1-800-741-7787 or 414-679-7207
Web: www.penzeys.com

Whole Foods

Shop for soy-based foods online.
www.WholeFoods.com

GLOBAL HERBS AND SPICES

Aniseed: Faintly sweet, with a distinctive licorice flavor. Often used in Italian sausage.
Basil: The spicy-sweet leaves of this member of the mint family are a frequent addition to Italian sauces.
Black Pepper: Freshly ground or cracked pepper has more punch. Use it liberally.
Cardamom: A member of the ginger family, cardamom has a warm, spicy-sweet flavor. *See page 56.*
Cayenne Pepper: Fiercely hot, this ground red pepper should be added in small amounts. *See page 56.*
Chili Powder: A blend of ground peppers, cumin, oregano, garlic and cloves.
Chives: Delivers a mild onion flavor without a harsh bite. Chives are best fresh and raw.
Cilantro: It's an herb you either love or hate. Fresh parsley is a good substitute.
Cinnamon: A favorite spice of Americans for flavoring baked goods; used in savory preparations in India and the Middle East.
Cumin: The aromatic, nutty seeds are available whole or ground. *See page 56.*
Ginger: The bulbous root of the ginger plant is loved the world around. Ground ginger is used in spiced desserts, such as gingerbread. Fresh ginger is an essential element of Asian cuisine. Freeze fresh ginger to make it easy to grate. Pickled ginger is a must with sushi. Candied or crystallized ginger is enjoyed as candy or as a flavoring for desserts.
Nutmeg: Buy whole and grate for best flavor.
Oregano: A must for Italian red sauces. The herb's pungency intensifies when dried.
Parsley: Always use fresh parsley — the dried version has no flavor. The Italian flat-leaf variety is tastier and easier to chop.
Red Pepper Flakes: An efficient means to add heat to a dish without having to chop hot peppers. Use sparingly.
Sea Salt: Preferred by chefs for its pure flavor, sea salt contains no additives.
Thyme: Another mint family relative, thyme is a basic herb of French cuisine.
Turmeric: This bitter yet aromatic spice lends a vibrant yellow color to foods. *See page 56.*
Vanilla: Use whole beans for an intense, pure vanilla flavor in desserts. When using extract, choose a high-quality pure extract for best flavor.

DRIED BEANS AND OTHER LEGUMES

Canned beans save time; be sure to rinse before using to rid them of excess salt. Dried beans offer more variety, better texture and often better flavor.
A few favorites: **Kidney beans** are long and dark red — excellent in chili and soups. **Cannellini beans** are large white Italian kidney beans. **Black beans** are popular in Latin American and Caribbean dishes. **Black-eyed peas** have long been a staple of Southern cooking. Nutty-flavored **Chickpeas**, a.k.a. garbanzos, are used in many Middle Eastern and Indian dishes. Quick-cooking **Lentils** are rich in folate. *See page 50.*

EVERYDAY CONDIMENTS

Balsamic Vinegar: Dark, sweet and mellow, this aged vinegar adds richness to dressings and marinades.
Catsup: America's favorite condiment contains the beneficial antioxidant lycopene. Buy a low-sodium version. *See page 37.*
Mayonnaise: Choose a fat-free soy brand.
Mustard: A naturally fat-free addition to sandwiches and salad dressing.
Red-Wine Vinegar: For best flavor, choose an imported vinegar.
Worcestershire Sauce: Made from garlic, soy sauce, tamarind, onions, molasses, anchovies and various seasonings; a small amount adds complexity to sauces and marinades.

INDEX

About CaP CURE 129

Appetizers
Baba Ghanoush 48
Bruschetta 33
Chinese Dumplings 60
Edamame 71
Egg Rolls 59
Hummus 47
Lima-Mole 102
Pico de Gallo 78
Pita Toast Points 48
Roasted Pepper Fillets 48
Samosas 52
Spanakopita 45
Vegetable Sushi 68

Apple Pie 99
Applesauce 81
Asian Diet 61

Baba Ghanoush 48
Baked Beans 75

Baked Goods
Banana Bread 86
Biscotti 42
Chapatis 52
Glazed Cinnamon Doughnuts 118
Cornbread 88
Crispy Brown Rice Cookies 103
Oatcakes 18
Scones 18
Suspiros 80

Banana Bread 86

Banana Cream Pie 108
Banana Pudding 92
Basmati Rice with Peas 54

Beans & Legumes
Baked Beans 75
Black Bean Soup 108
Black Beans and Rice 83
Black-Eyed Peas 92
Edamame 71
Enchilada Pie with Ranchero Sauce 58
Falafel 47
Hummus 47
Lentils and Folate 50
Lima-Mole 102
Minestrone 32
Pinto Bean Quesadillas 71
Red Lentil Dhal 50
Refried Beans 79
Senate Bean Soup 96
Three-Bean Chili 41
Tortilla Soup 74

Biscotti 42
Black Bean Soup 108
Black Beans and Rice 83
Black-Eyed Peas 92
Blueberry Banana Multi-Grain Pancakes 87
Blueberry Banana Shake 21

Breakfast
Blueberry Banana Multi-Grain Pancakes 87
Blueberry Banana Shake 21
Cherry Vanilla Granola 90
Chocolate Shake 84
Cinnamon Whole-Grain Waffles 88

Corn Tomato Omelet 90
Eggs Michael 85
Fruit Shake 84
Muesli 21
New English Breakfast 21
Oatcakes 18
Pannekoeken 22
Scones 18

Broccoli in Soy Cheese Sauce 78
Broccoli Potato Soup 22
Brownies with Cocoa Glaze 102
Bruschetta 33
Buddha's Feast 62

Cabbage Salad 78
Caesar Dressing 29
Caesar Salad with Herb Croutons 28

CaP CURE
About CaP CURE 129
CaP CURE, Nutritional Principles of 16

Caramel Sauce 86
Carrot Cake 100
Cauliflower au Gratin 79
Chapatis 52
Chef's Salad with Thousand Island Dressing 34
Cherry Vanilla Granola 90
Chicago Deep-Dish Pizza 114
Chiles Rellenos 56
Chili Lime Dressing 27
Chimichangas with Fresh Tomato Salsa 75
Chinese Dumplings 60
Chinese Roasted Tofu Salad 33
Chocolate Cupcakes 117

Chocolate Shake 84
Chocolate Tortilla Wraps with Strawberry Sauce 104
Chopped Vegetable Salad 36
Cinnamon Whole-Grain Waffles 88
Citrus Rice Pudding 95
Citrus Zests, Boost Flavor — and — Health with 28
Cloud Nine Frosting 96
Cocoa Frosting 104
Cocoa Glaze 102
Coleslaw 68
Collard and Mustard Greens 91
Corn and Butternut Squash 80
Corn Broth 16
Corn Chowder with Popcorn Croutons 16
Corn Dogs 112
Corn Tomato Omelet with Fresh Parsley 90
Cornbread 88
Cream of Tomato Soup 17
Creamed Spinach 76
Creamy French Dressing 88
Crème Brûlée 28
Crêpes Suzette 29
Crispy Brown Rice Cookies 103
Crispy Onion Rings 31
Croutons, Tortilla 104
Crucifers, Eat Your 90

Desserts (see also Baked Goods; Fruit; Sauces, Sweet)
Apple Pie 99
Banana Cream Pie 108
Banana Pudding 92
Brownies with Cocoa Glaze 102
Carrot Cake 100

NOTE: Entries in italics are from *The Taste for Living Cookbook* (CaP CURE, 1998).

Desserts (continued)

Chocolate Cupcakes 117
Chocolate Tortilla Wraps with Strawberry Sauce 104
Citrus Rice Pudding 95
Crème Brûlée 28
Crêpes Suzette 29
Devil's "Fool" Cake 104
Hot Fudge Sundaes 98
Key Lime Pie 110
Lemon Meringue Pie 94
Lemon Tartlets 26
Maple Flan 110
Old-Fashioned Chocolate Pudding 109
Pineapples and Oranges 66
Popcorn Balls 119
Roasted Plantains 82
Soy Nut Brittle 94
Strawberry Shortcake 96
Sweet Potato Pie 93
Tiramisù 41
Tofu Cheesecake 107
Tropical Fruits Scented with Vanilla and Cardamom 55
Zabaglione with Berries 42

Devil's "Fool" Cake 104
Doughnuts, Glazed Cinnamon 118

Dressings

Caesar Dressing 29
Chili Lime Dressing 27
Creamy French Dressing 88
Fire-Roasted Green Chile Dressing 103
Honey Mustard Dressing 36
Miso Shallot Dressing 35

Orange Ginger Dressing 33
Raspberry Vinaigrette 35
Sweet Onion Dressing 31
Thousand Island Dressing 35

Edamame 71
Egg Rolls 59
Eggplant Parmesan 36
Eggplant Parmesan Strudel with Marinara Sauce 64

Eggs

Eggs Benedict 85
Eggs Florentine 85
Eggs Michael 85
New English Breakfast 21
Quiche Lorraine 24
Zabaglione with Berries 42

Enchilada Pie with Ranchero Sauce 58

Entrées
(see also Sandwiches; Soups)

Buddha's Feast 62
Chicago Deep-Dish Pizza 114
Chiles Rellenos 56
Chimichangas with Fresh Tomato Salsa 75
Corn Dogs 112
Falafel 47
Eggplant Parmesan 36
Eggplant Parmesan Strudel with Marinara Sauce 64
Enchilada Pie with Ranchero Sauce 58
Fajitas 100
Granny G's Sweet and Sour Stuffed Cabbage 65
Greek Spinach Pie in a Phyllo Nest 61

Homemade Vegetable Pizza 62
Jerk Kebabs 84
Kung Pao Tofu 62
Lasagne with "Soysage" 46
Moussaka 44
Not-Meat Loaf with Shiitake Mushroom Gravy 52
Quiche Lorraine 24
Shepherd's Pie 90
Spaghetti Bolognese 38
Spaghetti Squash Manicotti 51
Spinach and Mushroom Enchiladas in Red Chili Sauce 76
Spinach Cannelloni 48
Spinach Ravioli with Fresh Tomato-Basil Sauce 35
Sukiyaki 71
Teriyaki Tofu Bowl with Chinese Vegetables 40
Three-Bean Chili 41
Tofu Cacciatore 40
Tofu Dog Casserole 42
Vegetable Curry 54
Vegetable Frittata with Roasted Tomato Salsa 54
Vegetable Gumbo 82
Vegetable Lo Mein 64

Exercise: You've Got to Move 106

Fajitas 100
Falafel 47
Fat: Evaulating Marketing Terms, 65
Fat-Free Whipped Topping 98
Fiber, Don't Forget 22
Fire-Roasted Green Chile Dressing 103
Folate 50

Food Guide Pyramid 9
French Fries 69
French Onion Soup 20
Fresh Tomato-Basil Sauce 35
Fresh Tomato Salsa 75
Fresh Tomato Sauce 49
Fried Rice 64
Fruit Shake 84

Fruit

Apples
  Apple Pie with an Oatmeal Cookie Crust 99
  Applesauce 81
  Pannekoeken 22
Bananas
  Banana Bread 86
  Banana Cream Pie 108
  Banana Pudding 92
  Blueberry Banana Multi-Grain Pancakes 87
  Blueberry Banana Shake 21
  Chocolate Tortilla Wraps with Strawberry Sauce 104
  Fruit Shake 84
  Tropical Fruits Scented with Vanilla and Cardamom 55
Berries
  Blueberry Banana Multi-Grain Pancakes 87
  Blueberry Banana Shake 21
  Chocolate Tortilla Wraps with Strawberry Sauce 104
  Cinnamon Whole-Grain Waffles with Strawberries and Raspberries 88
  Raspberry Sauce 28
  Strawberry Preserves 19
  Strawberry Shortcake 96

Tofu Cheesecake 107
Zabaglione with Berries 42
Dried Fruit
    Banana Bread 86
    Biscotti 42
    Carrot Cake 100
    Cherry Vanilla Granola 90
    Citrus Rice Pudding 95
    Muesli 21
    Scones 18
Lemons or Limes
    Key Lime Pie 110
    Lemon Meringue Pie 94
    Lemon Tartlets 26
    Sangría 79
Mangoes
    Mango Chutney 53
    Tropical Fruits Scented with Vanilla and Cardamom 55
Oranges
    Crêpes Suzette 29
    Orange-Ginger Dipping Sauce 61
    Orange Ginger Dressing 33
    Pico de Gallo 78
    Pineapples and Oranges 66
    Sangría 79
    Tropical Slaw 108
Papayas
    Tropical Fruits Scented with Vanilla and Cardamom 55
    Tropical Slaw 108
Pears
    Pear Sauce 90
Pineapple
    Pineapples and Oranges 66
    Tropical Fruits Scented with Vanilla and Cardamom 55

Plantains
    Roasted Plantains 82

Garlic, The Benefits of 83
Glazed Cinnamon Doughnuts 118

Grains
Oats
    Apple Pie 99
    Cherry Vanilla Granola 90
    Oatcakes 18
Rice
    Basmati Rice with Peas 54
    Black Beans and Rice 82
    Citrus Rice Pudding 95
    Crispy Brown Rice Cookies 103
    Fried Rice 64
    Mexican Rice 78
    Moussaka 44
    Not-Meat Loaf with Shiitake Mushroom Gravy 52
    Vegetable Sushi 68
Various
    Muesli 21
    Old-Fashioned Vegetable Barley Soup 18
Wheat
    Blueberry Banana Multi-Grain Pancakes 87
    Cinnamon Whole-Grain Waffles 88
    Tabbouleh 47

Granny G's Sweet and Sour Stuffed Cabbage 65
Greek Salad 45
Greek Spinach Pie in a Phyllo Nest 61
Grilled Brussels Sprouts 79

Grilled Cheese Sandwiches 97

Healthy World Pantry 121
Homemade Potato Chips 96
Homemade Vegetable Pizza 62
Honey Mustard Dressing 36
Hot and Sour Soup 59
Hot and Spicy Eggplant 65
Hot Fudge Sauce 98
Hot Fudge Sundaes 98
Hot Sauce 48
Hummus 47

Italian Greens with Roasted Onion and Lemon 38

Jerk Kebabs 84

Key Lime Pie 110
Kung Pao Tofu 62

Lasagne with "Soysage" 46
Lemon Meringue Pie 94
Lemon Tartlets 26
Lentils and Folate 50
Lima-Mole 102
Lycopene 37

Mango Chutney 53
Maple Flan 110
Marinara Sauce 37
Marketing Terms, Evaluating 65
Marinara Sauce 64
Mashed Potatoes 81
Medianoche Sandwiches 108
Mediterranean Message, The 32
Mexican Rice 78
Minestrone 32
Miso Shallot Dressing 35
Moussaka 44

Muesli 21

New Deli 75
New English Breakfast 21
Not-Meat Loaf with Shiitake Mushroom Gravy 52
Nutritional Principles of CaP CURE 16

Oatcakes 18
Old-Fashioned Chocolate Pudding 109
Old-Fashioned Vegetable Barley Soup 18
Orange-Ginger Dipping Sauce 60
Orange Ginger Dressing 33

Pannekoeken 22
Pasta Dough 51
Pea-Camole 71
Pear Sauce 90
Philly Cheese Steaks 112
Pico de Gallo 78
Pie Crust, Savory 26
Pineapples and Oranges 66
Pinto Bean Quesadillas 71
Pita Toast Points 48
Pizza, Chicago Deep-Dish 114
Pizza Dough 62
Pizza, Homemade Vegetable 62
Ponzu Sauce 69
Popcorn Balls 119
Portion Size: Sizing It All Up 120
Potato and Leek Soup 24

Quiche Lorraine 24

Ranchero Sauce 58
Raspberry Sauce 28

NOTE: Entries in italics are from *The Taste for Living Cookbook* (CaP CURE, 1998).

Raspberry Vinaigrette 35
Ratatouille 26
Red Chili Sauce 76
Red Lentil Dhal 50
Refried Beans 79
Restaurant Meals, Strategies for 30
Roasted Onion 76
Roasted Pepper Fillets 48
Roasted Plantains 82
Roasted Red Pepper 20
Roasted Tomato Salsa 54
Roasting Onions 40
Romaine, Tomato and Vidalia Salad with Creamy French Dressing 88

Salads
Cabbage Salad 78
Caesar Salad with Herb Croutons 28
Chef's Salad with Thousand Island Dressing 34
Chinese Roasted Tofu Salad 33
Chopped Vegetable Salad 36
Coleslaw 68
Greek Salad 45
Pico de Gallo 78
Romaine, Tomato and Vidalia Salad with Creamy French Dressing 88
Southwest Caesar Salad in a Fire-Roasted Green Chile Dressing 102
Spinach Salad with Crispy Onions 30
Tabbouleh 47
Taco Salad in a Chili Lime Dressing 26
Tropical Slaw 108

Samosas 52

Sandwiches
Grilled Cheese Sandwiches 97
Medianoche Sandwiches 108
New Deli 75
Philly Cheese Steaks 112
Pinto Bean Quesadillas 71
Tofu Egg Salad Sandwich 72
Vegetable Reuben 68
VLT with Herb Mustard 76

Sangría 79

Sauces, Savory
Fresh Tomato-Basil Sauce 35
Fresh Tomato Salsa
Fresh Tomato Sauce 49
Hot Sauce 48
Marinara Sauce 37
Marinara Sauce 64
Orange-Ginger Dipping Sauce 60
Ponzu Sauce 69
Ranchero Sauce 58
Red Chili Sauce 76
Shiitake Mushroom Gravy 52
Soy Cheese Sauce 78
Teriyaki Sauce 40
Three-Herb Marinara Sauce 51

Sauces, Sweet
Caramel Sauce 86
Cloud Nine Frosting 96
Cocoa Frosting 104
Fat-Free Whipped Topping 98
Hot Fudge Sauce 98
Pear Sauce 90
Raspberry Sauce 28

Strawberry Preserves 19
Savory Pie Crust 26
Scones 18

Seitan
Fajitas 100
Philly Cheese Steaks 112

Semolina Pasta Dough 36
Senate Bean Soup 96

Shakes
Blueberry Banana Shake 21
Chocolate Shake 84
Fruit Shake 84
Start the Day with a Shake 21

Shepherd's Pie 90
Shiitake Miso Soup 22
Shiitake Mushroom Gravy 53

Sides
Applesauce 81
Baked Beans 75
Basmati Rice with Peas 54
Black-Eyed Peas 91
Broccoli in Soy Cheese Sauce 78
Cauliflower au Gratin 79
Coleslaw 68
Collard and Mustard Greens 92
Corn and Butternut Squash 80
Creamed Spinach 76
Crispy Onion Rings 31
French Fries 69
Fried Rice 64
Grilled Brussels Sprouts 79
Italian Greens with Roasted Onion and Lemon 38
Mango Chutney 53

Mashed Potatoes 81
Mexican Rice 78
Pea-Camole 71
Red Lentil Dhal 50
Refried Beans 79
Roasted Pepper Fillets 48
Roasted Tomato Salsa 54
Samosas 52
Spicy Okra with Tomatoes 54
Stewed Tomatoes 80
Tabbouleh 47
Yam Brûlée 80

Sizing It All Up 120
Skillet-Roasting Chiles 76

Soups
Black Bean Soup 108
Broccoli Potato Soup 22
Corn Broth 16
Corn Chowder with Popcorn Croutons 16
Cream of Tomato Soup 17
French Onion Soup 20
Hot and Sour Soup 59
Minestrone 32
Old-Fashioned Vegetable Barley Soup 18
Potato and Leek Soup 24
Senate Bean Soup 96
Shiitake Miso Soup 22
Tomato Jalapeño Broth 57
Tortilla Soup 74
Vegetable Gumbo 82
Vegetable Stock 32
Vegetable Stock 18
Zucchini Soup with Roasted Red Pepper 20

Southwest Caesar Salad in a Fire-Roasted Green Chile Dressing 102

Soy (see also Tofu)
About 15
Edamame 71
Guide to Soyfoods 14
Soy Cheese
    Chicago Deep-Dish Pizza 114
    Eggplant Parmesan 36
    Fajitas 100
    Grilled Cheese Sandwiches 97
    Medianoche Sandwiches 108
    Philly Cheese Steaks 112
    Quiche Lorraine 24
    Soy Cheese Sauce 78
Soy "Meat"
    Chicago Deep-Dish Pizza 114
    Chimichangas with Fresh Tomato Salsa 75
    Chinese Dumplings 60
    Grilled Cheese Sandwiches 97
    Lasagne with "Soysage" 46
    Moussaka 44
    New Deli 75
    New English Breakfast 21
    Quiche Lorraine 24
    Shepherd's Pie 90
    Spaghetti Bolognese 38
    Taco Salad in a Chili Lime Dressing 26
Soy Nut Brittle 94
Tempeh
    About 15
    Fajitas 100
    Jerk Kebabs 83
    New English Breakfast 21
    Philly Cheese Steaks 112

Quiche Lorraine 24
Senate Bean Soup 96

Soy Nut Brittle 94
Spaghetti Bolognese 38
Spaghetti Squash Manicotti 51
Spanakopita 45
Spices: Health Benefits from the Spice Rack 56
Spicy Okra with Tomatoes 54
Spinach and Mushroom Enchiladas in Red Chili Sauce 76
Spinach Cannelloni 48
Spinach Ravioli with Fresh Tomato-Basil Sauce 35
Spinach Salad with Crispy Onions 30
Stewed Tomatoes 80
Strawberry Preserves 19
Strawberry Shortcake 96
Sukiyaki 71
Suspiros 80
Sweet Onion Dressing 31
Sweet Potato Pie 93

Tabbouleh 47
Taco Salad 26

Tea
Blueberry Banana Shake 21
Fruit Shake 84
Make Time for Tea 72

Teriyaki Sauce 40
Teriyaki Tofu Bowl with Chinese Vegetables 40
Thousand Island Dressing 35
Three-Bean Chili 41
Tiramisù 41

Tofu
About 15
Chinese Roasted Tofu Salad 33
Chocolate Cupcakes 117
Corn Dogs 112
Creamy French Dressing 88
Crème Brûlée 28
Fire-Roasted Green Chile Dressing 103
Glazed Cinnamon Doughnuts 118
Greek Salad 45
Hot and Sour Soup 59
Kung Pao Tofu 62
Quiche Lorraine 24
Spinach Ravioli with Fresh Tomato-Basil Sauce 35
Sukiyaki 71
Teriyaki Tofu Bowl with Chinese Vegetables 40
Tofu Cacciatore 40
Tofu Cheesecake 107
Tofu Dog Casserole 42
Tofu Egg Salad Sandwich 72
Vegetable Lo Mein 64

Tofu Cacciatore 40
Tofu Cheesecake 107
Tofu Dog Casserole 42
Tofu Egg Salad Sandwich 72
Tortilla Croutons 103
Tortilla Soup 74

Tortillas
Chimichangas with Fresh Tomato Salsa 75
Chocolate Tortilla Wraps with Strawberry Sauce 104
Fajitas 100

Spinach and Mushroom Enchiladas in Red Chili Sauce 76
Tortilla Croutons 104
Tortilla Soup 74

Tropical Fruits Scented with Vanilla and Cardamom 55
Tropical Slaw 108

Vegetable Curry 54
Vegetable Frittata with Roasted Tomato Salsa 54
Vegetable Gumbo 82
Vegetable Lo Mein 64
Vegetable Reuben 68
Vegetable Stock 32
Vegetable Stock 18
Vegetable Sushi 68

Vegetables
Broccoli
    Broccoli in Soy Cheese Sauce 78
    Buddha's Feast 62
Brussels Sprouts
    Grilled Brussels Sprouts 79
Cabbage & Bok Choy
    Buddha's Feast 62
    Cabbage Salad 78
    Coleslaw 68
    Egg Rolls 59
    Hot and Sour Soup 59
    Minestrone 32
    Sukiyaki 71
    Vegetable Lo Mein 64
Cauliflower
    Cauliflower au Gratin 79
    Vegetable Curry 54

NOTE: Entries in italics are from *The Taste for Living Cookbook* (CaP CURE, 1998).

Vegetables (continued)

Corn
- Corn and Butternut Squash 80
- Corn Broth 16
- Corn Chowder with Popcorn Croutons 16
- Corn Dogs 112
- Corn Tomato Omelet with Fresh Parsley 90
- Cornbread 88
- Samosas 52
- Shepherd's Pie 90
- Southwest Caesar Salad in a Fire-Roasted Green Chile Dressing 102
- Tortilla Soup 74
- Vegetable Gumbo 82

Crucifers 90

Eggplant
- Baba Ghanoush 48
- Eggplant Parmesan 36
- *Eggplant Parmesan Strudel with Marinara Sauce 64*
- Hot and Spicy Eggplant 65
- Moussaka 44
- Ratatouille 26

Greens
- Collard and Mustard Greens 92
- Italian Greens with Roasted Onion and Lemon 38

Jícama
- Pico de Gallo 78
- Tropical Slaw 108

Lima Beans
- Lima-Mole 102
- Shepherd's Pie 90

Mushrooms
- Buddha's Feast 62
- Chicago Deep-Dish Pizza 114
- Spinach and Mushroom Enchiladas in Red Chili Sauce 76

Okra
- Spicy Okra with Tomatoes 54
- Vegetable Gumbo 82

Onions
- *Crispy Onion Rings 31*
- Italian Greens with Roasted Onion and Lemon 38
- *Roasted Onion 76*
- Roasting Onions 40
- Romaine, Tomato and Vidalia Salad with Creamy French Dressing 88

Peas
- Basmati Rice with Peas 54
- Fried Rice 64

Peppers
- Fajitas 100
- Fire-Roasted Green Chile Dressing 103
- Greek Salad 45
- Hot Sauce 48
- Jerk Kebabs 83
- Kung Pao Tofu 62
- Mexican Rice 78
- Ratatouille 26
- Roasted Pepper Fillets 48
- *Roasted Red Pepper 20*
- Skillet-Roasting Fresh Chiles 76
- Tofu Cacciatore 40

Potatoes
- *French Fries 69*
- Greek Salad 45
- Homemade Potato Chips 96
- *Mashed Potatoes 81*
- Potato and Leek Soup 24
- Samosas 52
- Shepherd's Pie 90

Spinach
- Chicago Deep-Dish Pizza 114
- *Creamed Spinach 76*
- Spanakopita 45
- Spinach and Mushroom Enchiladas in Red Chili Sauce 76
- Spinach Ravioli with Fresh Tomato-Basil Sauce 35
- Sukiyaki 71

Sweet Potatoes/Yams
- Jerk Kebabs 83
- Shepherd's Pie 90
- Sweet Potato Pie 93
- *Yam Brûlée 80*

Tomatoes
- Bruschetta 33
- Cabbage Salad 78
- Chicago Deep-Dish Pizza 114
- Chimichangas with Fresh Tomato Salsa 75
- *Cream of Tomato Soup 17*
- Fresh Tomato-Basil Sauce 35
- Fresh Tomato Salsa 75
- *Fresh Tomato Sauce 49*
- Hot Sauce 48
- *Jalapeño Tomato Broth 57*
- Lycopene 37
- Marinara Sauce 37
- *Roasted Tomato Salsa 54*
- Romaine, Tomato and Vidalia Salad with Creamy French Dressing 88
- Spaghetti Bolognese 38
- Spicy Okra with Tomatoes 54
- Spinach Ravioli with Fresh Tomato-Basil Sauce 35
- *Stewed Tomatoes 80*
- Tabbouleh 47
- Tofu Cacciatore 40
- *VLT with Herb Mustard 76*

Various
- Buddha's Feast 62
- Fajitas 100
- Greek Salad 45
- *Homemade Pizza 62*
- Jerk Kebabs 83
- Minestrone 32
- *Old-Fashioned Vegetable Barley Soup 18*
- Ratatouille 26
- Shepherd's Pie 90
- Sukiyaki 71
- Vegetable Curry 54
- *Vegetable Frittata with Roasted Tomato Salsa 54*
- Vegetable Gumbo 82
- Vegetable Lo Mein 64
- Vegetable Stock 32
- *Vegetable Stock 18*
- Vegetable Sushi 68

Zucchini
- Fajitas 100
- Jerk Kebabs 83
- Ratatouille 26
- Zucchini Soup with Roasted Red Pepper 20
- *VLT with Herb Mustard 76*
- *Yam Brûlée 80*
- Zabaglione with Berries 42
- *Zucchini Soup with Roasted Red Pepper 20*

NOTE: Entries in italics are from *The Taste for Living Cookbook* (CaP CURE, 1998)

THE DEADLINE FOR CURING PROSTATE CANCER IS TODAY
HELP US MEET THAT DEADLINE

Every 14 minutes, another man dies of prostate cancer. That's 101 men every day whose lives are lost to the most commonly occurring non-skin cancer in America. We've missed the deadline for a cure for those men. Unless we act immediately, prostate cancer will take the lives of another 37,000 men this year alone. Every year, the toll grows.

These men, their wives and families, are not statistics. They are real people, whose greatest hope is to enjoy one more sunrise, to see their children grow up and to live long enough to hold a grandchild in their arms.

We have the scientific team in place to find cures and controls for prostate cancer. We've given them our all: By the end of 1999, CaP CURE will have contributed more than $80 million in awards to 550 cutting-edge research projects in nine countries. Our scientists are investigating every option, from vaccines and gene therapy to nutritional therapies, to extend the lives of men with prostate cancer. The scientists are doing their part.

We'd like to ask you to do your part. You've taken the first step by purchasing this cookbook. Take another step toward a cure by taking action:

- Purchase another *The Taste for Living World Cookbook* for someone you love and give the gift of a healthier life.
- Donate to CaP CURE, so we can beat the deadline facing 101 men every day — 37,000 men this year alone.
- Honor the memory of a loved one by making a contribution to CaP CURE.
- Designate a portion of your company's profits to CaP CURE.
- Provide in-kind goods or services.
- Host a fundraising event for CaP CURE.
- Volunteer your time and/or ideas.
- Ask your friends to join the circle of giving.
- Next time someone asks you what you would like for a present, ask him or her to make a donation to CaP CURE in lieu of a gift.
- Participate in workplace giving programs that match your contributions to CaP CURE.
- Participate in CaP CURE's Home Run Challenge with Major League Baseball, the SENIOR PGA TOUR for the CURE, or any of CaP CURE's fundraising programs.

> With your help, CaP CURE will find a cure for the most frequently diagnosed non-skin cancer in America.
>
> CaP CURE
> 1250 4th Street, Suite 360
> Santa Monica, CA 90401
> Phone: 800 757-2873 or 310 458-2873
> Fax: 310 458-8074
> E-mail: capcure@capcure.org
> World Wide Web: www.capcure.org

DON'T LET THE DEADLINE PASS. LIVES ARE AT STAKE. PLEASE ACT NOW.

CaP CURE is a not-for-profit 501(c)(3) public charity that funds research to find cures or controls for prostate cancer. The organization does not offer medical consultations or advice. For information about the diagnosis or treatment of prostate cancer or other cancers, please call the National Cancer Advisory Service, a toll-free number sponsored by the National Cancer Institute, 1-800-4-CANCER.

CREDITS

We would especially like to thank the following
establishments for the use of their tableware and accessories:

American Rag – Maison Midi
148 South LaBrea Avenue
Los Angeles, CA 90036
323-935-7293

Civilization
8884 Venice Boulevard
Los Angeles, CA 90034
310-202-8883

Crate & Barrel
10250 Santa Monica Boulevard
Los Angeles, CA 90067
310-551-1100

FreeHand
8413 West 3rd Street
Los Angeles, CA 90048
323-655-2607

Geary's of Beverly Hills
351 North Beverly Drive
Beverly Hills, CA 90210
310-273-4741

DO YOUR PART TO HELP US FIND A CURE FOR PROSTATE CANCER

CaP CURE, the Association for the Cure of Cancer of the Prostate, has the scientific team in place to find cures and controls for prostate cancer. We've given them our all: By the end of 1999, CaP CURE will have contributed more than $80 million in awards to 550 cutting-edge research projects in nine countries. Our scientists are investigating every option, from vaccines and gene therapy to nutritional therapies, to extend the lives of men with prostate cancer. The scientists are doing their part.

We'd like to ask you to do your part. You've taken the first step by purchasing this cookbook. Please take another step toward a cure:
- Donate to CaP CURE.
- Purchase either of the *Taste for Living* cookbooks for someone you love, and give the gift of a healthier life.

CaP CURE is a not-for-profit 501(c)(3) public charity that funds research to find cures or controls for prostate cancer. The organization does not offer medical consultations or advice. For information about the diagnosis or treatment of prostate cancer or other cancers, please call the National Cancer Advisory Service, a toll-free number sponsored by the National Cancer Institute, 1-800-4-CANCER.

For faster service on book orders:
Call toll free: 877-884-LIFE
Fax order to: 508-583-9904
E-mail order to: capcure@cfsmail.com

YES! YES! I/We want to help CaP CURE find a cure.

Enclosed is my check for:

❏ $1,000   ❏ $500   ❏ $100   ❏ Other

Please send to:
CaP CURE
1250 4th Street, Suite 360
Santa Monica, CA 90401

Name (*please print*) _____
Phone _____ Facsimile _____ e-mail _____
Street _____ City _____
State _____ Zip/Postal Code _____ Country _____

❏ Check/Money Order enclosed, payable to CaP CURE (US funds drawn on a US bank)
❏ Mastercard   ❏ Visa
Card Number _____ Expiration Date _____
Signature _____

If you would like additional information, please call: 1-800-757-2873 or visit our web site at http://www.capcure.org

---

YES! Please send me a copy of *The Taste for Living WORLD Cookbook* or *The Taste for Living Cookbook* (published in 1998).

Price: $27.50 plus $4.00 handling charge. Total: $31.50
For six or more copies please deduct 20% from the cover price.
Add $4.00 handling charge for each book ordered.

Please send to:
CaP CURE Books
P.O. Box 339
West Bridgewater, MA, 02379

Total *WORLD* books ordered _____ x $27.50 = _____
Total 1998 *Taste for Living* books ordered _____ x $27.50 = _____
Less 20% Discount (for 6 or more books) − _____
Plus Handling Charge ($4.00 per book) _____ x $4.00 + _____
TOTAL _____

Name (*please print*) _____
Street _____ City _____
State _____ Zip/Postal Code _____ Country _____

❏ Check/Money Order enclosed, payable to CaP CURE (US funds drawn on a US bank)
❏ Mastercard   ❏ Visa
Card Number _____ Expiration Date _____
Signature _____